# DOMESDAY BOOK

## Leicestershire

*History from the Sources*

# DOMESDAY BOOK

### A Survey of the Counties of England

*LIBER DE WINTONIA*

Compiled by direction of

## KING WILLIAM I

Winchester
1086

# DOMESDAY BOOK

General editor

JOHN MORRIS

## 22

# Leicestershire

edited by
**Philip Morgan**

*from a draft translation prepared by*
Michael Griffin

PHILLIMORE
Chichester
1979

1979

Published by

PHILLIMORE & CO. LTD.,
London and Chichester

*Head Office*: Shopwyke Hall,
Chichester, Sussex, England

© Mrs. Susan Morris, 1979

ISBN 0 85033 331 8 (case)
ISBN 0 85033 332 6 (limp)

*Printed in Great Britain by
Titus Wilson & Son Ltd.,
Kendal*

# LEICESTERSHIRE

---

Introduction

**The Domesday Survey of Leicestershire**

Notes
Index of Persons
Technical Terms
Index of Places
Systems of Reference
Maps

**History from the Sources**
*General Editor:* John Morris

The series aims to publish history
written directly from the sources
for all interested readers, both
specialists and others. The first
priority is to publish important
texts which should be widely
available, but are not.

## DOMESDAY BOOK

The contents, with the folio on which each county begins, are:

| | | | | | | | |
|---|---|---|---|---|---|---|---|
| 1 | Kent | I | 1 | 20 | Bedfordshire | | 209 |
| 2 | Sussex | | 16 | 21 | Northamptonshire | | 219 |
| 3 | Surrey | | 30 | 22 | Leicestershire | | 230 |
| 4 | Hampshire | | 37 | 23 | Warwickshire | | 238 |
| 5 | Berkshire | | 56 | 24 | Staffordshire | | 246 |
| 6 | Wiltshire | | 64 | 25 | Shropshire | | 252 |
| 7 | Dorset | | 75 | 26 | Cheshire | | 262 |
| 8 | Somerset | | 86 | 27 | Derbyshire | | 272 |
| 9 | Devon | | 100 | 28 | Nottinghamshire | | 280 |
| 10 | Cornwall | | 120 | 29 | Rutland | | 293 |
| 11 | Middlesex | | 126 | 30 | Yorkshire | | 298 |
| 12 | Hertfordshire | | 132 | 31 | Lincolnshire | | 336 |
| 13 | Buckinghamshire | | 143 | | Claims, Yorkshire | | 373 |
| 14 | Oxfordshire | | 154 | | Lincolnshire | | 375 |
| 15 | Gloucestershire | | 162 | | Yorkshire, summary | | 379 |
| 16 | Worcestershire | | 172 | | | | |
| 17 | Herefordshire | | 179 | 32 | Essex | II | 1 |
| 18 | Cambridgeshire | | 189 | 33 | Norfolk | | 109 |
| 19 | Huntingdonshire | | 203 | 34 | Suffolk | | 281 |

Domesday Book is termed *Liber de Wintonia* (The Book of Winchester) in column 332c

# INTRODUCTION

## The Domesday Survey

In 1066 Duke William of Normandy conquered England. He was crowned King, and most of the lands of the English nobility were soon granted to his followers. Domesday Book was compiled 20 years later. The Saxon Chronicle records that in 1085

> at Gloucester at midwinter ... the King had deep speech with his counsellors ... and sent men all over England to each shire ... to find out ... what or how much each landholder held ... in land and livestock, and what it was worth ... The returns were brought to him.[1]

William was thorough. One of his Counsellors reports that he also sent a second set of Commissioners 'to shires they did not know, where they were themselves unknown, to check their predecessors' survey, and report culprits to the King.'[2]

The information was collected at Winchester, corrected, abridged, chiefly by omission of livestock and the 1066 population, and fair-copied by one writer into a single volume. Norfolk, Suffolk and Essex were copied, by several writers, into a second volume, unabridged, which states that 'the Survey was made in 1086'. The surveys of Durham and Northumberland, and of several towns, including London, were not transcribed, and most of Cumberland and Westmorland, not yet in England, was not surveyed. The whole undertaking was completed at speed, in less than 12 months, though the fair-copying of the main volume may have taken a little longer. Both volumes are now preserved at the Public Record Office. Some versions of regional returns also survive. One of them, from Ely Abbey,[3] copies out the Commissioners' brief. They were to ask

> The name of the place. Who held it, before 1066, and now?
> How many *hides*?[4] How many ploughs, both those in lordship and the men's?
> How many villagers, cottagers and slaves, how many free men and Freemen?[5]
> How much woodland, meadow and pasture? How many mills and fishponds?
> How much has been added or taken away? What the total value was and is?
> How much each free man or Freeman had or has? All threefold, before 1066,
>    when King William gave it, and now; and if more can be had than at present?

The Ely volume also describes the procedure. The Commissioners took evidence on oath 'from the Sheriff; from all the barons and their Frenchmen; and from the whole Hundred, the priests, the reeves and six villagers from each village'. It also names four Frenchmen and four Englishmen from each Hundred, who were sworn to verify the detail.

The King wanted to know what he had, and who held it. The Commissioners therefore listed lands in dispute, for Domesday Book was not only a tax-assessment. To the King's grandson, Bishop Henry of Winchester, its purpose was that every 'man should know his right and not usurp another's'; and because it was the final authoritative register of rightful possession 'the natives called it Domesday Book, by analogy

---

[1] Before he left England for the last time, late in 1086.  [2] Robert Losinga, Bishop of Hereford 1079-1095 (see *E.H.R.* 22, 1907, 74).  [3] *Inquisitio Eliensis*, first paragraph.  [4] A land unit, reckoned as 120 acres.  [5] *Quot Sochemani.*

from the Day of Judgement'; that was why it was carefully arranged by Counties, and by landholders within Counties, 'numbered consecutively ... for easy reference'.[6]

Domesday Book describes Old English society under new management, in minute statistical detail. Foreign lords had taken over, but little else had yet changed. The chief landholders and those who held from them are named, and the rest of the population was counted. Most of them lived in villages, whose houses might be clustered together, or dispersed among their fields. Villages were grouped in administrative districts called Hundreds, which formed regions within Shires, or Counties, which survive today with minor boundary changes; the recent deformation of some ancient county identities is here disregarded, as are various short-lived modern changes. The local assemblies, though overshadowed by lords great and small, gave men a voice, which the Commissioners heeded. Very many holdings were described by the Norman term *manerium* (manor), greatly varied in size and structure, from tiny farmsteads to vast holdings; and many lords exercised their own jurisdiction and other rights, termed *soca*, whose meaning still eludes exact definition.

The Survey was unmatched in Europe for many centuries, the product of a sophisticated and experienced English administration, fully exploited by the Conqueror's commanding energy. But its unique assemblage of facts and figures has been hard to study, because the text has not been easily available, and abounds in technicalities. Investigation has therefore been chiefly confined to specialists; many questions cannot be tackled adequately without a cheap text and uniform translation available to a wider range of students, including local historians.

## Previous Editions

The text has been printed once, in 1783, in an edition by Abraham Farley, probably of 1250 copies, at Government expense, said to have been £38,000; its preparation took 16 years. It was set in a specially designed type, here reproduced photographically, which was destroyed by fire in 1808. In 1811 and 1816 the Records Commissioners added an introduction, indices, and associated texts, edited by Sir Henry Ellis; and in 1861-1863 the Ordnance Survey issued zincograph facsimiles of the whole. Texts of individual counties have appeared since 1673, separate translations in the Victoria County Histories and elsewhere.

## This Edition

Farley's text is used, because of its excellence, and because any worthy alternative would prove astronomically expensive. His text has been checked against the facsimile, and discrepancies observed have been verified against the manuscript, by the kindness of Miss Daphne Gifford of the Public Record Office. Farley's few errors are indicated in the notes.

[6]*Dialogus de Scaccario* 1,16.

The editor is responsible for the translation and lay-out. It aims at what the compiler would have written if his language had been modern English; though no translation can be exact, for even a simple word like 'free' nowadays means freedom from different restrictions. Bishop Henry emphasized that his grandfather preferred 'ordinary words'; the nearest ordinary modern English is therefore chosen whenever possible. Words that are now obsolete, or have changed their meaning, are avoided, but measurements have to be transliterated, since their extent is often unknown or arguable, and varied regionally. The terse inventory form of the original has been retained, as have the ambiguities of the Latin.

Modern English commands two main devices unknown to 11th century Latin, standardised punctuation and paragraphs; in the Latin, *ibi* ('there are') often does duty for a modern full stop, *et* ('and') for a comma or semi-colon. The entries normally answer the Commissioners' questions, arranged in five main groups, (i) the place and its holder, its hides, ploughs and lordship; (ii) people; (iii) resources; (iv) value; and (v) additional notes. The groups are usually given as separate paragraphs.

King William numbered chapters 'for easy reference', and sections within chapters are commonly marked, usually by initial capitals, often edged in red. They are here numbered. Maps, indices and an explanation of technical terms are also given. Later, it is hoped to publish analytical and explanatory volumes, and associated texts.

The editor is deeply indebted to the advice of many scholars, too numerous to name, and especially to the Public Record Office, and to the publisher's patience. The draft translations are the work of a team; they have been co-ordinated and corrected by the editor, and each has been checked by several people. It is therefore hoped that mistakes may be fewer than in versions published by single fallible individuals. But it would be Utopian to hope that the translation is altogether free from error; the editor would like to be informed of mistakes observed.

The maps are the work of Rosalind Brewer.

The preparation of this volume has been greatly assisted by a generous grant from the Leverhulme Trust Fund.

**Conventions**

* Refers to a note to the Latin text
[ ] enclose words omitted in the MS.

b. = bovate; c. = carucate.
( ) enclose editorial explanations.

230 a

CIVITAS de LEDECESTRE Tépore Regis EDWARDI.
reddeɓ p̄ annū regi . xxx . liɓ ad numerū de . xx̃ . in
ora . 7 xv . fextar mellis.

Quando rex ibat in exercitu p̄ terrã : de ipfo burgo
xii . burgenfes ibant cū eo . Si ū p̄ mare in hoftē ibat:
mittebant ei . iiii . equos de eoᵭ burgo ufqₜ Londoniã.
ad cōportanᵭ arma uel alia quæ opus . cet.

Modo h̃ Rex . W . p̄ oībz̧ redditibz̧ ciuitatis ejdem
7 comitat . xl.ii . liɓ 7 x . foliᵭ ad pond.

Pro uno accipitre : x . liɓ ad numeꝛ . p̄ fūmario : xx̃ . foł.

De monetarijs . xx . liɓ p̄ annū de . xx . in ora . De his
xx . liɓ . h̃ Hugo de Grentemaifnil tciū denariū.

Rex h̃ in LEDECESTRE . xxxix . domos.              ꟊlintone.
Archieꝑs eboracenfis . ii . dom cū faca 7 foca 7 ptiñ ad Cher
Hugo com . x . dom q̃ ptiñ ad Barhou . 7 vi . dom ptiñ
ad Cacheuuorde . 7 unā dom ptiñ ad Locteburne.
Abbatia de Couentreu h̃ . x . dom.              ꟊgelᵭ fuū.
Abbatia de Cruiland h̃ . iii . dom . De qbz̧ oībz̧ h̃ rex

# LEICESTERSHIRE

**C  The City of LEICESTER**

1  paid to the King £30 a year before 1066 at face value, at
20 [pence] to the *ora,* and 15 sesters of honey.

2  When the King went on campaign by land, 12 burgesses from
this Borough went with him; but if he went against the enemy by
sea, they sent him four horses from the Borough as far as London,
for bringing together weapons and anything else required.

3  Now King William has £42 10s, by weight, for all the payments
of the City and County.

4  For a hawk, £10 at face value; for a packhorse, 20s.

5  From the moneyers, £20 a year at 20 [pence] to the *ora;* of this
£20 Hugh of Grandmesnil has the third penny.

6  The King has 39 houses in Leicester.

7  The Archbishop of York, 2 houses, with full jurisdiction; they
belong to Tur Langton.

8  Earl Hugh, 10 houses which belong to Barrow (-on-Soar); 6 houses which
belong to Kegworth; and 1 house which belongs to Loughborough.

9  Coventry Abbey has 10 houses.

10  Crowland Abbey has 3 houses; from all of which the King has
his tax.

Hugo de Grentemaiſnil hĩ.c 7 x.domos.7 ii.æccĩas.

pter has hĩ in cõmune cũ rege.xxiiii.dom in eođ

Exceptis his hĩ iđ Hugo in Ledeceſtre ⌐burgo.

xxiiii.burgſes p̃tinent ad Hanſtigie.7 xiii.burgſes

p̃tinent ad Sigleſbie.7 iii.domos ptiñ ad Inuuareſbie.

7 x.domos ptiñ ad Merdegraue.7 iiii.dom ptiñ ad

Brohtone.7 ix.dom ptiñ ad Stotone.7 iiii.dom ptiñ

ad Wichingeſtone.7 vii.dom ptiñ ad Andreteſbie.7 iii.dom

ptiñ ad Sceltone.7 x.dom ptiñ ad Burſtelle.7 iii.dom

ptiñ ad Burtone.7 unã dom̃ ptiñ ad Bruneſtineſtorp.

7 ii.dom ptiñ ad Diresford.7 iii.dom ptiñ ad Leghã.quas

emit de Osbno.7 unã dom̃ ptiñ ad Letitone.7 i.dom̃ ptiñ

ad Turchiteleſtone. ⌐uaſtas.

In eođ burgo hĩ iđ Hugo.ii.æccĩas 7 ii.dom.7 iiii.dom

Hugo de Wituile teñ de ipſo Hug̃.v.dom cũ ſaca 7 ſoca.

Hæ ſunt de mutuatione de Wadford.

Robt de Veci hĩ.vi.dom cũ ſoca 7 ſoca ptiñ ad Niuuetone.

7 iii.alias cũ ſaca 7 ſoca ptiñ ad chiborne. ⌐Picheuuelle.

Goisfrid de Wirce.i.dom̃ ptiñ ad Dalbi.7 aliã ptiñ ad

In Ledeceſtre ſĩ.iiii.dom ptiñ ad Scepehefde.7 i.ptiñ

ad Sadintone.7 una ptiñ ad Torp.

★ ⌐In ipſo burgo hĩ Henric de Fereires 7 Robt̃⁹.i.burgſe.^(disñſator)

Jvdita comitiſſa hĩ in eođ burgo.xxviii.domos.

7 de medietate molini.v.ſoliđ 7 iiii.denar.

Ext̃ burgũ hĩ ipſa.vi.caruc træ ptiñ ad burgũ.

7 ibi hĩ.i.car.7 hões ej.iii.car.Ibi.viii.ac̃ p̃ti.Silua

vi.q̃rent lg̃.7 iii.q̃ẕ lat̃.Valet.xl.ſoliđ.totũ.


Silua toti⁹ Vicecomitat⁹ HERESWODE uocat̃ hĩ iiii.leu

in lg̃ 7.i.leu in lat̃.

11    Hugh of Grandmesnil has 110 houses and 2 churches. Besides
these he has in common with the King 24 houses in the Borough.
Apart from these, Hugh also has in Leicester
     24 burgesses who belong to Anstey and 13 burgesses who belong
to Sileby; and (these) houses which belong to

| | | | |
|---|---|---|---|
| Ingarsby | 3 | Birstall | 10 |
| Belgrave | 10 | Burton (Overy) | 3 |
| Broughton (Astley) | 4 | 'Bromkinsthorpe' | 1 |
| Stockerston | 9 | Desford | 2 |
| Wigston (Magna) | 4 | *Legham*, which he bought | |
| Enderby | 7 | from Osbern | 3 |
| (Earl) Shilton | 3 | *Letitone* | 1 |
| | | Thurcaston | 1 |

12    In this Borough Hugh also has 2 churches and 2 houses, and 4
derelict houses. Hugh of Gouville holds 5 houses from Hugh
himself with full jurisdiction. They are from exchange with Watford.

13    Robert of Vessey has 6 houses with full jurisdiction which belong
to Newton (Harcourt), and 3 others with full jurisdiction which
belong to Kibworth (Harcourt).

14    Geoffrey of La Guerche, 1 house which belongs to (Little) Dalby,
and another which belongs to Pickwell.

15    In Leicester there are 4 houses which belong to Shepshed, 1
which belongs to Saddington, and 1 which belongs to Thorpe (Acre).

16    In this Borough Henry of Ferrers and Robert the Bursar have
1 burgess.

17    Also in the Borough Countess Judith has 28 houses and from half
a mill 5s 4d. Outside the Borough she has 6 c. of land
which belong to the Borough; she has 1 plough there and her
men 3 ploughs. Meadow, 8 acres; woodland 6 furlongs long and
3 furlongs wide. Value of the whole, 40s.

18    The woodland of the whole Sheriffdom, called *Hereswode,* has
4 leagues in length and 1 league in width.

# HIC ANNOTANT TENENTES TRAS IN LEDECESKESCIRE.

## .I. REX WILLELMVS.

.II. Archieps Eboracenfis.

.III Eps Lincolienfis.

.IIII Eps Conftantienfis.

.V. Abbatia de Burgh.

.VI. Abbatia de Couentreu.

.VII Abbatia de Cruiland.

.VIII Goduin pbr 7 alij elemos.

.IX. Comes de Mellend.

.X. Comes Albericus.

.XI. Comitiffa Godeue.

.XII. Comitiffa Alueue.

★ .XIII Comes Hugo.

.XIIII. Hugo de Grentemaifnil.

.XV. Henricus de Ferieres.

.XVI. Robertus de Todeni.

.XVII. Robertus de Veci.

.XVIII Rogerius de Bufli.

.XIX. Robertus difpenfator.

.XX. Robertus Hoftiarius.

.XXI. Radulfus de Mortemer.

.XXII Radulfus filius Hubti.

.XXIII. Wido de Reinbodcurtn.

XXIIII. Wido de Credune.

.XXV. Willelmus Peurel.

.XXVI. Willelmus Buenuafleth.

.XXVII. Willelmus Loueth.

.XXVIII. Goisfridus Alfelin.

XXIX. Goisfridus de Wirce.

.XXX. Godefridus de Cambrai.

.XXXI. Gunfridus de Cioches.

.XXXII. Hunfridus camerarius.

.XXXIII. Giflebertus de Gand.

.XXXIIII Girbertus.

.XXXV. Durandus Maleth.

.XXXVI. Drogo de Beurere.

.XXXVII Maino brito.

.XXXVIII Ogerius brito.

.XXXIX. Nigellus de Albingi.

.XL. Judita comitiffa.

.XLI. Adeliz uxor Hugonis.

.XLII. Herbertus 7 alii feru regis. XLIII. Comes Hugo.

.XLIIII Homines comitis de Mellen.

# LIST OF LANDHOLDERS IN LEICESTERSHIRE

|     |     |     |     |
| --- | --- | --- | --- |
| 1 | King William | 23 | Guy of Raimbeaucourt |
| 2 | The Archbishop of York | 24 | Guy of Craon |
| 3 | The Bishop of Lincoln | 25 | William Peverel |
| 4 | The Bishop of Coutances | 26 | William Bonvallet |
| 5 | Peterborough Abbey | 27 | William Lovett |
| 6 | Coventry Abbey | 28 | Geoffrey Alselin |
| 7 | Crowland Abbey | 29 | Geoffrey of La Guerche |
| 8 | Godwin the Priest and other almsmen | 30 | Godfrey of Cambrai |
|   |  | 31 | Gunfrid of Chocques |
| 9 | The Count of Meulan | 32 | Humphrey the Chamberlain |
| 10 | Earl Aubrey | 33 | Gilbert of Ghent |
| 11 | Countess Godiva | 34 | Gerbert |
| 12 | Countess Aelfeva | 35 | Durand Malet |
| 13 | Earl Hugh | 36 | Drogo of La Beuvriere |
| (13) 14 | Hugh of Grandmesnil | 37 | Mainou the Breton |
| (14) 15 | Henry of Ferrers | 38 | Oger the Breton |
| (15) 16 | Robert of Tosny | 39 | Nigel of Aubigny |
| (16) 17 | Robert of Vessey | 40 | Countess Judith |
| [17 | Robert of Bucy ] | 41 | Adelaide wife of Hugh [of Grandmesnil] |
| 18 | Roger of Bully |  |  |
| 19 | Robert the Bursar | 42 | Herbert and others of the King's Servants |
| 20 | Robert Usher |  |  |
| 21 | Ralph of Mortimer | 43 | Earl Hugh |
| 22 | Ralph son of Hubert | 44 | The Count of Meulan's men |

Rex tenet *CROHTONE* . Ibi st̄ xxiiii . carc̄ træ . In dn̄io

sunt . ii . car̄ . 7 v . ſerui . 7 xxii . uilłi cū . ii . borđ hn̄t . ii . car̄

7 dimiđ . 7 xxx . ſocħi hn̄t . viii . car̄ . Ibi . xxx . ac̄ p̄ti . 7 ii . molini de . viii . ſoł.

Huic M̄ p̄tin *CNIPETONE* . Ibi st̄ . viii . care træ 7 vi . bo

uatæ . In dn̄io st̄ . ii . car̄ . 7 iiii . ſerui . 7 x . uilłi cū . iiii . borđ

7 x . ſocħis . hn̄t . iiii . car̄ . Ibi . vi . molini de . xiii . ſoliđ

7 iiii . den̄ . 7 xiii . ac̄ p̄ti .

Eiđ M̄ p̄tin̄ *HERSTAN* . Ibi st̄ . xii . caruc̄ træ . Ibi . xx .

ſocħi cū . v . uilłis 7 i . borđ hn̄t . vi . car̄ 7 dim . Ibi . xvii .

ac̄ p̄ti . Tot̄ valuit . x . liƀ . Modo . xvii . liƀ .

Rex ten̄ *BROCTONE* . Ibi st̄ . xii . caruc̄ træ . In dn̄io . ē

una car̄ . 7 xxiiii . ſocħi cū . ix . uilłis 7 ii . borđ hn̄t . xii .

car̄ . Ibi . c . ac̄ p̄ti . Valuit . iii . liƀ . Modo . viii . liƀ .

H̄ . ii . M̄ tenuit Morcar . Modo ten̄ Hugo ad firmā de rege .

Rex ten̄ *RODOLEI* . Rex . E . tenuit . Ibi st̄ . v . car̄ træ .

In dn̄io st̄ . ii . de his . 7 ibi . ii . car̄ . 7 xxix . uilłi cū p̄bro

7 xviii . borđ hn̄t . vi . car̄ . Ibi molin̄ de . iiii . ſoliđ .

7 xxx . vii . ac̄ p̄ti . Silua dn̄ica . i . leu l̄g . 7 dim̄ leu lat̄ .

Silua uillanoꝮ . iiii . q̄rent l̄g . 7 iii . q̄rent lat̄ .

H̄ uilla ualet p̄ annū . lxii . ſoliđ .

Huic M̄ p̄tin̄ ſubſequentia m̄ebra .

230 c

In *ADELACHESTONE* . st̄ . vi . bouatæ Træ . Vaſta . ē .

In Barneſbi . v . car̄ træ . i . bouata min̄ . 7 xv . ac̄ p̄ti .

In Setgraue , vi . car̄ træ . 7 iii . q̄ꝛ p̄ti in l̄g . 7 i . q̄ꝛ 7 dim̄ lat̄ .

In Seglebi . ii . car̄ træ 7 ii . bouatæ . 7 x . ac̄ p̄ti .    Γ lat̄ .

In Tochebi . vi . car̄ træ . 7 x . ac̄ p̄ti . Silua . ii . q̄ꝛ l̄g . 7 i . q̄ꝛ

In Sciftitone . xii . car̄ træ 7 molin̄ de . xii . den̄ . Silua . iii . q̄ꝛ

In Merdefelde . iii . car̄ træ . 7 viii . ac̄ p̄ti .   Γ l̄g . 7 ii . q̄ꝛ lat̄ .

[1]                          **LAND OF THE KING**

In FRAMLAND Wapentake

1a   The King holds CROXTON (Kerrial). 24 c. of land.
In lordship 2 ploughs; 5 slaves.
     22 villagers with 2 smallholders have 2½ ploughs.
         30 Freemen have 8 ploughs.
     Meadow, 30 acres; 2 mills at 8s.

1b   KNIPTON belongs to this manor. 8 c. and 6 b. of land.
In lordship 2 ploughs; 4 slaves.
     10 villagers with 4 smallholders and 10 Freemen have 4 ploughs.
     6 mills at 13s 4d; meadow, 13 acres.

1c   HARSTON belongs to this manor. 12 c. of land.
     20 Freemen with 5 villagers and 1 smallholder have 6½ ploughs.
     Meadow, 17 acres.
Value of the whole was £10; now £17.

2    The Kings holds (Nether) BROUGHTON. 12 c. of land.
In lordship 1 plough.
     24 Freemen with 9 villagers and 4 smallholders have 12 ploughs.
     Meadow, 100 acres.
The value was £3; now £8.
     Earl Morcar held these 2 manors. Hugh son of Baldric now
holds them at a revenue from the King.

[In GOSCOTE Wapentake]

3    The King holds ROTHLEY. King Edward held it. 5 c. of land.
In lordship 2 of them and 2 ploughs.
     29 villagers with a priest and 18 smallholders have 6 ploughs.
     A mill at 4s; meadow, 37 acres; the lord's woodland 1 league
         long and ½ league wide; the villagers' woodland 4 furlongs
         long and 3 furlongs wide.
Value of this village, 62s a year.

     The following members belong to this manor.
In ALLEXTON  6 b. of land. Waste.                             230 c
In BARSBY   5 c. of land less 1 b. Meadow, 15 acres.
In SEAGRAVE  6 c. of land.
     Meadow 3 furlongs in length and 1½ furlongs wide.
In SILEBY  2 c. and 2 b. of land. Meadow, 10 acres.
In TUGBY  6 c. of land.
     Meadow, 10 acres; woodland 2 furlongs long and 1 furlong wide.
In SKEFFINGTON  12 c. of land.
     A mill at 12d; woodland 3 furlongs long and 2 furlongs wide.
In (North) MAREFIELD  3 c. of land. Meadow, 8 acres.

In alia Merdefelde . III . car̃ træ̃.7 VIII . ãc p̃ti.　　г7 alia lat̃.

In Elſtede . III . car̃ træ̃ . II . bouat̃ min.7 I.ãc p̃ti.Silua . I . q̃ɂ lg̃.

In Caldeuuelle 7 Wiche . IIII . car̃ træ̃.7 II . molini de . II . ſot.

In Tiletone . II . car̃ træ̃ 7 IIII . ãc p̃ti.7 v . ãc ſiluæ.

In Offerdebie . XII . car̃ træ̃.7 II . molini de . VIII . ſot.7 XX.ãc p̃ti.

In Caihã . IIII . car̃ træ̃.7 VIII . ãc p̃ti.

In Worcnodebie . VI . car̃ træ̃.7 X.ãc p̃ti.

In Tuiuorde . IIII . car̃ træ̃ 7 dimid̃.7 VIII . ãc p̃ti.

In Sumerlidebie . I . car̃ træ̃ 7 dimid̃.7 VI . ãc p̃ti.г II . ſot.

In Friſebie . VIII . car̃ træ̃.7 IIII . ãc p̃ti.7 de parte molini

In Saxelbie . I . car̃ træ̃.7 v . ãc p̃ti.

In Grimeſtone . III . car̃ træ̃ . una bouata 7 dim̃ min.

In Badegraue . VI . car̃ træ̃ . III . bouat̃ min.7 X . ãc p̃ti.

In Gadeſbie . VIII . car̃ træ̃ 7 III . bouatæ.7 XII . ãc p̃ti.

In his ſunt . CC.7 IIII . ſocħi cũ . CLVII . uiłłis 7 nonaginta
IIII . borđ.hñtes. qt . XX . car̃ 7 II.7 reddt int om̃s XXXI . liƀ

г 7 VIII . ſot.7 I . den̄.

Rex ten̄ BVGEDONE Rex.E.tenuit.Ibi ſt̃ . IX . car̃ træ̃
7 dim̃ . In dñio ſt̃ . II . car̃.7 XIII . ſocħi cũ . VIII . uiłłis 7 XVI.
borđ hñt . XIII . car̃ 7 dim̃.7 reddt . XXX . ſot p annũ . Ibi
p̃ti acræ　　　Dñium ualet . XL . ſot p annũ.

In Medburne ſunt . II . car̃ træ̃.7 VI . ãc p̃ti 7 dimid̃.

★ In Graueho . I　　træ̃ . In Santone . II . car̃ træ̃.

★ In Carletone . v . . atæ træ̃ . In Nelueſtone . II . bouatæ træ̃.

In Galbi una car̃ træ̃ 7 dim̃.7 IIII . ãc p̃ti.

In Nortone . III . car̃ træ̃.7 v . ãc p̃ti.　　г træ̃.7 II . bouatæ.

In Stratone . IX . car̃ træ̃.7 X . ãc p̃ti. In Smitone . I . car̃

In Foxeſtone . II . car̃ træ̃.7 v . ãc p̃ti.

In his ſunt . LX . ſocħi cũ . II . uiłłis 7 XVI . borđ hñtes . XIII . car̃.
7 reddt . CL . ſot.7 XVIII . den̄.

Rex ħt Soca . II . carucatarũ in Blaueſtone 7 ptin ad Bu
gedone . Robt de Todeni ten̄ hanc tr̃a . Vat̃ . XI . ſot 7 obolũ.

In the other (South) MAREFIELD 3 c. of land. Meadow, 8 acres.
In HALSTEAD 3 c. of land less 2 b.
Meadow 1 acre; woodland 1 furlong long and another wide.
In CHADWELL and WYCOMB 4 c. of land. 2 mills at 2s.
In TILTON 2 c. of land. Meadow, 4 acres; woodland, 5 acres.
In ASFORDBY 12 c. of land. 2 mills at 8s; meadow, 20 acres.
In KEYHAM 4 c. of land. Meadow, 8 acres.
In WARTNABY 6 c. of land. Meadow, 10 acres.
In TWYFORD 4½ c. of land. Meadow, 8 acres.
In SOMERBY 1½ c. of land. Meadow, 6 acres.
In FRISBY 8 c. of land. Meadow, 4 acres; from part of a mill 2s.
In SAXELBY 1 c. of land. Meadow, 5 acres.
In GRIMSTON 3 c. of land less 1½ b.
In BAGGRAVE 6 c. of land less 3 b. Meadow, 10 acres.
In GADDESBY 8 c. and 3 b. of land. Meadow, 12 acres.
In these are 204 Freemen with 157 villagers and 94 smallholders who have 82 ploughs. Between all of them they pay £31 8s 1d.

[In GARTREE Wapentake]

The King holds (Great) BOWDEN. King Edward held it. 9½ c. of land. In lordship 2 ploughs.
13 Freemen with 8 villagers and 16 smallholders have 13½ ploughs; they pay 30s a year.
Meadow, ......acres.
Value of the lordship 40s a year.
In MEDBOURNE 2 c. of land. Meadow, 6½ acres.
In CRANOE 1 c. of land.
In SHANGTON 2 c. of land.
In CARLTON (Curlieu) 5 b. of land.
In ILLSTON 2 b. of land.
In GALBY 1½ c. of land. Meadow, 4 acres.
In (King's) NORTON 3 c. of land. Meadow, 5 acres.
In STRETTON 9 c. of land. Meadow, 10 acres.
In SMEETON (Westerby) 1 c. and 2 b. of land.
In FOXTON 2 c. of land. Meadow, 5 acres.
In these are 60 Freemen with 2 villagers and 16 smallholders who have 13 ploughs and pay 150s 18d.
The King has the jurisdiction of 2 c. in Blaston; they belong to (Great) Bowden. Robert of Tosny holds this land.
Value of this jurisdiction, 11s ½d.

Hunfrid camerari ten ad firmā de foca regis . ɪɪ . car̄ træ

in *ABEGRAVE* . 7 ibi hт̄ . ɪ . car̄ cū . ɪɪɪɪ . uiłłis 7 ɪɪ . borđ . q̄ hn̄t

unā car̄ . Ibi . vɪ . ac̄ p̄ti . Valuit . xɪɪ . den̄ . Modo . xx . fol.

*IN GERETREV WAP.*

Rex ten̄ *SETINTONE* . Ibi . ē una hida . ɪ . carucata min̄ .

In dn̄io . ē . ɪ . car̄ . 7 xɪ . fochi 7 xvɪɪ . uiłłi cū . v . borđ

hn̄tes . vɪɪɪ . car̄ . Ibi molin̄ de . ɪɪ . foliđ . 7 x . ac̄ p̄ti.

Valuit . ɪɪɪɪ . liƀ . Modo . ɪx . liƀ.

In *WETBERGE* . ſт̄ . ɪɪɪ . car̄ træ . In dn̄io . ē dimiđ car̄ .

7 ɪɪɪ . uiłłi cū . ɪ . focho 7 xɪ . borđ hn̄t . ɪɪɪɪ . car̄ . p̄tū una

q̄rent lḡ . 7 una lat̄ . Silua . v . q̄z lḡ . 7 ɪɪɪ . q̄z lat̄.

Valuit . x . foliđ . Modo . xl . foliđ.

230 d

Ad Wetberga p̄tin̄ : ɪ . car̄ træ 7 dim in Burḡo . 7 ibi . ē . ɪ . car̄

In *TORP* ſт̄ . v . car̄ træ . Ibi . xvɪ . uiłłi  ſcū . ɪ . uiłło.

cū . ɪɪɪ . fochis 7 vɪɪɪ . borđ hn̄t . vɪ . car̄ . Ibi . xxx . ac̄ p̄ti.

Valuit . ɪɪɪ . liƀ . Modo . vɪɪ : liƀ.

In *DISLEA* eſt . ɪ . hida . Ibi . xvɪ : uiłłi 7 xvɪ . fochi cū . ɪ.

borđ hn̄t . vɪɪɪ . car̄ . Ibi . ɪɪ . molini redđt . v . fol : 7 x . ac̄

p̄ti . Silua . ɪɪɪɪ . q̄z lḡ . 7 tn̄tđ lat̄ . Vaſta fuit : m̄ ual̄ . xl . fol.

Has t̄ras tenuit Edid regina . Modo hт̄ Goduin de

rege ad firmā . *DISLEA* ū ten de rege in feudo.

Idē Goduin ten de rege in feudo . ɪɪ . hiđ 7 dim in *SCEPES*

*HEFDE* . 7 ɪɪɪɪ . car̄ træ . Ofgot tenuit cū faca 7 foca.

In dn̄io hт̄ . ɪɪ . car̄ . 7 ɪɪ . feruos . 7 xxx uiłłi cū . xɪɪ . borđ

hn̄t . xv . car̄ . 7 xx . fochi cū . ɪɪ . militiƀ 7 vɪ . uiłłis 7 ɪɪɪɪ.

borđ hn̄t . xxɪ . car̄ . Ibi molin̄ de . v . foliđ . 7 l . ac̄ p̄ti.

Silua . ɪ . leu lḡ . 7 ɪɪɪɪ . q̄z lat̄ . Hanc t̄ra uaſta inuenit.

De hac t̄ra exeunt . vɪ . liƀ ad firmā p̄cepto ep̄i baioc̄fis.

p̄ feruitio infulæ de With.

230 c, d

5   In 'PRESTGRAVE' Humphrey the Chamberlain holds 2 c.
of land at a revenue from the King's jurisdiction.
He has 1 plough, with
    4 villagers and 2 smallholders who have 1 plough.
    Meadow, 6 acres.
The value was 12d; now 20s.

  In GARTREE Wapentake
6   The King holds SADDINGTON. 1 hide less 1 c. In lordship 1 plough and
    11 Freemen and 17 villagers with 5 smallholders who have 8 ploughs.
    A mill at 2s; meadow, 10 acres.
The value was £4; now £9.

  [In GOSCOTE Wapentake]
7   In WHATBOROUGH 3 c. of land. In lordship ½ plough.
    3 villagers with 1 Freeman and 11 smallholders have 4 ploughs.
    Meadow 1 furlong long and 1 wide; woodland 5 furlongs
      long and 3 furlongs wide.
    The value was 10s; now 40s.
    To Whatborough belong 1½ c. of land in 'THE BURGH'.      230 d
  1 plough, with
    1 villager.

8   In THORPE (Acre) 5 c. of land.
    16 villagers with 3 Freemen and 8 smallholders have 6 ploughs.
    Meadow, 30 acres.
The value was £3; now £7.

9   In DISHLEY 1 hide.
    16 villagers and 16 Freemen with 1 smallholder have 8 ploughs.
    2 mills pay 5s; meadow, 10 acres; woodland 4 furlongs long
      and as many wide.
It was waste; value now 40s.
  Queen Edith held these lands. Godwin now has them at a
revenue from the King. He also holds Dishley from the King
as a Holding.

10   In SHEPSHED Godwin also holds 2½ hides and 4 c. of land from
the King as a Holding. Osgot held it with full jurisdiction.
In lordship he has 2 ploughs; 2 slaves.
    30 villagers with 12 smallholders have 15 ploughs; 20 Freemen
      with 2 men-at-arms , 6 villagers and 4 smallholders
      have 21 ploughs.
    A mill at 5s; meadow, 50 acres; woodland, 1 league long
      and 4 furlongs wide.
  He found this land waste. From this land comes £6 at a revenue,
by command of the Bishop of Bayeux, for the service of the
Isle of Wight.

In *Nossitone* st̄.iii.car̄ træ p̃tiñ ad ſocā de *Ocheha*.

Ibi.xvii.ſocħi cū.vi.borđ hn̄t.vi.car̄.7 ibi.i.q̃ʒ ſiluæ
in lḡ.7 dim̄ q̃ʒ lat.Valet.xx.ſoliđ.Rex hr̄ in dn̄io. *In Gutlacis*
Rex teñ *Bichesbie*.Leuuiñ teneƀ T.R.E.Ibi st̄.v.car̄ træ. *Wapent*.
Tra.iiii.car̄.In dn̄io.ē una car̄.7 x.uiłłi cū.iiii.borđ hn̄t.ii.car̄.
Ibi.xx.ac̄ p̃ti.Valuit.xxx.ſoł.Modo.xl.ſoliđ.


.II. TERRA EP̄I EBORACENSIS. *In Gertrev Wapent*.

Archiep̄s Eboracenſis teñ *Terlintone*.7 Walcheliñ
de eo.Ibi ſunt.xiii.car̄ træ.cū *Lagintone*.q̃ ibi p̃tiñ.
In dn̄io ſunt.iii.car̄.7 iiii.ſerui.7 ii.ancillæ.7 xx.uiłłi cū
iiii.borđ hn̄t.vi.car̄.Ibi.xx.ac̄ p̃ti.Silua.iii.q̃ʒ lḡ.
7 ii.q̃ʒ lat. ⌊In eađ uilla teñ Herƀt de.W.iii.car̄ træ.
7 ibi hr̄.i.car̄ in dn̄io.7 v.uiłłi 7 ii.ſocħi cū.ii.borđ hn̄t.iii.
car̄.Ibi.xii.ac̄ p̃ti.Tot̄ ualuit.xx.ſoł.Modo.lx.ſoł.
Idē Walcheł teñ de Archiep̄o *Lvbanha*.7 Roƀt de eo.
Ibi st̄.viii.car̄ træ.In dn̄io st̄.ii.car̄.7 ii.ſerui.7 ii.an
cillæ.7 vi.uiłłi cū.iiii.borđ hn̄t.iii.car̄.
In eađ uilla teñ uñ miles de Roƀto.iii.car̄ træ.7 ibi
hr̄.i.car̄ in dn̄io.7 v.uiłłi cū.i.borđ hn̄t.i.car̄ 7 dimiđ.
Ibi.xxxvi.ac̄ p̃ti.Tot̄ ualuit,xx.ſoł.Modo.xl.ſoliđ
Archil 7 Oſmund 7 Oſlac tenuer̄ cū ſaca 7 ſoca.
Osƀn teñ de Arcħ in *Waleha*.ii.car̄ træ.In dn̄io.ē una
car̄ 7 iii.ſerui.7 iiii.uiłłi cū.i.borđ hn̄t.ii.car̄.
Ibi.xviii.ac̄ p̃ti.Valuit.iiii.ſoł.Modo.xx.ſoł.Archil tenuit.

[In GARTREE Wapentake]

11 In KNOSSINGTON 3 c. of land which belong to the
jurisdiction of Oakham.
>17 Freemen with 6 smallholders have 6 ploughs.
>Woodland 1 furlong in length and ½ furlong wide.
>
>Value 20s.
>>The King has it in lordship.

In GUTHLAXTON Wapentake

12 The King holds BITTESBY. Leofwin held it before 1066.
5 c. of land. Land for 4 ploughs. In lordship 1 plough.
>10 villagers with 4 smallholders have 2 ploughs.
>Meadow, 20 acres.
>
>The value was 30s; now 40s.

## 2     LAND OF THE (ARCH)BISHOP OF YORK

In GARTREE Wapentake

1 The Archbishop of York holds TUR LANGTON and Walkelin from him.
13 c. of land with LANGTON which belongs there.
In lordship 3 ploughs; 4 male and 2 female slaves.
>20 villagers with 4 smallholders have 6 ploughs.
>Meadow, 20 acres; woodland 3 furlongs long and 2 furlongs wide.

2 In the same village Herbert holds 3 c. of land from Walkelin.
In lordship he has 1 plough.
>5 villagers and 2 Freemen with 2 smallholders have 3 ploughs.
>Meadow, 12 acres.
>
>The value of the whole was 20s; now 60s.

3 Walkelin also holds LUBENHAM from the Archbishop and Robert
from him. 8 c. of land. In lordship 2 ploughs; 2 male and
2 female slaves.
>6 villagers with 4 smallholders have 3 ploughs.

4 In the same village a man-at-arms holds 3 c. of land from
Robert. In lordship he has 1 plough.
>5 villagers with 1 smallholder have 1½ ploughs.
>Meadow, 36 acres.
>
>The value of the whole was 20s; now 40s.
>>Arkell, Osmund, and Oslac held it with full jurisdiction.

5 Osbern holds 2 c. of land in WELHAM from the Archbishop.
In lordship 1 plough; 3 slaves.
>4 villagers with 1 smallholder have 2 ploughs.
>Meadow, 18 acres.
>
>The value was 4s; now 20s.
>>Arkell held it.

Idē.O.teñ de Arch in *CAITORP* ii.car̄ trǣ.In dñio hī.i.car̄
★ cū.i.feruo.7 i.franciḡ cū.ii.uiłłis 7 ii.bord̄ hñt.i.car̄.Ibi.xl.
ac̄ nemoris.Valuit.iiii.foł.Modo.xii.foł.Archil tenuit cū faca
Hugo teñ de Arch in *TILLINTONE*.i.car̄ trǣ.7 Friendai de eo.
Ibi.ē una car̄ cū.iiii.uiłłis 7 ii.bord̄.Valuit 7 uał.x.folid̄.
Ħ tra.ē de elemofina S̄ MARIǼ de Sudwelle.Getda tenuit T.R.E.

## .III. TERRA EP̄I LINCOLIENSIS.

Ēps LINCOLIENSIS teñ in *LEDECESTRE*.x.car̄ tre.In dñio
hī ibi.v.car̄.7 moliñ 7 dimid̄ de.x.foł 7 viii.deñ.7 ii.ǣccłas
de.xv.foł.7 xvii.burḡfes.xxxii.denar p̄ anñ redd̄tes.
De una parte trǣ ext̄ murū hī.v.foł 7 iiii.deñ.7 iii.uiłłi cū
p̄b̄ro 7 xii.bord̄ hñt.iiii.car̄.Ibi.xx.ac̄ p̄ti.
231 a
Idem eps teñ *CNIHTETONE*.Ibi sī.ii.partes.i.hidǣ.Tra.ē
vi.car̄.Ibi.xx.uiłłi cū.iiii.fochis hñt.vi.car̄.Ibi.xxx.ac̄
Idē eps teñ in *LEGRE*.i.car̄ trǣ.Ibi sī.ii.fochi      ⌐ p̄ti.
cū.i.bord̄ hñtes-dim car̄.
Hǣ trǣ S̄ MARIE Lincoliǣ ualent.vi.lib̄ 7 ii.foł.7 iiii.deñ.

Rob̄t teñ de epo in *SCERNEFORDE*.i.car̄ trǣ.Vna car̄
poteſt eē.Ibi sī.ii.bord̄.Valet.iiii.foł.
Radulf teñ de epo.ii.car̄ trǣ in *TONISCOTE*.Duǣ car̄
poſs.eē.7 ibi funt cū.iiii.fochis Valuit xx.deñ.M.x.folid̄.
Idē Rad̄ teñ de epo.iiii.car̄ trǣ in *PONTENEI*.Tra.ē.iiii.car̄.
In dñio sī.ii.7 iiii.ferui.7 i.ancilla.7 ix.uiłłi 7 ix.burḡfes
in ciuitate cū.v.bord̄ hñt.ii.car̄.Ibi.ii.ac̄ p̄ti.
Valuit.xx.foł.Modo.xxx.folid̄.

6 Osbern also holds 2 c. of land in KEYTHORPE from the Archbishop.
In lordship he has 1 plough, with 1 slave.
1 Frenchman with 2 villagers and 2 smallholders have 1 plough.
Wood, 40 acres.
The value was 4s; now 12s.
Arkell held it with full jurisdiction.

[In GOSCOTE Wapentake]

7 Hugh holds 1 c. of land in TILTON from the Archbishop, and
Frienday from him. 1 plough, with
4 villagers and 2 smallholders.
The value was and is 10s.
This land is of the alms (lands) of Saint Mary's Southwell.
Gytha held it before 1066.

## 3     LAND OF THE BISHOP OF LINCOLN

1 The Bishop of Lincoln holds 10 c. of land in LEICESTER.
In lordship he has 5 ploughs; 1½ mills at 10s 8d; 2 churches at 15s;
17 burgesses who pay 32d a year. From a piece of land outside
the wall he has 5s 4d.
3 villagers with a priest and 12 smallholders have 4 ploughs.
Meadow, 20 acres.

[In GUTHLAXTON Wapentake]

2 The Bishop also holds KNIGHTON. 2 parts of 1 hide.     231 a
Land for 6 ploughs.
20 villagers with 4 Freemen have 6 ploughs.
Meadow, 30 acres.

3 The Bishop also holds 1 c. of land in LEIRE.
2 Freemen with 1 smallholder who have ½ plough.
Value of these lands of St. Mary's of Lincoln £6 2s 4d.

4 Robert holds 1 c. of land in SHARNFORD from the Bishop.
1 plough possible.
2 smallholders.
Value 4s.

5 Robert holds 1 c. of land in COTES (de Val) from the Bishop.
2 ploughs possible. They are there, with
4 Freemen.
The value was 20d; now 10s.

6 Ralph also holds 4 c. of land in POULTNEY from the Bishop. Land
for 4 ploughs. In lordship 2; 4 male and 1 female slaves.
9 villagers and 9 burgesses in the City with
5 smallholders have 2 ploughs.
Meadow, 2 acres.
The value was 20s; now 30s.

Idē ten de epo in *MINISTONE*.iii.car træ.|7 unā car træ

q̃ redđ focā.Tra.ē.iii.car.Ibi.iiii.uiłłi cū.ii.fochis 7 i.uiłło

7 i.borđ hñt.ii.car.Ibi.vi.ać p̃ti.Valuit.xi.foł.m̃.x.foł.

Idē ten de epo in *WALECOTE*.iiii.car træ.7 ii.car tre q̃ redđt

focā.Tra.ē.iii.car.In dñio.ē una cū.i.feruo.7 iii.uiłłi cū

.i.borđ hñt.i.car.7 ii.fochi hñt.i.car.Ibi molin de.x.den.

7 xii.ać p̃ti.Valuit.x.folid.Modo.xx.folid.

Idē ten de epo in *CHENEMVNDESCOTE*.xiii.car træ 7 dim.

Tra.ē.viii.car.In dñio.ē una.7 vi.fochi 7 vi.uiłłi cū.vii.

borđ hñt.iiii.car.Ibi.x.ać p̃ti.Valuit.xxx.foł.m̃.xl.foł.

Vlf ten de eođ Rađ.ii.bouatas træ.in *SVINEFORD*.7 ualet

Has tras Radulfi tenuit Godric T.R.E. ⌐xii.den.

Rannulf ten de epo in *HALIACH* *IN GERETREV WAP*.

iii.car træ.In dñio st.ii.car.cū.i.feruo.7 iiii.uiłłi cū.ii.

borđ hñt.i.car.Ibi molin de.v.foł 7 iiii.den.Silua.iiii.

q̃rent lḡ.7 iii.q̃z lat.Valuit 7 uał.xx.foł.Bardi tenuit

Godefrid ten de epo.viii.car træ in *DALBI*. *IN GOSECOT WAP*.

Tra.ē.vi.car.In dñio st.iii.car.7 ii.ferui.7 vii.uiłłi 7 xvi.

fochi hñt.vi.car.Ibi.vi.q̃rent p̃ti in lḡ 7 in lat.

Valuit.lx.foł.Modo.lxx.Godric tenuit cū faca 7 foca.

In ipfa uilla ten un miles.i.car træ.7 uał.x.foł.

Roger ten de epo.iiii.car træ.in *CROCHESTONE*.In dñio

ē.i.car.7 iiii.uiłłi cū.ii.borđ hñt.i.car.Ibi molin de.xii.

den.7 vi.ać p̃ti.Valuit.v.foł.Modo.xx.foł.Godric tenuit.

7   He also holds 3½ c. of land in MISTERTON from the Bishop.
and 1 c. of land which pays jurisdiction. Land for 3 ploughs.
   4 villagers with 2 Freemen, 1 villager and
     1 smallholder have 2 ploughs.
   Meadow, 6 acres.
The value was 11s; now 10s.

8   He also holds 4 c. of land in WALCOTE from the Bishop and
2 c. of land which pays jurisdiction. Land for 3 ploughs.
In lordship 1, with 1 slave.
   3 villagers with 1 smallholder have 1 plough;
     2 Freemen have 1 plough.
   A mill at 10d; meadow, 12 acres.
The value was 10s; now 20s.

9   He also holds 13½ c. of land in KIMCOTE from the Bishop.
Land for 8 ploughs.   In lordship 1.
   6 Freemen and 6 villagers with 7 smallholders have 4 ploughs.
   Meadow, 10 acres.
The value was 30s; now 40s.

10  Ulf holds 2 b. of land in SWINFORD from the same Ralph.
Value 12d.
   Godric held these lands from Ralph before 1066.

In GARTREE Wapentake
11  Ranulf holds 3 c. of land in HOLYOAKS from the Bishop.
In lordship 2 ploughs, with 1 slave.
   4 villagers with 2 smallholders have 1 plough.
   A mill at 5s 4d; woodland 4 furlongs long and 3 furlongs wide.
The value was and is 20s.
   Bardi held it.

In GOSCOTE Wapentake
12  Godfrey holds 8 c. of land in (Great) DALBY from the Bishop.
Land for 6 ploughs.   In lordship 3 ploughs; 2 slaves.
   7 villagers and 16 Freemen have 6 ploughs.
   Meadow 6 furlongs in length and in width.
The value was 60s; now 70s.
   Godric held it with full jurisdiction.
   In the same village 1 man-at-arms holds 1 c. of land.
Value 10s.

13  Roger holds 4 c. of land in (South) CROXTON from the Bishop.
In lordship 1 plough.
   4 villagers with 2 smallholders have 1 plough.
   A mill at 12d; meadow, 6 acres.
The value was 5s; now 20s.
   Godric held it.

Radulf ten de epo in *Brantestone* *In Frandone Wap.*

vii.car træ 7 dimid.In dnio st.ii,car 7 iiii.serui.7 x.uilli
cu.i.bord 7 vi.sochis hnt.iiii.car. Ibi.ii.molini de.viii.
sol.7 xvi.ac pti.Valuit.xx.sol.Modo.l.sol.Leuenot te nuit.

★ R fili Walterii ten de epo in *Bvcheminstre*
.ix.car træ 7 dimid.Tra.e.viii.car.In dnio st.ii.7 viii.
uilli 7 xx.sochi cu.iii.bord hnt.viii.car.Ibi.lii.ac pti.
Valuit.iiii.sol.Modo.iiii.lib.Alden tenuit cu saca 7 soca.

Chetelbern ten de epo.i.car træ in *Holewelle*.Tra.e
.i.car.Hanc hnt ibi.iii.uilli cu.ii.bord.Ibi.x.ac pti.
Valuit.v.sol.Modo.vi.sol.Vlfiet tenuit cu saca 7 soca.


## IIII. TERRA EPI CONSTANTIENS. *In Gvtlacistan Wap.*

Eps Constantiensis ten in *Erendesberie*.ii.car træ
7 dimid.7 una bouat.Vlfric ten de eo.Tra.e.ii.car 7 dimid.
In dnio.e una.cu.i.seruo.7 iii.uilli 7 ii.bord hnt.i.car.
Valet.xx.solid.

231 b

## .V. TERRA SCI PETRI DE BVRG.

Abbatia De Bvrch ten in *Langetone*.v.car træ
ii.bouatas min.Tra.e.v.car.In dnio.e una.7 ix.uilli
cu.ii.bord hnt.iii.car.Ibi.viii.ac pti.7 v.ac siluæ.
Valuit.x.sol.Modo.xl.solid.Ailmar libe tenuit.T.R.E.
Ipsa abbatia ten in *Estone*.xii.car træ.Tra.e.xvi.car.
In dnio st.ii.car.7 x.uilli cu.v.bord 7 xii.sochis hnt
viii.car.Silua ibi dim leu lg.7 iiii.qrent lat.Ibi.xxx.
ac pti.Valuit.vi.lib.Modo.c.solid.Radulf comes
dedit S Petro.

In FRAMLAND Wapentake

14  Ralph holds 7½ c. of land in BRANSTON from the Bishop.
In lordship 2 ploughs; 4 slaves.
    10 villagers with 1 smallholder and 6 Freemen have 4 ploughs.
    2 mills at 8s; meadow, 16 acres.
The value was 20s; now 50s.
    Leofnoth held it.

15  R..... son of Walter holds 9½ c. of land in BUCKMINSTER from the
Bishop. Land for 8 ploughs. In lordship 2.
    8 villagers and 20 Freemen with 3 smallholders have 8 ploughs.
    Meadow, 52 acres.
The value was 4s; now £4.
    Haldane held it with full jurisdiction.

16  Ketelbern holds 1 c. of land in HOLWELL from the Bishop.
Land for 1 plough.
    3 villagers with 2 smallholders have it.
    Meadow, 10 acres.
The value was 5s; now 6s.
    Wulfgeat held it with full jurisdiction.

# 4    LAND OF THE BISHOP OF COUTANCES

In GUTHLAXTON Wapentake

1   In ARNESBY the Bishop of Coutances holds 2½ c. and 1 b.
of land. Wulfric holds from him. Land for 2½ ploughs.
In lordship 1, with 1 slave.
    3 villagers and 2 smallholders have 1 plough.
Value 20s.

# 5    LAND OF PETERBOROUGH (ABBEY)    231 b

[In GARTREE Wapentake]

1   Peterborough Abbey holds 5c. of land less 2 b. in (East) LANGTON.
Land for 5 ploughs. In lordship 1.
    9 villagers with 2 smallholders have 3 ploughs.
    Meadow, 8 acres; woodland, 5 acres.
The value was 10s; now 40s.
    Aelmer held it freely before 1066.

2   The Abbey also holds 12 c. of land in (Great) EASTON.
Land for 16 ploughs. In lordship 2 ploughs.
    10 villagers with 5 smallholders and 12 Freemen have 8 ploughs.
    Woodland ½ league long and 4 furlongs wide; meadow, 30 acres.
The value was £6; now 100s.
    Earl Ralph gave it to St. Peter's;

Duo milites teñ in hac uilla . ii . car̄ træ de abb̄e . Ibi . x . uilli
hñt . ii . car̄ . 7 x . ac̄s p̄ti . Valuit . xl . ſol . Modo . c . ſol .

## .VI. TERRA S̄ MARIE DE COVENTREV. *In Gvtlacistan Wap̄.*

Abbatia de Coventrev teñ *Bvrbece* . Ibi . e̅ . i . hida . 7 iiii.
pars . i . hidæ . Ibi s̄t . xxii . car̄ træ 7 dimid . In dñio s̄t . ii . car̄ .
7 xx . uilli cū . ii . bord 7 ii . ſeruis hñt . viii . car̄ . Ibi . p̄tū
una q̄rent l̄g . 7 tñtđ lat̄ . Silua dim leu l̄g . 7 iiii . q̄ʒ lat̄ .
Valuit . ii . ſoliđ q̄do abb̄ recepit . Modo . iiii . lib̄ .
Ipſa abbatia teñ . iii . car̄ træ in *Mersitone* . Tra . e̅ . ii . car̄ .
Has hñt ibi . iii . ſochi cū . v . bord . Ibi . viii . ac̄ p̄ti .
Valuit . xii . deñ . Modo . x . ſoliđ .
Ipſa abbatia teñ . iiii . car̄ træ in *Barewelle* . Valet . xxx . ſol ,
In dñio . e̅ . i . car̄ . 7 xiiii . uilli cū p̄bro 7 iii . bord hñt . ii . car̄ .
Ibi p̄tū . i . q̄rent l̄g . 7 tñtđ lat̄ . Silua . i . leu l̄g . 7 iii . q̄ʒ lat̄ .
In ipſa uilla s̄t . viii . ſochi hñtes . v . car̄ . ꝛ hic . e̅ ſup̄ſcripta .
Ad hanc uillā ptiñ . i . car̄ træ in *Stapletone* . cuj pecunia
Ipſa abbatia teñ *Scrapentot* . *In Geretrev Wapent̄.*
Ibi s̄t . xii . car̄ træ . In dñio s̄t . ii . car̄ . 7 iiii . ſerui . 7 vii . uilli
cū . vi . ſochis 7 iii . bord hñt . v . car̄ . Ibi . x . ac̄ p̄ti .
Valuit . ii . ſoliđ . Modo . xl . ſoliđ . *In Gosencote Wapent̄.*
Ipſa abbatia teñ . viii . car̄ træ 7 dim in *Pachintone* .
In dñio . e̅ . i . car̄ . 7 iii . uilli cū p̄bro 7 i . bord 7 v . ſochis hñt
iii . car̄ . Ibi moliñ de . xii . deñ . 7 iii . ac̄ p̄ti . Valet . xx . ſol .
In *Cherchebi* teñ Hugo . i . car̄ træ 7 dim de abb̄e .
Valet . ii . ſoliđ .

**39** In this village 2 men-at-arms hold 2 c. of land from the Abbot.
  10 villagers have 2 ploughs.
  Meadow, 10 acres.
The value was 40s; now 100s.

# 6 LAND OF ST. MARY'S COVENTRY

In GUTHLAXTON Wapentake

**1** Coventry Abbey holds BURBAGE. 1 hide and the fourth part
of 1 hide. 22½ c. of land. In lordship 2 ploughs.
  20 villagers with 2 smallholders and 2 slaves have 8 ploughs.
  Meadow 1 furlong long and as much wide; woodland ½ league
    long and 4 furlongs wide.
The value was 2s when the Abbey acquired it; now £4.

**2** The Abbey holds 3 c. of land itself in (Potters) MARSTON.
Land for 2 ploughs.
  3 Freemen with 5 smallholders have them.
  Meadow, 8 acres.
The value was 12d; now 10s.

**3** The Abbey holds 4 c. of land itself in BARWELL.
In lordship 1 plough.
  14 villagers with a priest and 3 smallholders have 2 ploughs.
  Meadow 1 furlong long and as much wide; woodland 1
    league long and 3 furlongs wide.
Value 30s.

**4** In the same village are 8 Freemen who have 5 ploughs.
To this village belongs 1 c. of land in Stapleton, whose stock is
entered above.

In GARTREE Wapentake

**5** The Abbey holds SCRAPTOFT itself. 12 c. of land.
In lordship 2 ploughs; 4 slaves.
  7 villagers with 6 Freemen and 3 smallholders have 5 ploughs.
  Meadow, 10 acres.
The value was 2s; now 40s.

In GOSCOTE Wapentake

**6** The Abbey holds 8½ c. of land itself in PACKINGTON.
In lordship 1 plough.
  3 villagers with a priest, 1 smallholder and 5
    Freemen have 3 ploughs.
  A mill at 12d; meadow, 3 acres.
Value 20s.

[In GUTHLAXTON Wapentake]

**7** In KIRBY (Mallory) Hugh holds 1½ c. of land from the Abbot.
Value 2s.

## .VII. Terra Æcclæ De Crviland. *In Gvtlacistan Wap.*

Abbatia De Crviland ten.ii.car træ in *Svtone.*

7 ii.car træ in *Stapletone.* Tra.ē.v.car. Ibi.vi.uitti

cū.ii.borđ hūt.i.car 7 dimiđ.Valuit.xxiiii.fot.M.xx.fot.

Ipfa abbatia ten in *Bebi*.x.car træ 7 dimiđ.Tra.ē.vii.

car.In dūio.ē una.7 ii.ferui.7 xxi.uitts cū.v.fochis

7 iii.borđ hūt.vi.car.Ibi.xxx.ač pti.

Valuit.lx.fot.Modo.xl.foliđ.


## .VIII.     Elemosinæ Regis.

Godvinvs pbr ten de rege in *Petlinge* dim car træ.7 ibi hĩ dim

car.7 i.ačm pti.7 dim.Valuit 7 uat.v.foliđ.

Vxor qntini ten de rege.ii.car træ in *Svesbi*.7 alias.ii in *Svton*

In his hĩ.ii.borđ.Tra.ē.ii.car.Valb.xv.fot.modo.iii.fot.

Ingald ten de rege in *Elvestone*.ii.car træ 7 unā v.Ibi hĩ.i.car.

7 ii.uitti cū.i.focħo hūt dim car.Valuit.x.foliđ.Modo.v.foliđ.

Ernebern pbr ten de rege.ii.car træ 7 dim in *Svinford*

7 ibi hĩ.i.car cū.ii.borđ.7 iii.ačs pti.Valet.v.foliđ.

Aluric pbr ten de rege in *Wicestan*.ii.car tre.ptin ad *Scene*

*ford*.Ibi hĩ.i.car.7 v.borđ ej hūt aliā.Ibi.iiii.ač pti.

Valuit 7 uat.xx.foliđ.

231 c

## IX. Terra Comitis De Mellend. *In Gvtlacistan Wap.*

Comes De Mellend tenet de rege *Ailestone.*

Ibi.ē.i.hida.7 vi.pars.i.hidæ.Ibi fuer.xiiii.car

T.R.E.In dūio st.ii.car.7 i.ancilla.7 xxiiii.uitti cū

.v.borđ hūt.v.car.Ibi.iiii.molini de.xlviii.fot.

.7 lv.ač pti.Valuit.iii.lib.Modo.iiii.lib.

# 7      LAND OF CROWLAND CHURCH

In GUTHLAXTON Wapentake
1    Crowland Abbey holds 2 c. of land in SUTTON (Cheney) and
2 c. of land in STAPLETON. Land for 5 ploughs.
    6 villagers with 2 smallholders have 1½ ploughs.
The value was 24s; now 20s.

[In GOSCOTE Wapentake]
2    The Abbey holds 10½ c. of land in BEEBY itself. Land for 7
ploughs. In lordship 1; 2 slaves.
    21 villagers with 5 Freemen and 3 smallholders have 6 ploughs.
    Meadow, 30 acres.
The value was 60s; now 40s.

# 8      THE KING'S ALMS (LANDS)

[In GUTHLAXTON Wapentake]
1    Godwin the priest holds ½ c. of land in PEATLING (Magna) from
the King. He has ½ plough.
    Meadow, 1½ acres.
The value was and is 5s.

2    Quentin's wife holds 2 c. of land in SHEARSBY from the King and
another 2 (c.) in SUTTON (-in-the-Elms). In them she has 2
smallholders. Land for 2 ploughs.
The value was 15s; now 3s.

[In GARTREE Wapentake]
3    Ingold holds 2 c. and 1 virgate of land in ILLSTON (-on-the-Hill)
from the King. He has 1 plough.
    2 villagers with 1 Freeman have ½ plough.
The value was 10s; now 5s.

[In GUTHLAXTON Wapentake]
4    Arnbern the priest holds 2½ c. of land in SWINFORD from the King.
He has 1 plough, with
    2 smallholders.
    Meadow, 3 acres.
Value 5s.

5    Aelfric the priest holds 2 c. of land in WIGSTON (Parva) from the
King which belongs to Sharnford. He has 1 plough.
    5 of his smallholders have another.
    Meadow, 4 acres.
The value was and is 20s.

# 9      LAND OF THE COUNT OF MEULAN      231 c

In GUTHLAXTON Wapentake
1    The Count of Meulan holds AYLESTONE from the King. 1 hide
and the sixth part of 1 hide. Before 1066 there were 14 ploughs.
In lordship 2 ploughs; 1 female slave.
    24 villagers with 5 smallholders have 5 ploughs.
    4 mills at 48s; meadow, 55 acres.
The value was £3; now £4.

Saxi tenuit.7 Leuuin de eo tr̄a.vi.car̄       ita q̄d ★

de.iiii.ex his poterat facere q̄d uoleƀ.De.ii.̄ non ita.

Ipſe cōm ten̄ FRELLESWORDE.Ibi.ē dim car̄ træ.Ibi

ii.ſocħi hn̄t dimid car̄.Valuit.ii.ſot.Modo.v.ſolid.

Idē.Co.ten̄.vi.car̄ træ in HVNECOTE.Tra.ē.vi.car̄.

In dn̄io ſt̄.iii.7 ii.ſerui 7 i.ancilla.7 xx.uiłti cū.viii.

borđ hn̄t.iii.car̄.7 ii.ſocħi.cū pƀro ſt̄ ibi.7 molinū

de.x.ſot.7 xv.ac̄ pti.Silua dim leu l̄g.7 iiii.q̄ƶ lat̄.

Valuit.xv.ſot.Modo.iiii.liƀ.

In COSBI.ē una car̄ tre.quæ jacet in HVNECOTE.

Idē.Co.ten̄.vi.car̄ træ in BOSEWORDE.In dn̄io ſt̄

iii.car̄.7 ii.ſerui.7 vii.ſocħi cū.x.uiłtis 7 vii.borđ

hn̄t.ii.car̄.Silua.i.leu l̄g.7 dim leu lat̄.

Valuit.iiii.liƀ.Modo.L.ſolid.

Has tras ōms tenuit Saxi.7 potuit ire quó uoluit.

## X. TERRA ALBERICI COMITIS. *In GVTLACISTAN WAP.*

Comes ALBERICVS tenuit CNAPETOT.Ibi ſt̄

ii.partes uni hiđæ.Tra.ē.vi.car̄.In dn̄io.ē una.

7 iii.ſerui.7 x.uiłti cū pƀro 7 vi.borđ hn̄t.v.car̄. *7 ii.ſocħis*

Ibi ptū.iii.q̄rent l̄g.7 ii.q̄ƶ lat̄.Valuit.xx.ſolid.

Modo.L.ſolid.

Idē tenuit SCEPECOTE.Ibi.ē.i.car̄ træ 7 dim.Ibi.ē

una car̄ 7 dim cū.ii.ſocħis 7 ii.borđ.Vluric tenet.

Valuit.ii.ſot.Modo.x.ſolid.

Idē.Co.tenuit HINCHELIE.Ibi ſt̄.xiiii.car̄ træ.In

dn̄io ſt̄.iiii.car̄.7 viii.ſerui.7 xlii.uiłti cū.xvi.borđ

7 iii.ſocħis hn̄t.ix.car̄ 7 dim.Ibi ptū.vi.q̄ƶ in l̄g.

7 iii.q̄ƶ lat̄.Silua.i.leu l̄g.7 iii.q̄ƶ lat̄.

Valuit.vi.liƀ.Modo.x.liƀ.

Saxi held it and Leofwin (held) land for 6 ploughs from him
so that with 4 of them he could do what he wished; with 2 not so.

2   The Count holds FROLESWORTH himself. ½ c. of land.
      2 Freemen have ½ plough.
      The value was 2s; now 5s.

3   The Count also holds 6 c. of land in HUNCOTE.   Land for 6 ploughs.
      In lordship 3; 2 male and 1 female slaves.
        20 villagers with 8 smallholders have 3 ploughs.
          2 Freemen with a priest.
        A mill at 10s; meadow, 15 acres; woodland ½ league long
          and 4 furlongs wide.
      The value was 15s; now £4.

4   In COSBY 1 c. of land which lies in Huncote.

5   The Count also holds 6 c. of land in in (Market) BOSWORTH.
      In lordship 3 ploughs; 2 slaves.
        7 Freemen with 10 villagers and 7 smallholders have 2 ploughs.
        Woodland 1 league long and ½ league wide.
      The value was £4, now 50s.
        Saxi held all these lands and could go where he would.

# 0           LAND OF EARL AUBREY

In GUTHLAXTON Wapentake

1   Earl Aubrey held KNAPTOFT.   2 parts of 1 hide.   Land for 6 ploughs.
      In lordship 1; 3 slaves.
        10 villagers with a priest, 2 Freemen and 6 smallholders
          have 5 ploughs.
        Meadow 3 furlongs long and 2 furlongs wide.
      The value was 20s; now 50s.

2   He also held SAPCOTE. 1½ c. of land. 1½ ploughs, with
        2 Freemen and 2 smallholders.
        Wulfric holds it.
      The value was 2s; now 10s.

3   The Earl also held HINCKLEY.   14 c. of land.   In lordship
      4 ploughs; 8 slaves.
        42 villagers with 16 smallholders and 3 Freemen have
          9½ ploughs.
        Meadow 6 furlongs in length and 3 furlongs wide;
          woodland 1 league long and 3 furlongs wide.
      The value was £6; now £10.

Idē.Co.tenuit.ix.car̄ træ in *SIBETESDONE*.In dñio

st̄.ii.car̄.7 i.ancilla.7 xxx.uilti 7 xvii.bord̄ hn̄t.vii.

car̄.p̄tu.iii.q̄ȝ lḡ.7 ii.q̄ȝ lat̄.In ead̄ uilla st̄ adhuc

ii.car̄ træ.Tot̄ ualuit.lx.solid̄.Modo.c.solid̄.

Idē.Co.tenuit.i.car̄ træ in *SCENTONE*.Ibi st̄.iii.bord̄.

Valuit.xii.den̄.Modo.iii.solid̄.Harding tenuit has

                        Ł tras.

Normann ten.iiii.car̄ træ 7 dim in *SVEVESBI*.In dñio

st̄.ii.car̄.7 iiii.uilti cū.ii.sochis 7 iii.bord̄ hn̄t.ii.car̄.

p̄tū.iiii.q̄ȝ lḡ.7 ii.q̄ȝ lat̄.Valuit.xv.sot̄.Modo.xl.sot̄.

Radulf ten in *CREBRE*.iiii.car̄ tre 7 dim.7 i.bouat̄ā.

In dñio.ē.i.car̄.7 ii.serui.7 viii.uilti cū.i.socho 7 iiii.

bord̄ hn̄t.ii.car̄.Ibi molin de.iiii.sot̄.7 xii..ac̄ p̄ti.

Valuit.lxviii.denar̄.Modo.xl.solid̄.

Huic M̄ p̄tin.i.car̄ træ.Pars ej in Brotone 7 pars in

Sutone.Vasta fuit.Modo uat̄.v.solid̄.

231 d

Almar ten.v.car̄ tre 7 dim in *DRAITONE*.Tra.ē.v.car̄.

In dñio st̄.ii.7 xiiii.uilti cū.viii.bord̄ hn̄t.iiii.car̄.

Valuit.xxx.solid̄.Modo.xl.sot̄.

Robt ten.viii.car̄ træ 7 dim in *BETMESWEL*.Tra.ē

vi.car̄.In dñio.ē una.7 ii.uilti cū p̄bro 7 xiiii.bord̄ hn̄t

iii.car̄.p̄tū.iiii.q̄ȝ lḡ.7 una q̄ȝ lat̄.Valuit.x.sot̄.

Idē ten.i.car̄ træ 7 dimid in *SVINFORD*.  Ł m̄.xl.sot̄.

Tra.ē.ii.car̄.Ibi.ē molin de.iiii.sot̄.cū.i.seruo.7 iii.

ac̄ p̄ti.Valuit.ii.sot̄.Modo.v.solid̄.

Normann ten.iiii.car̄ tre 7 dim in *WALTONE*.Tra.ē

ii.car̄.Has hn̄t ibi.x.sochi.p̄tū.i.q̄ȝ lḡ.7 una lat̄.

Valuit.x.sot̄.Modo.xxv.solid̄.

Idē ten.vi.car̄ træ 7 dim in *TEVLINGORDE*.Tra.ē.vi.

car̄.In dñio st̄.ii.7 viii.uilti cū.x.bord̄ hn̄t.ii.car̄.

Ibi molin de.ii.solid̄.Valuit.xx.sot̄.Modo.xl.sot̄.

4 The Earl also held 9 c. of land in SIBSON.
In lordship 2 ploughs; 1 female slave.
   30 villagers and 17 smallholders have 7 ploughs.
   Meadow 3 furlongs long and 2 furlongs wide.
   In the same village are a further 2 c. of land.
The value of the whole was 60s; now 100s.

5 The Earl also held 1 c. of land in SHENTON.
   3 smallholders.
The value was 12d; now 3s.
   Harding held these lands.

6 Norman holds 4½ c. of land in SHEARSBY. In lordship 2 ploughs.
   4 villagers with 2 Freemen and 3 smallholders have 2 ploughs.
   Meadow 4 furlongs long and 2 furlongs wide.
The value was 15s; now 40s.

7 Ralph holds 4½ c. and 1 b. of land in CROFT.
In lordship 1 plough; 2 slaves.
   8 villagers with 1 Freeman and 4 smallholders have 2 ploughs.
   A mill at 4s; meadow, 12 acres.
The value was 68d; now 40s.
   To this manor belongs 1 c. of land; part of it is in Broughton
(Astley) and part in Sutton (in the Elms).
It was waste; value now, 5s.

8 Aelmer holds 5½ c. of land in (Fenny)DRAYTON.                231 d
Land for 5 ploughs. In lordship 2.
   14 villagers with 8 smallholders have 4 ploughs.
The value was 30s; now 40s.

9 Robert holds 8½ c. of land in BITTESWELL.   Land for 6 ploughs.
In lordship 1.
   2 villagers with a priest and 14 smallholders have 3 ploughs.
   Meadow 4 furlongs long and 1 furlong wide.
The value was 10s; now 40s.

0 He also holds 1½ c. of land in SWINFORD.   Land for 2 ploughs.
   A mill at 4s, with 1 slave.
   Meadow, 3 acres.
The value was 2s; now 5s.

1 Norman holds 4½ c. of land in WALTON (by Kimcote). Land for 2 ploughs.
   10 Freemen have them.
   Meadow 1 furlong long and 1 wide.
The value was 10s; now 25s.

[In GARTREE Wapentake]

12 He also holds 6½ c. of land in THEDDINGWORTH. Land for 6 ploughs.
In lordship 2.
   8 villagers with 10 smallholders have 2 ploughs.
   A mill at 2s.
The value was 20s; now 40s.

231 c, d

Idē ten̄. iii. car̄ træ 7 ii. bouat̄ in *TEVLINGORDE*. Tra.ē
iii. car̄. Ibi. vii. foc̄hi hn̄t. i. car̄ 7 dimiđ.

Valuit. x. fot. Modo. xx. foliđ.

Radulf⁹ ten̄. ii. car̄ træ in *TORP*. Tra.ē. ii. car̄. Has
hn̄t ibi. ii. uitti cū. i. borđ. 7 moliñ ibi de. ii. foliđ.

Valuit. x. fot. Modo. xx. foliđ.

Radulf⁹ carnot ten̄. iiii. car̄ træ in *ANELEPE*.
Tra.ē. iiii. car̄. In dn̄io.ē una. 7 viii. uitti cū. iii. borđ
hn̄t. iii. car̄. Ibi moliñ de. viii. foliđ. 7 xxii. ac̄ p̄ti.

Valuit. x. fot. Modo. xxv. foliđ.

Idē ten̄. xi. car̄ træ in *SEOLDESBERIE*. Tra.ē. xi. car̄.
In dn̄io.ē una. 7 iiii. uitti 7 viii. foc̄hi cū. ii. borđ hn̄t
ix. car̄. p̄tū. v. q̄rent lḡ. 7 iii. q̄ɀ lat̄. Valuit. xx. foliđ.

Idē ten̄. vii. ear̄ træ in *WALETONE*. ⌐ Modo. xxx. fot.
In dn̄io.ē una car̄. 7 vii. foc̄hi cū. ii. uittis 7 i. borđ hn̄t
iiii. car̄. Ibi. xxx. ac̄ p̄ti. Valuit. xxxii. den̄. M̊. xxx. fot.
Has tras tenuit ōms Harding cū hōibɀ fuis. 7 Albicus
poftea habuit. Modo ſt̄ in manu regis.

## .XI. TERRA GODEVÆ COMITISSÆ.

Comitissa GODEVA tenuit *NORTONE*. Ibi. vi. car̄ træ.
Tra.ē. vii. car̄. In dn̄io ſt̄. iii. car̄. Ibi p̄br cū. i. uitto
7 ii. borđ hn̄t. i. car̄. Ibi. viii. ac̄ p̄ti. Valuit. v. fot. M̊. vi. fot.
Ipfa. Co. tenuit. iii. car̄ træ in *APLEBI*. Tra.ē. iii. car̄.
In dn̄io ſt̄. ii. car̄. 7 viii. uitti cū. vi. borđ hn̄t. ii. car̄.

Valuit 7 ualet. xx. foliđ.

Ipfa Co. tenuit. i. car̄ træ 7 dim̄ in *BILDESTONE*. Ibi
funt. iii. foc̄hi cū. i. car̄. T.R.E. erant. ii. car̄ ibi.

Valuit 7 uat̄. v. foliđ.

13  He also holds 3 c. and 2 b. of land in THEDDINGWORTH.
Land for 3 ploughs.
    7 Freemen have 1½ ploughs.
The value was 10s; now 20s.

[In GUTHLAXTON Wapentake]

14  Ralph holds 2 c. of land in (Little) THORPE.  Land for 2 ploughs.
    2 villagers with 1 smallholder have them.
    A mill at 2s.
The value was 10s; now 20s.

[In GOSCOTE Wapentake]

15  Ralph of Chartres holds 4c. of land in WANLIP. Land for 4 ploughs.
In lordship 1.
    8 villagers with 3 smallholders have 3 ploughs.
    A mill at 8s; meadow, 32 acres.
The value was 10s; now 25s.

16  He also holds 11 c. of land in SHOBY.  Land for 11 ploughs.
In lordship 1.
    4 villagers and 8 Freemen with 2 smallholders have 9 ploughs.
    Meadow  5 furlongs long and 3 furlongs wide.
The value was 20s; now 30s.

17  He also holds 7 c. of land in WALTON (on the Wolds).
In lordship 1 plough.
    7 Freemen with 2 villagers and 1 smallholder have 4 ploughs.
    Meadow, 30 acres.
The value was 32d; now 30s.
    Harding held all these lands with his men. Earl Aubrey
held them later; they are now in the King's hands.

# 11         LAND OF COUNTESS GODIVA

[In GUTHLAXTON Wapentake]

1  Countess Godiva held NORTON (juxta Twycross).  6 c. of land.
Land for 7 ploughs.  In lordship 3 ploughs.
    A priest with 1 villager and 2 smallholders have 1 plough.
    Meadow, 8 acres.
The value was 5s; now 6s.

2  The Countess held 3 c. of land herself in APPLEBY.  Land for 3 ploughs.
In lordship 2 ploughs.
    8 villagers with 6 smallholders have 2 ploughs.
The value was and is 20s.

3  The Countess held 1½ c. of land herself in BILSTONE.
    3 Freemen with 1 plough.  Before 1066, 2 ploughs.
The value was and is 5s.

## .XII. TERRA ALVEVE COMITISSÆ.

COMITISSA ALVEVA tenuit.v.car̆ træ in *AILESTONE*.

T.R.E.erant ibi.xii.car̆.In dn̄io st̄ m̆.ii.cū.i.feruo.

7 xviii.uitti cū.i.focħo 7 viii.bord hn̄t.vi.car̆.

Valuit 7 uat.c.7 x.fot.     *IN GOSECOTE WAPENT̆*.

Ipfa.Co.tenuit *DVNITONE*.Ibi xxii.car̆ træ 7 dimid̆.

T.R.E.erant xx.car̆ ibi.Modo in dn̄io st̄.iii.7 xxx.uitti

cū pb̆ro 7 v.fochis 7 xi.bord hn̄t.xii.car̆.Ibi molin̄

de x.fot 7 viii.den̆.Silua.xii.q̃ʒ lḡ.7 viii.lat̆.

Valuit.c.fot.Modo.xi.lib̆.

232 a

## .XIII TERRA HVGON̆ DE GRENTEMAIS IN GVTLACISTAN WAP̆.

HVGO De Grentemaifnil ten̆ de rege *WICHINGES*

*TONE*.Ibi.ē.i.hida 7 tcia pars.i.hidæ.Tra.ē.xvi.car̆.

De hac tra.ē in dn̄io.i.hidæ.7 ibi.iiii.car̆.7 ii.ferui

7 una ancilla.7 xxxii.uitti cū pb̆ro 7 xii.bord hn̄t.v.car̆.

Ibi.xxxi.focħ cū.i.clerico 7 ii.militib̆ 7 iiii.franciğ hōib̆

hn̄t.viii.car̆.Ibi.l.ac̆ p̆ti.Valuit 7 uat.viii.lib̆.

Radulf comes tenuit.

Ide ten̆.i.car̆ træ in *SAPECOTE*.Tra.ē.ii.car̆.In dn̄io

ē una.7 iii.uitti cū.iii.focħ 7 ii.bord hn̄t dim̆ car̆.Ibi

.ii.ac̆ p̆ti.Valet.x.fot.     ꝼIbi st̄.iii.bord.Vat.v.fot.

Ibi p̆tin̆.i.car̆ træ in *FRELESWORDE*.Tra.ē dim car̆.

Ide ten̆ de feudo reginæ ut dicit.ii.car̆ træ in *SCERNEFORD*.

Tra.ē.i.car̆.Ibi.i.focħs cū.iii.bord ht̄ dim̆ car̆.Valuit

xii.den̆.Modo.x.folid̆.Aluuin̆ tenuit cū faca 7 foca.

Ide ten̆.v.car̆ træ in *SCELTONE*.In dn̄io st̄.iii.car̆.

cū.i.feruo.7 x.uitti cū pb̆ro 7 iiii.focħ 7 v.bord hn̄t.iii.

car̆.Ibi.xii.ac̆ p̆ti.7 molin̄ de.xvi.den̆.Silua.viii.

q̆rent̆ lḡ.7 iii.lat̆.Valuit.v.fot.Modo.lxx.folid̆.

# 12 LAND OF COUNTESS AELFEVA

1 Countess Aelfeva held 5 c. of land in AYLESTONE.
Before 1066, 12 ploughs. In lordship now 2, with 1 slave.
18 villagers with 1 Freeman and 8 smallholders have 6 ploughs.
The value was and is 110s.

In GOSCOTE Wapentake

2 The Countess held (Castle) DONINGTON herself. 22½ c. of land.
Before 1066, 20 ploughs. Now in lordship 3.
30 villagers with a priest, 5 Freemen and 11 smallholders
have 12 ploughs.
A mill at 10s 8d; woodland 12 furlongs long and 8 wide.
The value was 100s; now £11.

# 13 LAND OF HUGH OF GRANDMESNIL 232 a

In GUTHLAXTON Wapentake

1 Hugh of Grandmesnil holds WIGSTON (Magna) from the King.
1 hide there and the third part of 1 hide. Land for 16 ploughs.
Of this land the third part of 1 hide in lordship. 4 ploughs;
2 male and 1 female slaves.
32 villagers with a priest and 12 smallholders have 5 ploughs;
31 Freemen with 1 cleric, 2 men-at-arms and 4 French men
have 8 ploughs.
Meadow, 50 acres.
The value was and is £8.
Earl Ralph held it.

He also holds

2 in SAPCOTE 1 c. of land. Land for 2 ploughs. In lordship 1.
3 villagers with 3 Freemen and 2 smallholders have ½ plough.
Meadow, 2 acres.
Value 10s.
1 c. of land in FROLESWORTH belongs there. Land for ½ plough.
3 smallholders.
Value 5s.

3 in SHARNFORD 2 c. of land from the Queen's Holding as he states.
Land for 1 plough.
1 Freeman with 3 smallholders has ½ plough.
The value was 12d; now 10s.
Alwin held it with full jurisdiction.

4 in (Earl) SHILTON 5 c. of land. In lordship 3 ploughs, with 1 slave.
10 villagers with a priest, 4 Freemen and 5 smallholders
have 3 ploughs.
Meadow, 12 acres; a mill at 16d; woodland 8 furlongs long
and 3 wide.
The value was 5s; now 70s.

Idē ten in *ROTERIE* . vi . car træ . iii . bouat min . Tra.ē.vi.

car . In dñio st . ii . car cū . i . seruo . 7 x . uilli cū pbro . 7 v .

bord hñt . iiii . car . Ibi moliñ de . xxviii . den . Valuit . xx .

sol . Modo . lx . solid .

De soca har . ii . car træ st in Brunechinestorp . 7 iii . in Deres

ford . 7 dimid in Clanefelde . 7 dim in Brantestone .

Idē ten in *GROBI* . vi . car træ . iii . bouat min . Tra . ē . iiii .

car . In dñio st . ii . 7 x . uilli cū . i . socho 7 v . bord hñt . iiii .

car . Silua ibi . ii . leu lg . 7 dim leu lat . Valuit . xx . sol .

Modo . lx . solid . Vlf tenuit has . ii . tras cū saca 7 soca .

Idē ten in *CHEREBI* . ii . car træ . Tra . ē . i . car . Hec ibi . ē

in dñio cū . i . uitto 7 v . bord . 7 iiii . ac pti . Valuit . v . sol .

Idem ten . iii . car træ in *DERESFORD* . iii . bo Modo . x . sol .

uat min . Tra . ē . iiii . car . Ibi . i . uitts ht . i . car . 7 iiii . ac

pti ibi . Silua dimid leu lg . 7 tntd lat . Valuit . v . solid .

Idē ten in *STAPLETONE* . i . car træ . Tra . ē . i . car . modo . xx . sol .

Ibi . ii . uilli cū . iii . bord hñt dim car . Valuit . v . sol . m . x . sol .

Idē ten . ii . car træ . 7 dim in *CHERCHEBI* . Tra . ē . i . car .

Ibi . ii . uilli 7 ii . sochi hñt . i . car 7 dim . Valuit . xii . den .

Idē ten de feudo reginæ . ii . car træ in Modo . x . sol .

*NIWEBOLD* 7 *BROCARDESCOTE* . Tra . ē . iii . car . Ibi . iii . uilli

hñt . i . car . Valuit . v . sol . Modo . xx . solid .

Idē ten . vi . car træ in *PECHINTONE* . Tra . ē . iiii . car . In dñio

ē una cū . i . seruo 7 iii . bord . Valuit . v . sol . Modo . lx . solid .

Idē ten in *ELVESTONE* . ix . car træ *IN GERETREV WAP* .

una v min . Tra . ē . vi . car . Ibi . xiii . sochi cū . i . uitto 7 ii . bord

hñt . iiii . car . Ibi . xx . ac pti . Valuit . xx . sol . Modo . xxx . solid .

5    in RATBY  6 c. of land less 3 b. Land for 6 ploughs.
In lordship 2 ploughs, with 1 slave.
    10 villagers with a priest and 5 smallholders have 4 ploughs.
    A mill at 28d.
The value was 20s; now 60s.
    2 c. of land of the jurisdiction of these are in 'Bromkinsthorpe';
3 in Desford; ½ in Glenfield; ½ in Braunstone.

6    in GROBY 6 c. of land less 3 b. Land for 4 ploughs. In lordship 2.
    10 villagers with 1 Freeman and 5 smallholders have 3 ploughs.
    Woodland 2 leagues long and ½ league wide.
The value was 20s; now 60s.
    Ulf held these two lands with full jurisdiction.

7    in KIRKBY (Mallory) 2 c. of land. Land for 1 plough.
It is there in lordship, with
    1 villager and 5 smallholders.
    Meadow, 4 acres.
The value was 5s; now 10s.

8    in DESFORD 3 c. of land less 3 b. Land for 4 ploughs.
    1 villager has 1 plough.
    Meadow, 4 acres; woodland ½ league long and as much wide.
The value was 5s; now 20s.

9    in STAPLETON 1 c. of land. Land for 1 plough.
    2 villagers with 3 smallholders have ½ plough.
The value was 5s; now 10s.

10    in KIRKBY (Mallory) 2½ c. of land. Land for 1 plough.
    2 villagers and 2 Freemen have 1½ ploughs.
The value was 12d; now 10s.

11    from the Queen's Holding 2 c. of land in NEWBOLD (Verdon) and
BRASCOTE. Land for 3 ploughs.
    3 villagers have 1 plough.
The value was 5s; now 20s.

12    in PECKLETON 6 c. of land. Land for 4 ploughs.
In lordship 1, with 1 slave;
    3 smallholders.
The value was 5s; now 60s.

  In GARTREE Wapentake

13    in ILLSTON (on the Hill) 9 c. of land less 1 virgate.
Land for 6 ploughs.
    13 Freemen with 1 villager and 2 smallholders have 4 ploughs.
    Meadow, 20 acres.
The value was 20s; now 30s.

Idē ten in *TORP* dim car træ.Tra.ē dim car̄.Ibi st̄.ii.hōes

Idē ten *STOCTONE*.Ibi st̄.xxviii.car træ.  ⌠ Val.iii.sol.

Tra.ē.xxii.car̄.In dn̄io st̄.iii.car̄.7 iiii.serui.7 xix.uilli

7 xxxiii.sochi cū.v.bord hn̄t.xxii.car̄.Ibi.lx.ac̄ p̄ti.

Valuit.viii.lib.Modo.ix.lib.Radulf⁹ comes tenuit.

232 b

Idē Hugo ten̄.xii.car træ in *BVRTONE*.Tra.ē.viii.car̄.

In dn̄io st̄.iii.car̄.7 viii.serui.7 xv.uilli 7 vi.sochi cū.v.

bord hn̄t.vi.car̄.Ibi.xiiii.ac̄ p̄ti.Valuit.iiii.lib.m̄.vi.lib.

Idē ten.xi.car træ 7 unā bouat in *CARLINTONE*.Tra.ē

vii.car̄.In dn̄io st̄.iii.car̄.7 v.serui.7 ix.uilli cū p̄bro

7 viii.bord 7 i.francig hn̄t.v.car̄.Ibi.xvi.ac̄ p̄ti.

Valuit.iii.lib.Modo.iiii.lib.

Idē ten.xii.car træ in *NOVESLEI*.Tra.ē.viii.car̄.

In dn̄io st̄.ii.7 iii.serui.7 xvi.uilli cū p̄bro 7 viii.

bord hn̄t.vi.car̄.Ibi.xx.ac̄ broce.Valuit

xxx.sol.Modo.lx.sol.     *IN GOSECOTE WAPENT.*

Idē ten.ix.car træ in *TVRCHITELESTONE*.Tra.ē.iiii.car̄.

In dn̄io st̄.ii 7 iiii.serui.7 xxii.uilli cū.iiii.bord.hn̄t.vi.

car̄.Ibi molin̄ de.iii.sol.Silua.ii.leu lḡ.7 dim leu lat̄.

Valuit.xxx.sol.Modo.iiii.lib.Leuuin lib̄e tenuit.

Idē ten.vii.car træ in *MERDEGRAVE*.Tra.ē.vi.car̄.

In dn̄io st̄.iii.car̄.7 iii.serui.7 viii.uilli cū.v.bord 7 vii.

soch hn̄t.iiii.car̄.Ibi molin̄ de.xii.sol.7 xxiiii.ac̄ p̄ti.

Silua.v.q̄rent lḡ.7 iii.q̄ꝝ lat̄.Valuit.lx.sol.M̄.c.solid.

Idē ten.vi.car træ in *BVRSTELLE*.Tra.ē.v.car̄.In

dn̄io.ē una.cū.i.seruo.7 iii.uilli 7 ix.soch cū.xi.bord

hn̄t.iii.car̄.Ibi molin̄ de.x.sol.7 xxx.vi.ac̄ p̄ti.Silua

iii.q̄ꝝ lḡ.7 ii.q̄ꝝ lat̄.Valuit.xl.sol.M̄.v.uncias auri.

Aluuin p̄bochestan teneb̄.ſꝗ Hugo dic̄ q̄a rex sibi ded̄.

14    in THORPE (Langton ) ½ c. of land. Land for ½ plough.
2 men.
Value 3s.

15    STOCKERSTON. 28 c. of land. Land for 22 ploughs.
In lordship 3 ploughs; 4 slaves.
19 villagers and 33 Freemen with 5 smallholders have 22 ploughs.
Meadow, 60 acres.
The value was £8; now £9.
Earl Ralph held it.

16    Hugh also holds 12 c. of land in BURTON (Overy). Land for    232 b
8 ploughs. In lordship 3 ploughs; 8 slaves.
15 villagers and 6 Freemen with 5 smallholders have 6 ploughs.
Meadow, 14 acres.
The value was £4; now £6.

He also holds

17    in CARLTON (Curlieu) 11 c. and 1 b. of land. Land for 7 ploughs.
In lordship 3 ploughs; 5 slaves.
9 villagers with a priest, 8 smallholders and 1 Frenchman
have 5 ploughs.
Meadow, 16 acres.
The value was £3; now £4.

18    in NOSELEY 12 c. of land. Land for 8 ploughs. In lordship 2; 3 slaves.
16 villagers with a priest and 8 smallholders have 6 ploughs.
Water meadow, 20 acres.
The value was 30s; now 60s.

In GOSCOTE Wapentake

19    in THURCASTON 9 c. of land. Land for 4 ploughs.
In lordship 2; 4 slaves.
22 villagers with 4 smallholders have 6 ploughs.
A mill at 3s; woodland 2 leagues long and ½ league wide.
The value was 30s; now £4.
Leofwin held it freely.

20    in BELGRAVE 7 c. of land. Land for 6 ploughs.
In lordship 3 ploughs; 3 slaves.
8 villagers with 5 smallholders and 7 Freemen have 4 ploughs.
A mill at 12s; meadow, 24 acres; woodland 5 furlongs
long and 3 furlongs wide.
The value was 60s; now 100s.

21    in BIRSTALL 6 c. of land. Land for 5 ploughs.
In lordship 1, with 1 slave.
3 villagers and 9 Freemen with 11 smallholders have 3 ploughs.
A mill at 10s; meadow, 36 acres; woodland 3 furlongs long
and 2 furlongs wide.
The value was 40s; now 5 ounces of gold.
Alwin Buxton held it, but Hugh states that the King gave it to him.

Idē teñ . ii . caŕ tr̄ae in *ANSTIGE* . Tra . ē . iiii . caŕ . In dñio
ē una . 7 iiii . ſerui . 7 xiii . uilłi cū . iiii . borđ hñt . ii . caŕ.
Ibi . viii . āc p̄ti . Silua . i . leū l̄g . 7 dim leū lat̄ . 7 alia Silua
ii . q̃ɼ l̄g . 7 . i . q̃ɼ lat̄ . Valuit . x . ſoł . Modo . xl . ſoliđ.
Idē teñ . x . caŕ tr̄ae in *TVRMODESTONE* . Tra . ē . vii . caŕ.
In dñio ſt̄ . iii . caŕ . 7 v . ſerui . 7 xv . uilłi cū . ii . ſocħ 7 vii . borđ
hñt . iiii . caŕ 7 dimiđ . Ibi moliñ de . vi . ſoł 7 viii . deñ . 7 xxiiii.
āc p̄ti . Valuit 7 uał . lx . ſoliđ . Hanc ht̄ . H . p̄ uno C̃D . ſed ſcira
Idē teñ . ix . caŕ tr̄ae in *HVMERSTANE* . Soca p̄tiñ      ſ negat.
ad Sceltone . Tra . ē . vi . caŕ . Ibi . xiiii . ſocħi cū . vi . borđ hñt
vii . caŕ 7 dim . Ibi . xii . āc p̄ti . Valuit . xx . ſoł . Modo . xl . ſoł.
Idē teñ . v . bouat tr̄ae in *SVINFORD* . Tra . ē dim caŕ . Hanc
ht̄ ibi . i . uilłs cū . ii . borđ . Valuit . v . ſoł . Modo . x . ſoł.
Idē teñ . vi . caŕ tr̄ae in *BRVNESTANESTORP* . Tra . ē . iiii . caŕ.
In dñio . ē una . 7 iii . ſerui . 7 vi . uilłi cū . iii . borđ hñt . ii . caŕ.
Ibi moliñ de . xx . ſoł . ſ Ad hoc C̃D p̄tiñ . iiii . ſocħi in *SMITETONE*.
Hi hñt . i . caŕ . 7 viii . ac̃s p̄ti . Silua . iii . q̃ɼ l̄g . 7 iii . q̃ɼ lat̄.
Valuit . xx . ſoliđ . Modo . xl . ſoliđ . H̄ tra jac̃ ad Ledeceſtre.
cū om̃ibɼ c̃ſuetudinibɼ ſuis.
Rotbt de Buci teñ de Hugone . vi . caŕ tr̄ae in *LESTONE*.
Tra . ē . iiii . caŕ . In dñio . ē . i . caŕ . cū . i . ſeruo . 7 ix . uilłi cū . i.
borđ hñt . iii . caŕ . Valuit . xx . ſoł . Modo . xl . ſoliđ.
Idē . Ro . teñ . vi . caŕ tr̄ae in eađ uilla . Tra . ē . iiii . caŕ.
In dñio . ē una . cū . i . ſeruo . 7 vi . uilłi hñt . ii . caŕ . Ibi . xx.
āc p̄ti . Valuit 7 uał . xx . ſoliđ . Balduin 7 Aluuin tenueŕ.
Idē teñ . v . caŕ tr̄ae una bouata miñ in *SMITONE* . Tra . ē
. iii . caŕ . In dñio . ē . i . caŕ . 7 ii . ſocħ cū . i . uilło 7 iii . borđ hñt . i . caŕ.
                                 ſ Valuit 7 uał . xx . ſoł.

22   in ANSTEY 2 c. of land.  Land for 4 ploughs.
In lordship 1; 4 slaves.
13 villagers with 4 smallholders have 2 ploughs.
Meadow, 8 acres; woodland 1 league long and ½ league wide;
additional woodland 2 furlongs long and 1 furlong wide.
The value was 10s; now 40s.

23   in THURMASTON 10 c. of land.  Land for 7 ploughs.
In lordship 3 ploughs; 5 slaves.
15 villagers with 2 Freemen and 7 smallholders have 4½ ploughs.
A mill at 6s 8d; meadow, 24 acres.
The value was and is 60s.
Hugh has this as one manor but the Shire denies it.

24   in HUMBERSTONE 9 c. of land. The jurisdiction belongs to
Shilton.  Land for 6 ploughs.
14 Freemen with 6 smallholders have 7½ ploughs.
Meadow, 12 acres.
The value was 20s; now 40s.

[In GUTHLAXTON Wapentake]
25   in SWINFORD 5 b. of land.  Land for ½ plough.
1 villager has it with 2 smallholders.
The value was 5s; now 10s.

26   in BRUNTINGTHORPE 6 c. of land.  Land for 4 ploughs.
In lordship 1; 3 slaves.
6 villagers with 3 smallholders have 2 ploughs.
A mill at 20s.
To this manor belong 4 Freemen in SMEETON.  They have 1 plough.
Meadow, 8 acres; woodland 3 furlongs long and 3 furlongs wide.
The value was 20s; now 40s.
This land lies in Leicester with all its customary dues.

27   Robert of Bucy holds 6 c. of land in THURLASTON  from Hugh.
Land for 4 ploughs.  In lordship 1 plough, with 1 slave.
9 villagers with 1 smallholder have 3 ploughs.
The value was 20s; now 40s.

28   Robert also holds 6 c. of land in the same village.
Land for 4 ploughs.  In lordship 1, with 1 slave.
6 villagers have 2 ploughs.
Meadow, 20 acres.
The value was and is 20s.
Baldwin and Alwin held it.

[In GARTREE Wapentake]
29   He also holds 5 c. of land less 1 b. in SMEETON (Westerby).
Land for 3 ploughs. In lordship 1 plough.
2 Freemen with 1 villager and 3 smallholders have 1 plough.
The value was and is 20s.

Idē Robt ten de Hugone . ii . car træ in *TAIWORDE* .

Tra . ē . i . car . Hæc ibi . ē in dñio cū iii . borđ . 7 v . ac pti .

Valuit . v . fot . 7 iiii . den . Modo . xx . foliđ .

Roger ten de . H . in *OLDEBI* . i . car træ 7 dim . Tra . ē

. i . car . Valuit 7 uat . v . foliđ .

Huard ten de . H . in alia *PETLINGE* . iii . car træ

7 dimiđ Tra . ē . ii . car . In dñio . ē ūna . 7 viii . uitti

cū . ii . borđ hñt aliā . Ibi moliñ de . xvi . denar .

7 ii . fochi cū dim car . 7 v . ac pti . Valuit 7 uat

Idē . H . ten . i . car træ in *SEVESBI* ſ xx . foliđ .

de elemofina regis q̄ ht in uadimonio .

Tra . ē dimiđ car . Hanc ht ibi un miles

Valuit 7 uat . v . foliđ .

Fulbt ten . ii . car træ in *SAPECOTE* . de . H . Tra . ē . ii .

car . In dñio . ē una . 7 ii . uitti cū . ii . borđ . 7 ii . fochis

hñt car 7 dim . Ibi moliñ de . iii . fot . 7 xvi . ac pti .

Valuit . v . foliđ . Modo . xxv . foliđ .

Iuo ten de . H . in *WILEBI* . iii . car træ . Tra . ē . i . car

7 dim . In dñio . ē . i . car . 7 iii . fochi cū . i . uitto 7 iiii .

borđ 7 i . feruo hñt . i . car . Valuit . lxiiii . deñ . Modo

Vlf ten de . H . i . car træ in ead uilla . ſ xx . foliđ .

Tra . ē dim car . Valuit . iii . fot . Modo . v . foliđ .

Uxor Robti ten de . H . in *CREC* . v . car træ 7 dimiđ

una bouata mī . Tra . ē . iii . car 7 dim . In dñio . ē . i . car .

cū . i . feruo . 7 iiii . uitti 7 iiii . borđ 7 iii . foch cū . iii . francig

hñt . iii . car . Ibi moliñ de . iii . foliđ . Valuit . v . fot . Modo

Osbn ten de . H . iii . car træ in *BROSTONE* . ſ xl . foliđ .

Tra . ē . iii . car . In dñio ſt . ii . 7 vi . uitti cū . ii . borđ hñt

. i . car . Ibi moliñ de . ii . foliđ . 7 vii . ac pti . Valuit . x .

foliđ . Modo . xxx . foliđ .

[In GOSCOTE Wapentake]

30   Robert also holds 2 c. of land in TWYFORD from Hugh.
Land for 1 plough. It is there in lordship, with
   3 smallholders.
   Meadow, 5 acres.
The value was 5s 4d; now 20s.

[In GUTHLAXTON Wapentake]

31   Roger holds 1½ c. of land in OADBY from Hugh. Land for 1 plough.
The value was and is 5s.

32   Howard holds 3½ c. of land from the other PEATLING (Parva) from Hugh.
Land for 2 ploughs. In lordship 1.
   8 villagers with 2 smallholders have the other.
   A mill at 16d; 2 Freemen with ½ plough; meadow, 5 acres.
The value was and is 20s.

33   Howard also holds 1 c. of land in SHEARSBY from the alms(lands)
of the King which he has in pledge. Land for ½ plough.
   A man-at-arms has it.
The value was and is 5s.

34   Fulbert holds 2 c. of land in SAPCOTE from Hugh.
Land for 2 ploughs. In lordship 1.
   2 villagers with 2 smallholders and 2 Freemen have 1½ ploughs.
   A mill at 3s; meadow, 16 acres.
The value was 5s; now 25s.

35   Ivo holds 3 c. of land in WILLOUGHBY (Waterless) from Hugh.
Land for 1½ ploughs. In lordship 1 plough.
   3 Freemen with 1 villager, 4 smallholders and 1 slave have 1 plough.
The value was 64d; now 20s.

36   In the same village Ulf holds 1 c. of land from Hugh.
Land for ½ plough.
The value was 3s; now 5s.

37   Robert's wife holds 5½ c. of land less 1 b. in CROFT from Hugh.
Land for 3½ ploughs. In lordship 1 plough, with 1 slave.
   4 villagers, 4 smallholders and 3 Freemen with 3 Frenchmen
    have 3 ploughs.
   A mill at 3s.
The value was 5s; now 40s.

38   Osbern holds 3 c. of land in BROUGHTON (Astley) from Hugh.
Land for 3 ploughs. In lordship 2.
   6 villagers with 2 smallholders have 1 plough.
   A mill at 2s; meadow, 7 acres.
The value was 10s; now 30s.

Vlf ten de.H.in *ENDREBIE* .vi. car træ.iii.bouat
min.Tra.ē.iiii.car. In dnio st.ii.cū.i.feruo.7 x.uilti
cū.i.borđ hnt.ii.car. Ibi molin de.v.fol.7 xx.ac pti.
Silua.vi.q̃ɀ lḡ.7 iiii.q̃ɀ lat. Valuit.xx.fol.m.lv.fol.

Erneifus ten de.H.in *CLANEFELDE* .vi.car træ.iii.bouat
min.Tra.ē.iiii.car. In dnio st.ii.7 ii.ferui.7 iii.uilti
cū pbro 7 ii.borđ 7 iiii.foch hnt.iii.car. Ibi molin
de.xvi.den.7 viii.ac pti.Silua.viii.q̃ɀ lḡ.7 iiii.q̃ɀ
lat. Valuit.x.fol.Modo xl.fol.

★ Filius Robti burdel ten de.H.in *BRANTESTONE*.
vi.car træ.v.bouat min.Tra.ē.iiii.car. In dnio.ē
una.7 iiii.ferui.7 ii.fochi 7 iiii.uilti cū.i.borđ hnt
ii.car.Ibi.v.ac pti.Silua.v. q̃ɀ lḡ.7 iii.q̃ɀ lat.
Valuit.xx.fol.Modo.lx.folid.

Serlo ten de.H.v.bouat tre in *CHEREBI*.Tra.ē dim
car. Ibi.ē.i.borđ.Silua dim leu lḡ.7 iii.q̃ɀ lat.
Valuit.ii.fol.Modo.iii.folid.

Ernald ten de.H.i.car træ in *SVTONE*.Tra.ē dim car.
Hæc ibi.ē in dnio.Valuit.iii.fol.Modo.x.folid.

Iuo ten de.H.ii.car træ in *CATEBI*.Tra.ē.i.car. In
dnio tam.ē.i.car.7 vii.uilti cū pbro 7 iii.borđ hnt.i.
car.Silua ibi.iii.q̃ɀ lḡ.7 ii.q̃ɀ lat.Valuit.v.fol.M.xx.

Ernald ten de.H.i.car træ in *NEVLEBI*.7 est 𝑓 folid.
de feudo reginæ.Tra.ē dim car.Ibi st.iii.uilti. Silua
iii.q̃rent lḡ.7 ii.q̃ɀ lat.Valuit.ii.fol.Modo.x.fol.

Radulf 7 Ernald ten de.H.in *BERVLVESTONE*.iii.car
træ.una v min.Tra.ē.ii.car.Has hnt ibi.vi.uilti cū
iiii.borđ.Silua.iii.q̃ɀ lḡ.7 ii.q̃ɀ lat.Valuit.x.folid.

𝑓 Modo.xl.fol.

39     Ulf holds 6 c. of land less 3 b. in ENDERBY from Hugh.
Land for 4 ploughs. In lordship 2, with 1 slave.
   10 villagers with 1 smallholder have 2 ploughs.
   A mill at 5s; meadow, 20 acres; woodland 6 furlongs long
     and 4 furlongs wide.
The value was 20s; now 55s.

40     Erneis holds 6 c. of land less 3 b. in GLENFIELD from Hugh.
Land for 4 ploughs. In lordship 2; 2 slaves.
   3 villagers with a priest; 2 smallholders and 4 Freemen have
     3 ploughs.
   A mill at 16d; meadow, 8 acres; woodland 8 furlongs long
     and 4 furlongs wide.
The value was 10s; now 40s.

41     Robert Burdet's son holds 6 c. of land less 5 b. in BRAUNSTONE
from Hugh.   Land for 4 ploughs. In lordship 1; 4 slaves.
   2 Freemen and 4 villagers with 1 smallholder have 2 ploughs.
   Meadow, 5 acres; woodland 5 furlongs long and 3 furlongs wide.
The value was 20s; now 60s.

42     Serlo holds 5 b. of land in KIRKBY (Mallory) from Hugh.
Land for ½ plough.
   1 smallholder.
   Woodland ½ league long and 3 furlongs wide.
The value was 2s; now 3s.

43     Arnold holds 1 c. of land in SUTTON (Cheney) from Hugh.
Land for ½ plough. It is there in lordship.
The value was 3s; now 10s.

44     Ivo holds 2 c. of land in CADEBY from Hugh.
Land for 1 plough. In lordship however, 1 plough.
   7 villagers with a priest and 3 smallholders have 1 plough.
   Woodland 3 furlongs long and 2 furlongs wide.
The value was 5s; now 20s.

45     Arnold holds 1 c. of land in NEVLEBI from Hugh.
It is of the Queen's Holding. Land for ½ plough.
   3 villagers.
   Woodland 3 furlongs long and 2 furlongs wide.
The value was 2s; now 10s.

46     Ralph and Arnold hold 3 c. of land less 1 virgate in BARLESTONE
from Hugh.   Land for 2 ploughs.
   6 villagers with 4 smallholders have them.
   Woodland 3 furlongs long and 2 furlongs wide.
The value was 10s; now 40s.

Walter ten de.H.ı.car̄ træ in *Scepehe*.Tra.ē.ı.car̄.

In dñio.ē una.7 ııı.uiłłi cū.ıı.borđ hñt.ı.car̄.Ibi moliñ

de.x.soł.Valuit.ıı.soł.Modo.xx.soliđ.

Gulbt̃ ten de.H.ıx.car̄ træ in *Cotesbece*.Tra.ē

vı.car̄.In dñio.ē.ı.7 x.uiłłi cū.ıı.borđ hñt.ıııı.car̄.

Ibi moliñ de.ııı.soł.Valuit.xx.soł.Modo.xxx.soł.

Eduiñ ten de.H.in eađ uilla.ı.car̄ træ 7 dim.Tra.ē.ı.car̄.

Ibi.ıı.hõẽs hñt dim car̄.Valet.x.soł. *In Gertrev Wap.*

Iuo ten de H.in *Avintone*.x.car̄ træ 7 dim.Tra.ē.vıı.car̄.

In dñio st̃.ııı.car̄.7 vı.serui.7 xxv.uiłłi cū.ıı.borđ hñt.v.

car̄ 7 dim.Ibi moliñ de.ıı.soł.7 xx.ãc p̃ti.Valuit xl.soliđ

★ Idem ten de.H.in *Gerberie*.xıı.car̄ træ.     ⎰Modo.c.soł.

Tra.ē.vııı.car̄.In dñio st̃.ıı.7 ıııı.serui.7 ı.ancilla.7 xvı.

uiłłi cū.vıı.borđ 7.ı.miles cū.ııı.francig hñt.v.car̄.

Ibi moliñ de.ıııı.soł.Valuit.xl.soł.Modo.ıııı.libb.

Huard 7 Erneis ten de.H.ıııı.car̄ træ in *Stoctone*.

Tra.ē.ıı.car̄.Ibi.st̃.ıı.car̄ 7 dim.Valuit.xv.soł.Modo

Filius Robt̃i burdet ten de.H.in *Galbi*     ⎰xx.soliđ.

xııı.car̄ træ 7 ıı.bouat.Tra.ē.x.car̄.In dñio.ē.ı.car̄.

7 v.serui.7 ıı.ancillæ.7 xıııı.uiłłi cū.ıı.borđ 7 xı.socħ

hñt.vıı.car̄.7 ı.francig cū.ı.car̄.Ibi moliñ de.ıı.soł.

7 xxx.ãc p̃ti.Valuit 7 uał.ııı.libb.

De hac tra ten.ıı.milites.ı.car̄ træ 7 ııı.bouat.7 ibi

hñt.ı.car̄ 7 dim.Valet.xx.soliđ.

Fulco ten de.H.ıı.car̄ træ in *Frisebi*.Tra.ē.ı.car̄.

In dñio.ē una.cū.ı.seruo.7 ıı.uiłłi cū.ı.socħ 7 ııı.borđ

hñt.ı.car̄.Ibi.v.ãc p̃ti.Valuit.x.soł.Modo.xx.soliđ.

47   Walter holds 1 c. of land in SHEEPY (Parva) from Hugh.     
Land for 1 plough. In lordship 1.
   3 villagers with 2 smallholders have 1 plough.
   A mill at 10s.
The value was 2s; now 20s.

48   Wulfbert holds 9 c. of land in COTESBACH from Hugh.
Land for 6 ploughs. In lordship 1.
   10 villagers with 2 smallholders have 4 ploughs.
   A mill at 3s.
The value was 20s; now 30s,

49   In the same village Edwin holds 1½ c. of land from Hugh.
Land for 1 plough.
   2 men have ½ plough.
Value, 10s.

In GARTREE Wapentake

50   Ivo holds 10½ c. of land in EVINGTON from Hugh.
Land for 7 ploughs. In lordship 3 ploughs; 6 slaves.
   25 villagers with 2 smallholders have 5½ ploughs.
   A mill at 2s; meadow, 20 acres.
The value was 40s; now 100s.

51   He also holds 12 c. of land in INGARSBY from Hugh.
Land for 8 ploughs. In lordship 2; 4 male and 1 female slaves.
   16 villagers with 7 smallholders and 1 man-at-arms with
      3 Frenchmen have 5 ploughs.
   A mill at 4s.
The value was 40s; now £4.

52   Howard and Erneis hold 4 c. of land in STOUGHTON from Hugh.
Land for 2 ploughs. 2½ ploughs there.
The value was 15s; now 20s.

53   Robert Burdet's son holds 13 c. and 2 b. of land in GALBY from
Hugh.   Land for 10 ploughs. In lordship 1 plough; 5 male
and 2 female slaves.
   14 villagers with 2 smallholders and 11 Freemen have 7 ploughs;
     1 Frenchman with 1 plough.
   A mill at 2s; meadow, 30 acres.
The value was and is £3.
   Of this land 2 men-at-arms hold 1 c. and 3 b. of land.
They have 1½ ploughs.
Value, 20s.

54   Fulk holds 2 c. of land in FRISBY from Hugh. Land for 1 plough.
In lordship 1, with 1 slave.
   2 villagers with 1 Freeman and 3 smallholders have 1 plough.
   Meadow, 5 acres.
The value was 10s; now 20s.

Hugo ten de.H.IIII.car træ in SANCTONE.Tra.ē.III.

car.In dnĩo sť.II.cũ.I.feruo.7 IIII.uiłłi 7 IIII.borđ cũ.II.focħ

hñt.I.car 7 dim.Ibi.x.ac pti.Valuit.xvI.foł.M̊.xL.foł.

Idē ten de.H.vI.car træ in STANTONE.Tra.ē.IIII.car.

In dnĩo sť.II.7 II.ferui.7 xv.uiłłi cũ pƀro 7 II.borđ

hñt.IIII.car.Ibi.II.molini de.v.foł 7 IIII.den.7 vIII.

ac pti.Silua.vI.qrent lḡ.7 IIII.q̃ẓ lať.Valuit.xL.foł.

Osƀn ten de.H.xI.car træ in LANGTONE.ꟻModo.Lx.foł.

Tra.ē.vIII.car.In dnĩo sť.II.7 III.ferui.7 xII.uiłłi cũ

pƀro 7 I.milite 7 v.borđ 7 I.focħ hñt.vII.car.Ibi

moliñ de.II.foł.7 xII.ac pti.Valuit 7 uał.xL.foł.

Louet ten de.H.in GLEN.xvII.car træ 7 II.bouať.

Tra.ē.xII.car.In dnĩo sť.III.car.7 II.ferui 7 III.ancillæ.

7 xII.uiłłi cũ.vI.borđ 7 xx.fochis hñt.vI.car.Ibi mo

linũ de.III.foł.7 xxx.ac pti.Valuit 7 uał.vI.liƀ.

Aluuin ten de.H.I.car træ in eađ uilla.Tra.ē dim car.

Ħ ibi.ē cũ.II.uiłłis Valuit.II.foł.Modo.v.foł.

Suain ten de.H.in SITESTONE IN GOSECOTE WAPENť.

ix.car træ.Tra.ē.vI.car.In dnĩo.ē una.7 xvII.uiłłi

cũ pƀro 7 I.borđ 7 xI.fochis hñt.vI.car.Ibi molinũ

de.vIII.foł.7 xxx.ac pti.Valuit.xxx.foł.Modo.xL.foł.

Widard ten de H.II.car træ in BVRSTELE.Tra.ē.I.car.

In dnĩo.ē una.7 II.ferui.7 vIII.uiłłi cũ.IIII.borđ hñt.I.car.

Ibi moliñ de.xII.den.7 xvI.ac pti.Valuit.x.foł.Modo

Wiłłs ten de.H.in TVRMODESTONE ꟻIII.uncias auri.

III.car træ 7 dim.Tra.ē.II.car 7 dim.In dnĩo.ē una.

7 III.uiłłi hñt alia.Ibi.vII.ac pti.Valuit.x.foł.M̊.xL.

55 Hugh holds 4 c. of land in SHANGTON from Hugh.
Land for 3 ploughs. In lordship 2, with 1 slave.
    4 villagers and 4 smallholders with 2 Freemen have 1½ ploughs.
    Meadow, 10 acres.
The value was 16s; now 40s.

56 He also holds 6 c. of land in STONTON (Wyville) from Hugh.
Land for 4 ploughs. In lordship 2; 2 slaves.
    15 villagers with a priest and 2 smallholders have 4 ploughs.
    2 mills at 5s 4d; meadow, 8 acres; woodland 6 furlongs long
      and 4 furlongs wide.
The value was 40s; now 60s.

57 Osbern holds 11 c. of land in (Thorpe) LANGTON from Hugh.
Land for 8 ploughs. In lordship 2; 3 slaves.
    12 villagers with a priest, 1 man-at-arms, 5 smallholders
      and 1 Freeman have 7 ploughs.
    A mill at 2s; meadow, 12 acres.
The value was and is 40s.

58 Lovett holds 17 c. and 2 b. of land in (Great) GLEN from Hugh.
Land for 12 ploughs. In lordship 3 ploughs ; 2 male and 2 female slaves.
    12 villagers with 6 smallholders and 20 Freemen have 6 ploughs.
    A mill at 3s; meadow, 30 acres.
The value was and is £6.

59 In the same village Alwin holds 1 c. of land from Hugh.
Land for ½ plough. It is there, with
    2 villagers.
The value was 2s; now 5s.

In GOSCOTE Wapentake
60 Swein holds 9 c. of land in SYSTON from Hugh.
Land for 6 ploughs. In lordship 1.
    17 villagers with a priest, 1 smallholder and 11 Freemen
      have 6 ploughs.
    A mill at 8s; meadow, 30 acres.
The value was 30s; now 40s.

61 Widhard holds 2 c. of land in BIRSTALL from Hugh.
Land for 1 plough. In lordship 1; 2 slaves.
    8 villagers with 4 smallholders have 1 plough.
    A mill at 12d; meadow, 16 acres.
The value was 10s; now 3 ounces of gold.

62 William holds 3½ c. of land in THURMASTON from Hugh.
Land for 2½ ploughs. In lordship 1.
    3 villagers have another.
    Meadow, 7 acres.
The value was 10s; now 40s.

Roḃt 7 Serlo ten de.H.ix.car̂ tre 7 v.bouat̂ ꝼſolid̂.

in *WIMVNDEWALLE*.Tra.ē.vi.car̂.In dñio ſt̂.ii.car̂.

cū.i.ſeruo.7 xi.uilli 7 iiii.ſocħi cū.iiii.bord̂ 7 ix.francig

233 a
ſeruientiḃ hñt.x.car̂ int ōms.Ibi.xv.ac̄ p̃ti.

Valuit.xx.ſol̂.Modo.c.ſolid̂.Hanc tr̃a tenuer̂.ii.frs

ꝑ.ii.ĉ 7 poſtea emit alter ab altero part̃e ſu̅a.7 fecit

unū ĉ de duobʒ.T.R.E.

Ernald ten de.H.in *SIGLEBI*.viii.car̂ træ 7 dimid̂.

Tra.ē.v.car̂.In dñio ſt̂.iii.car̂.7 iiii.ſerui.7 xviii.

uilli cū.iiii.socħ 7 iiii.bord̂ hñt.vi.car̂.Ibi.ii.molini

de.xxx.ſol̂.7 lx.ac̄ p̃ti.Valuit.lx.ſol̂.Modo.cx.ſol̂.

Iuo ten de.H.xiiii.car̂ træ in *ASCEBI*.Tra.ē.x.car̂.

In dñio.ē una.7 ii.ſerui.7 viii.uilli cū pḃro 7 vi.ſocħis

7 iiii.bord̂ hñt.vi.car̂.Silua.i.leu lḡ.7 iiii.q̃ʒ lat̂.

ad.c.porc̄.Valuit.x.ſolid̂.Modo.xl.ſolid̂.

Ernald ten de.H.vi.car̂ træ 7 dim in *HELETONE*.

Tra.ē.iiii.car̂.In dñio ſt̂.ii.7 iiii.ſerui.7 xxv.uilli

cū.i.milite 7 iiii.bord̂ hñt.viii.car̂.Ibi moliñ

de.ii.ſol̂.7 iiii.ac̄ p̃ti.Silua.i.leu lḡ.7 dim leu lat̂.

Valuit.x.ſolid̂.Modo.lx.ſolid̂.

Idē ten.ii.car̂ træ de.H.in *STANTONE*.Tra.ē.i.car̂.

In dñio.ē una.7 vi.uilli cū.i.bord̂ hñt.i.car̂.Silua

v.q̃ʒ lḡ.7 iii.q̃ʒ lat̂.7 ex altera parte.iiii.ac̄ ſiluæ.

Valuit.ii.ſol̂.Modo.x.ſolid̂.He.ii.træ Ernaldi ſt̂

de feudo.W.comitis.Suain utraſqʒ liḃe tenuit.T.R.E.

Hugo ten de.H.dimid̂ car̂ træ in *WITEWIC*.Tra.

ē dimid̂ car̂.Ibi.ē.i.bord̂ Silua.i.q̃ʒ lḡ.7 dim q̃ʒ lat̂.

Walter ten de.H.xvi.car̂ træ ꝼValet.ii.ſol̂.

7 dim in *WALTHA*.Tra.ē.xi.car̂.In dñio ſt̂.ii.car̂.

7 xxiiii.ſocħi cū.i.uillo 7 i.bord̂ hñt.vi.car̂.

Ibi.i.miles cū.vii.bord̂ 7 iii.ſeruis 7 i.ancilla ht̂.i.

car̂ 7 dimid̂.Ibi.c.ac̄ p̃ti.Valuit.iii.liḃ.Modo.vi.liḃ.

53   Robert and Serlo hold 9 c. and 5 b. of land in WYMESWOLD from Hugh.
Land for 6 ploughs. In lordship 2 ploughs with 1 slave.
>11 villagers and 4 Freemen with 4 smallholders and 9
>French servants have 10 ploughs amongst
>them all.                         233 a
>Meadow, 15 acres.

The value was 20s; now 100s.
>Two brothers held this land as two manors. One later bought
the other's part from him and made one manor of the two before 1066.

54   Arnold holds 8½ c. of land in SILEBY from Hugh. Land for 5 ploughs.
In lordship 3 ploughs; 4 slaves.
>18 villagers with 4 Freemen and 4 smallholders have 6 ploughs.
>2 mills at 30s; meadow, 60 acres.

The value was 60s; now 110s.

55   Ivo holds 14 c. of land in ASHBY (de la Zouch) from Hugh.
Land for 10 ploughs. In lordship 1; 2 slaves.
>8 villagers with a priest, 6 Freemen and 4 smallholders
>have 6 ploughs.
>Woodland 1 league long and 4 furlongs wide for 100 pigs.

The value was 10s; now 40s.

66   Arnold holds 6½ c. of land in ALTON from Hugh.
Land for 4 ploughs. In lordship.2; 4 slaves.
>25 villagers with 1 man-at-arms and 4 smallholders have 8 ploughs.
>A mill at 2s; meadow, 4 acres; woodland 1 league long and
>½ league wide.

The value was 10s; now 60s.

67   He also holds 2 c. of land from Hugh in STAUNTON (Harold).
Land for 1 plough. In lordship 1.
>6 villagers with 1 smallholder have 1 plough.
>Woodland 5 furlongs long and 3 furlongs wide; from
>another part, woodland, 4 acres.

The value was 2s; now 10s.
>These two lands of Arnold's are from Earl Waltheof's Holding.

Swein held both freely before 1066.

68   Hugh holds ½ c. of land in WHITWICK from Hugh. Land for ½ plough.
>1 smallholder.
>Woodland 1 furlong long and ½ furlong wide.

Value, 2s.

[In FRAMLAND Wapentake]

69   Walter holds 16½ c. of land in WALTHAM (on-the-Wolds)
from Hugh. Land for 11 ploughs. In lordship 2 ploughs.
>24 Freemen with 1 villager and 1 smallholder have 6 ploughs.
>1 man-at-arms with 7 smallholders and 3 male and 1
>female slaves has 1½ ploughs.
>Meadow, 100 acres.

The value was £3; now £6.

Idē ten de.H.in *Torp*.xv.car̄ træ.Tra.ē.x.car̄.

In dn̄io s̄t.v.car̄ 7 ii.ſerui.7 xvi.uilti cū.xi.ſochis

7 viii.borđ hn̄t.vii.car̄.Ibi molin̄ de.v.ſol 7 iiii.

denar̄.p̄tū.iiii.q̊ʒ lḡ.7 tn̄tđ lat̄.Valuit.xx.ſolid.

Idē ten de.H.iii.car̄ træ in eađ uilla.⌈Modo.vii.lib.

Tra.ē.ii.car̄.Has hn̄t ibi.viii.uilti cū.iii.borđ.

Valuit.iii.ſot.Modo.xx.ſolid

Hugo ten de H.ii.car̄ træ in *Boseworde*.Tra.ē

.i.car̄.Hanc hn̄t ibi p̄br cū diacono 7 iiii.borđ.7 ii.

ſeruis.Ibi.xii.ac̄ p̄ti.Silua.i.q̊ʒ lḡ.7 dim q̊ʒ lat̄.

Valuit.x.ſolid.Modo.xx.ſolid.

Idē ten de.H.tciā part̄e.i.car̄ træ in *Bartone*.

Tra.ē dim̄ car̄.Hanc h̄t ibi cū.i.uilto 7 ii.borđ.

Ibi.ii.ac̄ p̄ti.Valuit.xii.den̄.Modo.iii.ſolid.

Hæ.ii.træ s̄t de feudo reginæ.Aluuin libe tenuit T.R.E.

Huard ten in *Niwebold*.ii.car̄ træ.Tra.ē.ii.car̄.

Nc̄ ibi.i.car̄ in dn̄io cū.ii.borđ.Val.x.ſot.

.XIIII. TERRA HENRICI DE FERIERES.

Henricvs De Fereires ten de rege *Stapeford*.

Ibi.xiiii.car̄ træ.T.R.E.erant ibi.xvii.car̄.

De hac tra s̄t.iiii.carucatæ in dn̄io.7 ibi.v.car̄.7 iiii.ſerui.

Ibi.xxiii.uilti cū.iiii.borđ 7 xxiii.ſoch hn̄t.xiii.car̄.

Ibi.ii.molini de.viii.ſolid.7 c.xxx.ac̄ p̄ti.

Valuit.iiii.lib.Modo.x.lib.

Idē.H.ten *Tvnge*.cū om̄ibʒ appendic.Ibi s̄t.xxi.car̄

træ 7 dim.T.R.E.erant ibi.xi.car̄.De hac tra s̄t in dn̄io

iii.carucatæ.                  Ibi.xx.vii.uilti cū.ii.ſochis

7 viii.borđ hn̄t.xiii.car̄.Ibi.vi.ac̄ p̄ti.Silua.i.leu

lḡ.7 dimiđ leu lat̄.Valuit.v.ſolid.Modo.vi.lib.

70     He also holds 15 c. of land in THORPE (Arnold) from Hugh.
Land for 10 ploughs. In lordship 5 ploughs; 2 slaves.
    16 villagers with 11 Freemen and 8 smallholders have 7 ploughs.
    A mill at 5s 4d; meadow 4 furlongs long and as many wide.
The value was 20s; now £7.

71     In the same village he also holds 3 c. of land from Hugh.
Land for 2 ploughs.
    8 villagers with 3 smallholders have them.
The value was 3s; now 20s.

[In GUTHLAXTON Wapentake]

72     Hugh holds 2 c. of land in (Market) BOSWORTH from Hugh.
Land for 1 plough.
    A priest with a deacon, 4 smallholders and 2 slaves have it.
    Meadow, 12 acres; woodland 1 furlong long and ½ furlong wide.
The value was 10s; now 20s.

73     He also holds the third part of 1 c. of land in BARTON (-in-the-Beans)
from Hugh. Land for ½ plough. He has it, with
    1 villager and 2 smallholders.
    Meadow, 2 acres.
The value was 12d; now 3s.
    These two lands are of the Queen's Holding. Alwin held them
freely before 1066.

74     Howard holds 2 c. of land in NEWBOLD (Verdon). Land for 2
ploughs. Now in lordship 1 plough, with
    2 smallholders.
Value, 10s.

14        **LAND OF HENRY OF FERRERS**        233 b

[In FRAMLAND Wapentake]

1     Henry of Ferrers holds STAPLEFORD from the King. 14 c. of land.
Before 1066, 17 ploughs. In lordship 4 c. of this land; 5 ploughs;
4 slaves.
    23 villagers with 4 smallholders and 23 Freemen have 13 ploughs.
    2 mills at 8s; meadow, 130 acres.
The value was £4; now £10.

[In GOSCOTE Wapentake]

2     Henry also holds TONGE with all its dependencies. 21½ c. of land.
Before 1066, 11 ploughs. In lordship 3 c. of this land.
    27 villagers with 2 Freemen and 8 smallholders have 13 ploughs.
    Meadow, 6 acres; woodland 1 league long and ½ league wide.
The value was 5s; now £6.

In *WERDITONE* st̄ . iiii . car̄ trǣ . T.R.E. fueř ibi . v . car̄.

Ibi . iiii . socħi cū . vi . uiłłis 7 ii . borđ hn̄t . iii . car̄.

Silua . iiii . q̄rent l̄g . 7 una q̄ȝ lat̄ . Valuit . xii . den̄.

Modo . xx . sol̄ . Aluuin̄ calūniat̄ Soca uni carucatæ

huj trǣ . dicens eā ad *SCEPESHEFDE* regis ptinere.

In *SAXEBI* st̄ . v . car̄ trǣ ptinent ad *STAPEFORD*.

Ibi . ix . uiłłi hn̄t . iii . car̄ . 7 molin̄ de . ii . sol̄ . 7 lx . ac̄s p̄ti.

p̄ciū ej in *STAPEFORD*.

Idē . H . ten̄ . ix . car trǣ in *CASTONE* . T.R.E. erant ibi

. x . car̄ . In dn̄io . ē . i . car̄ . 7 dim̄ . 7 ii . serui . 7 xii . socħi

7 x . uiłłi cū . i . borđ hn̄t . vii . car̄ . Ibi molin̄ de . x . solid̄.

7 c . ac̄ p̄ti . Valuit . xl . sol̄ . Modo . vii . lib̄.

Idē . H . ten̄ *EDMERESTORP* 7 *WITMEHA* . Ibi st̄ . xxvii.

car̄ trǣ 7 dimiđ . T.R.E. erant ibi . xvi . car̄ . De hac tra

st̄ . ii . car̄ . 7 In dominio 7 ibi . vii . car̄ . 7 . iiii . serui . 7 xxviii . uiłłi cū

p̄bro 7 xv . socħis 7 iiii . borđ hn̄t . xiiii . car̄ . Ibi . ccc . ac̄

p̄ti . Valuit . iiii . lib̄ . Modo . xiii . lib̄.

In *SATGRAVE* . ē dim̄ car trǣ . Ibi un̄ uiłłs cū . i . borđ

hn̄t . i . car̄ . 7 iiii . ac̄ p̄ti . Valuit . vi . den̄ . Modo . ii . solid̄.

In *WERDEBI* . ē dim̄ car trǣ vasta . Tam̄ ual̄ . viii . denar̄.

Idē . H . ten̄ . vi . car trǣ in *WORTONE*.

T.R.E. fueř ibi . vi . car̄ . In dn̄io st̄ . iiii . car̄ . cū . i . seruo.

7 xv . uiłłi cū . xiii . borđ hn̄t . v . car̄ . Valuit . xl . sol̄ . Modo

**N**IGELLVS ten̄ de Henrico . vi . car trǣ in *TVICROS* . T.R.E. c . solid̄

erant ibi . vi . car̄ . In dn̄io . ē . i . car̄ . cū . i . seruo . 7 xi . uiłłi

cū . vi . borđ hn̄t . vi . car̄ . Valuit . iii . sol̄ . Modo . xl . sol̄.

**R**oald ten̄ 9 de Henrico . iii . car trǣ in *GOPESHILLE* . T.R.E. erant . iii . car̄

ibi . In dn̄io . ē . i . car̄ . 7 viii . uiłłi cū . v . borđ hn̄t . ii . car̄.

Valuit . xii . denar̄ . Modo . xxx . solid̄.

**I**pse . H . ten̄ . ii . car trǣ in *SCEPA* . T.R.E. erant ibi . iii . car̄.

Has hn̄t ibi . viii . uiłłi cū . vi . borđ . Ibi molin̄ de . ii . solid̄.

7 vi . ac̄ p̄ti . Valuit . ii . solid̄ . Modo . xxx . solid̄.

3　In WORTHINGTON 4 c. of land. Before 1066, 5 ploughs.
　　4 Freemen with 6 villagers and 2 smallholders have 3 ploughs.
　　Woodland 4 furlongs long and 1 furlong wide.
　　The value was 12d; now 20s.
　　Alwin claims the jurisdiction of 1 c. of this land saying
　　that it belongs to King's Shepshed.

4　In SAXBY 5 c. of land which belongs to Stapleford.
　　9 villagers have 3 ploughs.
　　A mill at 2s; meadow, 60 acres.
　　Its assessment is in Stapleford.

[In FRAMLAND Wapentake]
5　Henry also holds 9 c. of land in COSTON. Before 1066, 10 ploughs.
　　In lordship 1½ ploughs; 2 slaves.
　　12 Freemen and 10 villagers with 1 smallholder have 7 ploughs.
　　A mill at 10s; meadow, 100 acres.
　　The value was 40s; now £7.

6　Henry also holds EDMONDTHORPE and WYMONDHAM. 27½ c. of land.
　　Before 1066, 16 ploughs. In lordship 2 c. of this land; 7 ploughs;
　　4 slaves.-
　　28 villagers with a priest, 15 Freemen and 4 smallholders
　　　　have 14 ploughs.
　　Meadow, 300 acres.
　　The value was £4; now £13.

[In GOSCOTE Wapentake]
7　In SEAGRAVE ½ c. of land.
　　1 villager with 1 smallholder have 1 plough.
　　Meadow, 4 acres.
　　The value was 6d; now 2s.

[In FRAMLAND Wapentake]
8　In WYFORDBY ½ c. of land. Waste.
　　Value however, 8d.

[In GUTHLAXTON Wapentake]
9　Henry also holds 6 c. of land in ORTON (on-the-Hill). Before 1066,
　　6 ploughs. In lordship 4 ploughs, with 1 slave.
　　15 villagers with 13 smallholders have 5 ploughs.
　　The value was 40s; now 100s.

10　Nigel holds 6 c. of land in TWYCROSS from Henry. Before 1066,
　　6 ploughs. In lordship 1 plough, with 1 slave.
　　11 villagers with 6 smallholders have 6 ploughs.
　　The value was 3s; now 40s.

11　Roald holds 3 c. of land in GOPSALL from Henry. Before 1066,
　　3 ploughs. In lordship 1 plough.
　　8 villagers with 5 smallholders have 2 ploughs.
　　The value was 12d; now 30s.

12　Henry holds 2 c. of land in SHEEPY (Magna) himself. Before 1066, 3 ploughs.
　　8 villagers with 6 smallholders have them.
　　A mill at 2s; meadow, 6 acres.
　　The value was 2s; now 30s.

Roger ten de.H.in *CVNINGESTONE*.ii.car træ.T.R.E.
erant ibi.ii.car.In dñio.e.i.car.7 x.uilti cũ.vi.borđ
hñt.ii.car.Ibi moliñ 7 iii.a̅c p̃ti.Valuit.ii.fot.M̃.xx.fot.

Wazelin ten in *SNOCHANTONE*.i.car træ 7 dim de.H.
T.R.E.erant ibi.ii.car.In dñio.e una car cũ.i.feruo.
7 vi.uilti cũ.ii.borđ hñt.ii.car.Ibi.iiii.a̅c p̃ti.
Valuit.ii.fot.Modo.xx.foliđ.

Roger ten de.H.in *SCENTONE*.ii.bouat træ.Ibi.e un
uilts.Valet.ii.foliđ.     *IN GERETREVVES WAPENT.*

Godric ten de.H.ix.car træ in *HOHTONE*.T.R.E.erant
ibi.v.car.In dñio.e dimiđ car.7 ii.ferui.7 v.uilti cũ.iii.
borđ hñt.iii.car 7 dimiđ.Ibi.xx.a̅c p̃ti.Valuit 7 uat
xx.foliđ.Wallef com̃ tenuit.Judita calũniat̃.

Hugo ten de.H.i.car træ in *ASCBI*.7 p̃tiñ ad Niuuebold.
T.R.E.erat ibi.i.car.Ibi sf.ii.uilti.Valuit 7 uat.iii.foliđ.

233 c
Mechenta ten de.H.in *OVERTONE*.i.car træ.Ibi hĩ.i.car
cũ.i.uilto 7 ii.borđ Silua.i.q̃ʒ lg̃.7 altera in lat.
Valuit.vi.den.Modo.v.fot.

Robt ten *SCELLA*.de.H.Ibi sf.vii.car træ.T.R.E.erañ
ibi.v.car.Ibi.iiii.fochi cũ.ii.uiltis hñt.ii.car.Silua
vi.q̃rent lg̃.7 iiii.q̃ʒ lat.Valuit 7 uat.xx.foliđ.

Idẽ ten de.H.alia *SCELA*.Ibi sf.vi.car træ.T.R.E.
erant ibi.iii.car.In dñio sf.iii.car.7 xxi.uilts cũ.xii.
borđ hñt.iii.car.Ibi moliñ de.v.foliđ.7 xii.a̅c p̃ti.
Valuit.xx.foliđ.Modo.lx.foliđ.

Idẽ ten de.H.i.car træ in *BORTROD*.Ibi un uilts hĩ
unã car.Valuit.viii.denar.Modo.iiii.foliđ.

13   Roger holds 2 c. of land in CONGERSTONE from Henry.
Before 1066, 2 ploughs. In lordship 1 plough.
   10 villagers with 6 smallholders have 2 ploughs.
   A mill; meadow, 3 acres.
The value was 2s; now 20s.

14   Wazelin holds 1½ c. of land in SMOCKINGTON from Henry.
Before 1066, 2 ploughs. In lordship 1 plough, with 1 slave.
   6 villagers with 2 smallholders have 2 ploughs.
   Meadow, 4 acres.
The value was 2s; now 20s.

15   Roger holds 2 b. of land in SHENTON from Henry.
   1 villager.
Value, 2s.

In GARTREE Wapentake
16   Godric holds 9 c. of land in HOUGHTON (-on-the-Hill) from Henry.
Before 1066, 5 ploughs. In lordship ½ plough; 2 slaves.
   5 villagers with 3 smallholders have 3½ ploughs.
   Meadow, 20 acres.
The value was and is 20s.
   Earl Waltheof held it. Countess Judith claims it.

[In GOSCOTE Wapentake]
17   Hugh holds 1 c. of land in ASHBY (Folville) from Henry; it belongs to
Newbold (Folville). Before 1066, 1 plough.
   2 villagers.
The value was and is 3s.

18   Meginta holds 1 c. of land in COLEORTON from Henry.       233 c
She has 1 plough, with
   1 villager and 2 smallholders.
   Woodland 1 furlong long and another in width.
The value was 6d; now 5s.

19   Robert holds (Nether) SEAL from Henry. 7 c. of land.
Before 1066, 5 ploughs.
   4 Freemen with 2 villagers have 2 ploughs.
   Woodland 6 furlongs long and 4 furlongs wide.
The value was and is 20s.

20   He also holds the other (Over) SEAL from Henry. 6 c. of land.
Before 1066, 3 ploughs. In lordship 3 ploughs.
   21 villagers with 12 smallholders have 3 ploughs.
   A mill at 5s; meadow, 12 acres.
The value was 20s; now 60s.

21   He also holds 1 c. of land in BOOTHORPE from Henry.
   1 villager has 1 plough.
The value was 8d; now 4s.

Idē ten de.H.1.car̄ træ in *APLEBERIE*.Ibi.1111.fochi

hñt.11.car̄.7 111.acs p̄ti.Valuit.x11.den.Modo.x.fot.

Nigell ten de.H.x.car̄ træ in *SCOPESTONE*.

T.R.E.erant ibi.x.car̄.In dñio ſt.11.car̄.7 xv.uilli

cū p̄bro 7 111.bord hñt.v1.car̄.Ibi.x11.ac p̄ti.

Valuit.x11.den.Modo.xl.folid.            ſ potuit.

De hac tr̄a T.R.E.tenuit Sbern.11.car̄ træ.7 q̄ uoluit ire

Reliq̄ tr̄a tenuit Leuric.cuj tr̄a ten Ofmund ep̄s

Gleduin ten de.H.in *NEVTONE* dimid car̄ træ ſ de rege.

In dñio.ē.1.car̄.cū.1.bord.7 11.acs p̄ti

Roger ten de.H.1.car̄ træ in ead uilla.Valet.11.fot.

Johs ten de.H.in *VDECOTE*.11.car̄ træ.T.R.E.erant

ibi.11.car̄.In dñio.ē una.Silua.111.q̄rent lḡ.7 111.lat.

Valuit.x11.den.Modo.x.folid.

Ardulf ten de.H.1.car̄ træ in *OSGODTORP*.In dñio

ht dimid car̄.7 111.uilli cū.v.bord hñt.1.car̄.

Valuit.x11.den.Modo.v.folid.

Roger ten de H.in *STRETONE*.1.car̄ træ uaſta.7 alia

in *DVRANDESTORP* fimilit uaſta.7 tcia in *OVRETONE*

fimilit uaſta.Valent tam.11.fot.Aluric 7 Leuenot

libe tenuer̄.duas har̄.tcia tenuit Cari.fed cū ea difcede

Robt ten de.H.1.car̄ træ 7 una bouata  ſ ñ potuit.

in *BVRTONE*.Ibi.ē.1.car̄ in dñio 7 uñ uillm cū dimid

car̄.Ibi.11.ac p̄ti.Valuit.v.fot.Modo.x.folid.

Nigell ten de.H.in *WINDESERS*.111.car̄ træ uaſtas.

T.R.E.erant ibi.11.car̄.Aluric libe tenuit.

22 He also holds 1 c of land in APPLEBY from Henry.
    4 Freemen have 2 ploughs.
    Meadow, 3 acres.
The value was 12d; now 10s.

23 Nigel holds 10 c of land in SWEPSTONE from Henry.
Before 1066, 10 ploughs. In lordship 2 ploughs.
    15 villagers with a priest and 3 smallholders have 6 ploughs.
    Meadow, 12 acres.
The value was 12d; now 40s.
    Before 1066 Esbern held 2 c of this land; he could go where he
would. Leofric, whose land Bishop Osmund holds from the King,
held the rest of the land.

24 Gladwin holds ½ c of land in NEWTON (Burgoland) from Henry.
In lordship 1 plough, with
    1 smallholder.
    Meadow, 2 acres.

25 In the same village Roger holds 1 c of land from Henry.
Value, 2s.

26 John holds 2 c of land in WOODCOTE from Henry.
Before 1066, 2 ploughs. In lordship 1.
    Woodland 3 furlongs long and 3 wide.
The value was 12d; now 10s.

27 Ardwulf holds 1 c of land in OSGATHORPE from Henry.
In lordship he has ½ plough.
    3 villagers with 5 smallholders have 1 plough.
The value was 12d; now 5s.

28 Roger holds 1 c of land in STRETTON from Henry; waste.
Another in DONISTHORPE; likewise waste.
A third in COLEORTON; likewise waste.
Value however, 2s.
    Aelfric and Leofnoth held two of these freely; Kari held
the third but could not leave with it.

  [In FRAMLAND Wapentake]

29 Robert holds 1 c and 1 b of land in BURTON (Lazars) from Henry.
In lordship 1 plough;
    1 villager with ½ plough.
    Meadow, 2 acres.
The value was 5s; now 10s.

30 Nigel holds 3 c. of land in WINDESERS from Henry; waste.
Before 1066, 2 ploughs.
    Aelfric held it freely.

Roger ten de.H.in *SV̄MERDEBI*.iii.car̄ træ 7 ii.

bouat̄.T.R.E.erant ibi.iiii.car̄.In dn̄io.ē una.7 v.

uilli cū pb̄ro 7 ii.bord hn̄t.ii.car̄.Ibi.xx.ac̄ p̄ti.

Valuit.xv.folid̄.Modo.xl.folid̄.

Huic M̄ ptin.v.car̄ træ in *DALBI*.T.R.E.erant ibi

iiii.car̄.Ibi.xvi.fochi cū pb̄ro hn̄t.vi.car̄.Ibi.xl.

ac̄ p̄ti.Valuit.x.folid̄.Modo.xx.folid̄.Aluuold̄

Idē.R.ten̄ de.H.in *BVRC*.ii.car̄ træ 𝄐 libe tenuit.

7 iii.bouat̄.T.R.E.erant ibi.iiii.car̄.In dn̄io.ē.i.car̄.

7 iiii.uilli hn̄t.i.car̄.cū.i.bord.Ibi.xx.ac̄ p̄ti.

Valuit.v.folid̄.Modo.xx.folid̄.Aluuold libe tenuit.

Hugo ten̄ de.H.iii.car̄ træ in *NEVBOLD*.T.R.E.erant

ibi.iiii.car̄.In dn̄io.ē una car̄ 7 dim.7 iiii.uilli hn̄t

iii.car̄.Ibi.viii.ac̄ p̄ti.7 molin̄ de.xii.denar̄.

Valuit.iii.folid̄.Modo.x.folid̄.Game libe tenuit.

Nigell ten̄ de.H.in *LINTONE*.i.car̄ træ uaftā.

.XV TERRA ROBERTI DE TODENI. *IN GERETREV WAPENT̄.*

Rotbert̄ De Todeni ten̄ de rege in *HORNIWALE*

iii.car̄ træ.T.R.E.erant ibi.v.car̄.Ih dn̄io funt.ii.car̄.

Ibi.viii.uilli 7 iii.fochi cū.ii.bord hn̄t.iii.car̄.Ibi.xii.

ac̄ p̄ti.Silua.ii.q̊ẕ lḡ.7 una q̊ẕ lat̄.Valuit.x.fot.M̄.xxx.

Idem.R.ten̄.iiii.car̄ træ in *METORNE*.        𝄐 folid̄.

T.R.E.erant ibi.viii.car̄.In dn̄io ft.iiii.car̄.7 iii.ferui.

7 xiii.uilli cū.vi.bord hn̄t.iiii.car̄.      𝄐 hn̄t.iii.car̄.

Huic M̄ ptin.ii.car̄ træ in *BLASTONE*.Ibi.xv.fochi

In M̄ ft xx.ac̄ p̄ti.Silua.iii.q̊ẕ lḡ.7 ii.q̊ẕ lat̄.

Valuit.xxx.folid̄.Modo.iiii.lib̄.

31 Roger holds 3 c and 2 b of land in SOMERBY from Henry.
Before 1066, 4 ploughs. In lordship 1.
5 villagers with a priest and 2 smallholders have 2 ploughs.
Meadow, 20 acres.
The value was 15s; now 40s.
To this manor belong 5 c of land in (Little) DALBY.
Before 1066, 4 ploughs.
16 Freemen with a priest have 6 ploughs.
Meadow, 40 acres.
The value was 10s; now 20s.
Alfwold held it freely.

32 Roger also holds 2 c and 3 b of land in BURROUGH (-on-the-Hill) from
Henry. Before 1066, 4 ploughs. In lordship 1 plough.
4 villagers have 1 plough with 1 smallholder.
Meadow, 20 acres.
The value was 5s; now 20s.
Alfwold held it freely.

33 Hugh holds 3 c of land in NEWBOLD (Saucey) from Henry.
Before 1066, 4 ploughs. In lordship 1½ ploughs.
4 villagers have 3 ploughs.
Meadow, 8 acres; a mill at 12d.
The value was 3s; now 10s.

[In GOSCOTE Wapentake]
34 Nigel holds 1 c. of land in LINTON from Henry; waste.

15        **LAND OF ROBERT OF TOSNY**        233 d

In GARTREE Wapentake
1 Robert of Tosny holds 3 c of land in HORNINGHOLD from the King.
Before 1066, 5 ploughs. In lordship 2 ploughs.
8 villagers and 3 Freemen with 2 smallholders have 3 ploughs.
Meadow, 12 acres; woodland 2 furlongs long and 1 furlong wide.
The value was 10s; now 30s.

2 Robert also holds 4 c of land in MEDBOURNE.
Before 1066, 8 ploughs. In lordship 3 ploughs; 3 slaves.
13 villagers with 6 smallholders have 4 ploughs.
To this manor belong 2 c of land in BLASTON.
15 Freemen.
In the manor are meadow, 20 acres; woodland 3 furlongs long
and 2 furlongs wide.
The value was 30s; now £4.

Idē.R.teñ.xvii.car̄ træ in *HERDEBI*.T.R.E.erant ibi
xiiii.car̄.In dñio st.iii.7 viii.ſerui.7 xxiiii.ſochi cū
vii.uiſtis 7 iii.borđ hñt.xiii.car̄.Ibi p̄tū.v.q̄rent lḡ.
7 iiii.q̄rent lat.Valuit.iiii.liƀ.Modo.c.ſoliđ.

Idē.R.teñ.xv.car̄ træ in *BARCHESTONE*.T.R.E.erant
ibi.xv.car̄.In dñio st.iii.car̄.7 vii.ſerui.7 xiiii.uiſti
cū.ii.borđ 7 p̄ro 7 aliis.iiii.uiſtis 7 xxv.ſochis hñt.xi.
car̄.Valuit.iiii.liƀ.Modo.c.ſoliđ.

Idē.R.teñ.ix.car̄ træ in *BOTESFORD*.T.R.E.erant ibi
xxv.car̄.In dñio st.v.car̄.7 vi.ſerui.7 xii.uiſti 7 lx.
ſochi cū.v.borđ hñt.xv.car̄.Ibi p̄br cū.i.car̄.
Ibi.iiii.molini de.xl.ſot.Valuit.xii.liƀ.m̂.xv.liƀ.

Idē.R.teñ.iii.car̄ træ in *REDMELDE*.T.R.E.erant
ibi.iiii.car̄.H̄ ptiñ ad Botesford.Ibi.ii.ſochi cū.ii.
borđ hñt dimiđ.car̄.Valuit 7 uat.xx.ſoliđ.

Eiđ m̄ Botesford ptiñ.iii.car̄ træ 7 ii.bouatæ in
*GNIPTONE*.T.R.E.erant ibi.iii.car̄.Ibi.v.ſochi hñt
ii.car̄.7 moliñ de.v.ſoliđ.7 iiii.ac̄s p̄ti.Valet.xx.ſot.
Has tras tenuer̄.iiii.taini Oſulf Oſmund Roulf 7 Leuric
7 quo uoluer̄ cū eis ire potuer̄.

Walter teñ.ii.car̄ træ de Roƀto in *LACHESTONE*.
T.R.E.erant ibi.iii.car̄.In dñio.ē una car̄.7 ii.ſerui.
7 iii.uiſti cū.ii.borđ hñt.i.car̄.Ibi.viii.ac̄ p̄ti.
Valuit.vi.ſot.Modo.xx.ſoliđ.

Osƀn teñ de.R.ii.car̄ træ in *LVBEHA*.Tra.ē.iii.car̄.
In dñio.ē.i.car̄ 7 dim.7 vi.uiſti cū.ii.borđ hñt.i.car̄.
Ibi.x.ac̄ p̄ti.Valuit.x.ſot.Modo.xx.ſot.

[In FRAMLAND Wapentake]

3 Robert also holds 17 c. of land in HARBY. Before 1066, 14 ploughs. In lordship 3; 8 slaves.
24 Freemen with 7 villagers and 3 smallholders have 13 ploughs.
Meadow 5 furlongs long and 4 furlongs wide.
The value was £4; now 100s.

4 Robert also holds 15 c. of land in BARKESTONE. Before 1066, 15 ploughs. In lordship 3 ploughs; 7 slaves.
14 villagers with 2 smallholders, a priest and another 4 villagers and 25 Freemen have 11 ploughs.
The value was £4; now 100s.

5 Robert also holds 9 c. of land in BOTTESFORD. Before 1066, 25 ploughs. In lordship 5 ploughs; 6 slaves.
12 villagers and 60 Freemen with 5 smallholders have 15 ploughs.
A priest with 1 plough.
4 mills at 40s.
The value was £12; now £15.

6 Robert also holds 3 c. of land in REDMILE. Before 1066, 4 ploughs. It belongs to Bottesford.
2 Freemen with 2 smallholders have ½ plough.
The value was and is 20s.

7 To this manor of Bottesford belong 3 c. and 2 b. of land in KNIPTON. Before 1066, 3 ploughs.
5 Freemen have 2 ploughs.
A mill at 5s; meadow, 4 acres.
Value, 20s.
4 thanes, Oswulf, Osmund, Rolf and Leofric held these lands and could go with them where they would.

[In GARTREE Wapentake]

8 Walter holds 2 c. of land in LAUGHTON from Robert. Before 1066, 3 ploughs. In lordship 1 plough; 2 slaves.
3 villagers with 2 smallholders have 1 plough.
Meadow, 8 acres.
The value was 6s; now 20s.

9 Osbern holds 2 c. of land in LUBENHAM from Robert. Land for 3 ploughs. In lordship 1½ ploughs.
6 villagers with 2 smallholders have 1 plough.
Meadow, 10 acres.
The value was 10s; now 20s.

Wills ten de.R.xviii.car͛ træ in *Barcheberie*.

Tra.e̅.xvi.car͛.In dn̅io st̅.iii.car͛.⁊ iii.serui.⁊ vii.

uilli cu̅.iii.bord ⁊ x.sochis ⁊ iiii.francig hn̅t.x.car͛

De hac tra.vi.carucat ten un miles in *Hvngretone*.

⁊ ibi ht̅.i.car͛ in dn̅io.⁊ ii.seruos.⁊ vii.soch cu̅.iii.car͛.

Ibi.xvi.ac̅ p̅ti.Valuit.xxx.solid.Modo.iiii.lib̅.

Roger͛ ten de Will̅o.v.car͛ træ in *Croptone*.⁊ Walter͛

ii.car͛ træ ⁊ dimid in *Qveneberie*.⁊ in dn̅io hn̅t.iii.car͛.

⁊ iiii.seruos.⁊ vii.uillos cu̅.iiii.bord hn̅tes.i.car͛.

Ibi.xxiiii.ac̅ p̅ti.Valuit.xv.sol.Modo.xxx.solid.

In ead uilla ten un francig trā.i.car͛.Valet.v.solid.

Iuo ten͛ de.R.xvii.car͛ træ *In Franelvnd Wapent͛*.

iii.bouat͛ ⁊ dimid min in *Clachestone*.Tra.e̅.xvii.car͛.

In dn̅io st̅.iiii.car͛.⁊ xii.serui.⁊ xiiii.uilli cu̅.ii.bord

⁊ xxx.sochis hn̅t.xii.car͛.Ibi.xx.ac̅ p̅ti.Valuit ⁊ ual

Gisleb̅t ten.vi.car͛ træ de.R.in *Hoches*.  ⌐vi.lib̅.

Tra.e̅.vii.car͛.In dn̅io st̅.ii.car͛.⁊ ii.serui.⁊ v.uilli

⁊ viii.sochi cu̅.i.francig hn̅t.ii.car͛ ⁊ dim.Ibi.xviii.

ac̅ p̅ti.Valuit ⁊ ual.xl.solid.

234 a

Osmund ⁊ Roger͛ ten͛ de.R.iiii.car͛ træ.

Tra.e̅.iiii.car͛.In dn̅io st̅.iii.car͛.⁊ iiii.serui.⁊ iiii.uilli

cu̅ iii.bord hn̅t dimid car͛.Valuit ⁊ ual.xl.solid.

Odard ten de.R.i.car͛ træ in *Bothesford* ⁊ Baldricus

ii.car͛ træ.⁊ Clarebald.ii.car͛ træ.⁊ Rob̅t.i.car͛ træ.

Helduin.i.car͛ træ ⁊ dim.Gisleb̅t.i.car͛ træ.⁊ alii.iiii.

francig.iii.car͛ træ ⁊ dimid.Int tot.xii.car͛ træ.

Tra.e̅.xii.car͛.In dn̅io st̅.ix.car͛.⁊.iiii.serui.⁊ vii.sochi

cu̅.ii.uiltis ⁊ xiii.bord hn̅tes.ii.car͛ int om̅s.Aliq̅ nil hn̅t.

Ibi.ii.molini ⁊ dim de.v.sol ⁊ vi.denar͛.

Totu̅ valuit.vi.lib̅ q̅do recepunt.Modo.xvi.lib̅.

Leuric tenuit ⁊ q̅ uoluit ire potuit.

[In GOSCOTE Wapentake]

10 William holds 18 c. of land in BARKBY from Robert.
Land for 16 ploughs. In lordship 3 ploughs; 3 slaves.
    7 villagers with 3 smallholders, 10 Freemen and 4 Frenchmen
        have 10 ploughs.
    A man-at-arms holds 6 c. of this land in HUNGERTON.
He has 1 plough in lordship; 2 slaves.
    7 Freemen with 3 ploughs.
    Meadow, 16 acres.
The value was 30s; now £4.

11 Roger holds 5 c. of land in (South) CROXTON from William.
Walter (holds) 2½ c. of land in QUENBY. In lordship they have
3 ploughs; 4 slaves.
    7 villagers with 4 smallholders have 1 plough.
    Meadow, 24 acres.
The value was 15s; now 30s.
    In the same village a Frenchman holds land for 1 plough.
Value 5s.

In FRAMLAND Wapentake

12 Ivo holds 17 c. of land less 3½ b. in (Long) CLAWSON from Robert.
Land for 17 ploughs. In lordship 4 ploughs; 12 slaves.
    14 villagers with 2 smallholders and 30 Freemen have 12 ploughs.
    Meadow, 20 acres.
The value was and is £6.

13 Gilbert holds 6 c. of land in HOSE from Robert. Land for 7
ploughs. In lordship 2 ploughs; 2 slaves.
    5 villagers and 8 Freemen with 1 Frenchman have 2½ ploughs.
    Meadow, 18 acres.
The value was and is 40s.

14 Osmund and Roger hold 4 c. of land from Robert.        234 a
Land for 4 ploughs. In lordship 3 ploughs; 4 slaves.
    4 villagers with 3 smallholders have ½ plough.
The value was and is 40s.

15 In BOTTESFORD Odard holds 1 c. of land from Robert; Baldric 2 c.
of land; Clarebald 2 c. of land; Robert 1 c. of land; Heldwin 1½ c.
of land; Gilbert 1 c. of land; another 4 Frenchmen 3½ c. of land.
Between them 12 c. of land. Land for 12 ploughs.
In lordship 9 ploughs; 4 slaves.
    7 Freemen with 2 villagers and 13 smallholders have 2 ploughs
        amongst them all. Some (of them) have nothing.
    2½ mills at 5s 6d.
Total value when acquired £6; now £16.
    Leofric held it; he could go where he would.

In STACHEDIRNE teñ Wilts de.R.IIII.car tre 7 dim̄.7 III.bo.

7 Roger.IIII.car træ 7 VII.bouat.Tra.ē.IX.car.

In dñio st̄.II.car̄.7 XII.fochi cū.II.uilłis 7 III.bord hñt.v.

car̄.Ibi.XL.ac̄ p̄ti.Valuit.XL.fot.Modo.L.folid.p̄dict

Leuric libe tenuit Soca 7 faca p̄tiñ ad HOLESFORD. ★


.XVI TERRA ROBERTI DE VECI. *IN GVTLACISTAN WAPENT̄.*

ROTBERT dé VECI teñ de rege MORTONE 7 Godefrid

de eo.Ibi st̄.XIIII.car̄ træ.T.R.E.erant ibi.IX.car̄.

In dñio st̄.II.car̄.cū.I.feruo.7 XXIIII.fochi 7 IIII.francig

hñt.v.car̄.Valuit X.fot.modo.XL.folid.

Norman teñ de.R.VI.car̄ træ.II.bouat min iñ

SCENTONE.T.R.E.erant ibi.v.car̄.In dñio.ē una.

7 VII.uilłi cū.III.bord hñt.II.car̄.Valuit.XII.den̄.M

DURAND teñ de.R.IIII.car̄ træ in CLEVE ⌠XXX.folid.

LIORDE.T.R.E.erant ibi.v.car̄.In dñio st̄.III.car̄.7 II.

ferui.7 v.uilłi cū.III.bord hñt.I.car̄.Ibi.XII.ac̄ pti.

Valuit.VI.folid.Modo.XXX.folid. *IN GERTREV WAPENT̄.*

GOISFRID teñ de.R.IIII.car̄ træ in GODMVNDELAI.

T.R.E.erant ibi.II.car̄.In dñio.ē una.7 II.ferui.7 III.

fochi hñt aliā.Ibi.VIII.ac̄ pti.Valuit.XII.den̄.Modo

GOISFRID teñ de.R.II.car̄ træ iñ SANCTONE. ⌠x.folid.

Tra.ē.I.car̄.quæ ibi.ē in dñio cū.II.feruis.Valuit XII.den̄.

MORILAND teñ de.R.III.car̄ træ 7 VI.bouat ⌠Modo.v.fot.

in TORP.T.R.E.erant ibi.IIII.car̄.In dñio st̄.II.car̄.

7 VI.ferui.7 VII.uilłi cū.III.bord hñt.I.car̄ 7 dimid.

Ibi.III.ac̄ pti.Valuit.IIII.folid.Modo.XX.folid.

16  In STATHERN William holds 4½ c. and 3 b. of land from Robert;
    Roger (holds) 4 c. and 7 b. of land. Land for 9 ploughs.
    In lordship 2 ploughs.
        12 Freemen with 2 villagers and 3 smallholders have 5 ploughs.
        Meadow, 40 acres.
    The value was 40s; now 50s.
        The said Leofric held it freely.
    The full jurisdiction belongs to Bottesford.

## 16        LAND OF ROBERT OF VESSEY

In GUTHLAXTON Wapentake
1   Robert of Vessey holds (GIL)MORTON from the King and Godfrey
    from him. 14 c. of land. Before 1066, 9 ploughs.
    In lordship 2 ploughs, with 1 slave.
        24 Freemen and 4 Frenchmen have 5 ploughs.
    The value was 10s; now 40s.

2   Norman holds 6 c. of land less 2 b. in SHENTON from Robert.
    Before 1066, 5 ploughs. In lordship 1.
        7 villagers with 3 smallholders have 2 ploughs.
    The value was 12d; now 30s.

3   Durand holds 4 c. of land in (South) KILWORTH from Robert.
    Before 1066, 5 ploughs. In lordship 3 ploughs; 2 slaves.
        5 villagers with 3 smallholders have 1 plough.
        Meadow, 12 acres.
    The value was 6s; now 30s.

In GARTREE Wapentake
4   Geoffrey holds 4 c. of land in GUMLEY from Robert.
    Before 1066, 2 ploughs. In lordship 1; 2 slaves.
        3 Freemen have the other (plough).
        Meadow, 8 acres.
    The value was 12d; now 10s.

5   Geoffrey holds 2 c. of land in SHANGTON from Robert. Land
    for 1 plough which is there in lordship, with 2 slaves.
    The value was 12d; now 5s.

6   Moriland holds 3 c. and 6 b. of land in THORPE (Langton) from
    Robert. Before 1066, 4 ploughs. In lordship 2 ploughs; 6 slaves.
        7 villagers with 3 smallholders have 1½ ploughs.
        Meadow, 3 acres.
    The value was 4s; now 20s.

Ipſe Rotbt̃ ten̄ de rege.iiii.car̃ træ.7 Laurenti de eo.
in *BASVRDE*.T.R.E.erant ibi.iii.car̃.In dñio ſt̃.iii.car̃.
7 iii.ſerui.7 iiii.uiłłi cũ.i.bord̃.hñt.i.car̃.Ibi moliñ
de.iii.ſolid̃.7 xvi.ãc p̃ti.Valuit.iiii.ſoł.Modo.xxx.ſoł
In ipſa uilla.xx.ſochi cũ.v.bord̃ hñt.vi.car̃.7 xx.ac̃s
p̃ti.Vał.xx.ſolid̃.

Ipſe.R.ten̄.xii.car̃ træ in *CLIBORNE*.T.R.E.erant ibi.x.
car̃.In dñio ſt̃.iii.car̃.7 vi.ſerui.7 x.uiłłi cũ.vi.ſochis
7 vi.bord̃ 7 i.francig hñt.v.car̃.Ibi.xvi.ãc p̃ti.
Valuit.xl.ſolid̃.Modo.lx.ſolid̃.

Ipſe.R.ten̄ *NEVTONE*.Ibi ſt̃.x.car̃ træ.
In dñio ſt̃.iii.car̃.7 xi.uiłłi cũ.viii.ſochis|7 v.bord̃ 7 vi.ſerũ
hñt.v.car̃.De hac tra ht̃ un̄ miles.ii.car̃ træ.7 ibi ht̃.i.
car̃.Ibi.xii.ãc p̃ti.7 moliñ de.ii.ſolid̃.
Valuit.xxx.ſolid̃.Modo.lx.ſolid̃.

Has tras Rob̃ti.tenuit Æilric fili Meriet T.R.E.7 lib̃ hõ fuit.

234 b

.XVII. TERRA ROB̃TI DE BVCI. *IN GVTLACISTAN* F.WAPENT.

ROTBERT de Bvci ten̄ de rege.iii.car̃ træ
in *PETLINGE*.Tra.ē.ii.car̃.Ibi.ē.i.uiłłs.
7 viii.ãc p̃ti.Valuit.ii.ſolid̃.Modo.v.ſolid̃.
Idē.R.ten̄.ii.car̃ træ in *LEGRE*.Tra.ē.ii.car̃.
IIas hñt ibi.viii.uiłłi cũ.i.bord̃.Valuit.ii.ſoł.m̃.xv.ſoł.
Idem.R.ten̄ dim̄ car̃ træ in *FRELESWORDE*.Tra.ē dim̄
car̃.Ibi.ē.i.bord̃.Valuit.xii.den̄.Modo.ii.ſolid̃.
Has tras tenuit lib̃e Aluuin T.R.E.

7 Robert holds 4 c. of land himself in (Husbands) BOSWORTH from
the King and Laurence from him. Before 1066, 3 ploughs.
In lordship 3 ploughs; 3 slaves.
    4 villagers with 1 smallholder have 1 plough.
    A mill at 3s; meadow, 16 acres.
The value was 4s; now 30s.
    In the same village 20 Freemen with 5 smallholders have 6 ploughs.
    Meadow, 20 acres.
Value 20s.

8 Robert holds 12 c. of land himself in KIBWORTH (Harcourt).
Before 1066, 10 ploughs. In lordship 3 ploughs; 6 slaves.
    10 villagers with 6 Freemen, 6 smallholders and 1 Frenchman
        have 5 ploughs.
    Meadow, 16 acres.
The value was 40s; now 60s.

9 Robert holds NEWTON (Harcourt) himself. 10 c. of land.
In lordship 3 ploughs.
    11 villagers with 8 Freemen, a priest, 5 smallholders and 6
        slaves have 5 ploughs.
    From this land a man-at-arms has 2 c. of land. He has 1 plough.
    Meadow, 12 acres; a mill at 2s.
The value was 30s; now 60s.
    Alric son of Mergeat held these lands of Robert's before 1066;
he was a free man.

17          LAND OF ROBERT OF BUCY          234 b

In GUTHLAXTON Wapentake
1 Robert of Bucy holds 3 c. of land in PEATLING (Magna) from
the King. Land for 2 ploughs.
    1 villager.
    Meadow, 8 acres.
The value was 2s; now 5s.

Robert also holds
2 in LEIRE 2 c. of land. Land for 2 ploughs.
    8 villagers with 1 smallholder have them.
The value was 2s; now 15s.

3 in FROLESWORTH ½ c. of land. Land for ½ plough.
    1 smallholder.
The value was 12d; now 2s.
    Alwin held these lands freely before 1066.

Idē.R.ten.vii.car̄ træ 7 dimid in *Donitone*.T.R.E.
erant ibi.vi.car̄.In dnio st.ii.7 vii.uitti 7 ix.focħi
cū.iiii.bord hnt.iiii.car̄ 7 dimid.Ibi.xvi.ac pti.
Valuit.xx.folid.Modo.lx.folid.Leuuin libe tenuit.
Idē.R.ten.ii.car̄ træ in parua *Essebi*.T.R.E.erant
ibi.ii.car̄ 7 dim.Ibi.vi.uitti cū.i.bord hnt.i.car̄.
Ibi.viii.ac pti.Valuit.vi.fot.Modo.x.folid.
Goduin libe tenuit.      *In Geretrev Wapent.*
Idē.R.ten.i.car̄ træ in *Avintone*.Ibi ħt dim car̄.
in dnio.7 iiii.uitti hnt.i.car̄.Valuit 7 uat.v.folid.
Hugo ten de.Robto.ii.car̄ træ *In Gvtlacistan Wap.*
7 dim in *Svinford*.In dnio.ē ibi.i.car̄.7 uitti hnt dim
car̄.Valuit.vi.folid.Modo.x.folid.
Idē.H.ten de.R.in *Walecote*.ii.car̄ træ.Tra.ē.ii.car̄
In dnio.ē una.7 Vlf cū fuis hoib ħt alia.Valuit.xx.
den.Modo.vi.folid.Oflac libe tenuit has.ii.tras
Rotbt ten de.R.iii.car̄ træ in *Cossebi*.Tra.ē.iii.
car̄.In dnio.ē una.cū.i.feruo.7 iii.uitti cū.iii.francig
7 v.bord hnt.ii.car̄.Valuit.v.fot.Modo.xx.folid.
Goisfrid ten de.R.una car̄ træ 7 una virg in *Bervl*
*vestone*.Tra.ē.i.car̄ 7 dimid.Ibi st.ii.uitti cū.iiii.
bord hntes.i.car̄.Valuit.viii.fot.Modo.x.folid.
Warin ten de R.iii.car̄ træ 7 dim in *Svinesford*.
T.R.E.erant ibi.iiii.car̄ 7 dim.Ibi.ii.hoēs ej hnt.ii.
car̄.Valuit.xxi.folid.Modo.xx.fot.Tres taini tenuer.
Hugo ten de R.iii.car̄ træ 7 dim.una virg min.
T.R.E.erant ibi.v.car̄.In dnio.ē una car̄ cū.i.feruo.
7 iii.uitti cū.iii.bord hnt.i.car̄.Valuit.x.fot.Modo.xx.

4   in DUNTON (Bassett) 7½ c. of land. Before 1066, 6 ploughs.
In lordship 2.
   7 villagers and 9 Freemen with 4 smallholders have 4½ ploughs.
   Meadow, 16 acres.
The value was 20s; now 60s.
   Leofwin held it freely.

5   in ASHBY PARVA  2 c. of land. Before 1066, 2½ ploughs.
   6 villagers with 1 smallholder have 1 plough.
   Meadow, 8 acres.
The value was 6s; now 10s.
   Godwin held it freely.

In GARTREE Wapentake
6   in EVINGTON 1 c. of land. He has ½ plough in lordship.
   4 villagers have 1 plough.
The value was and is 5s.

In GUTHLAXTON Wapentake
7   Hugh holds 2½ c. of land in SWINFORD  from Robert.
In lordship 1 plough.
   The villagers have ½ plough.
The value was 6s; now 10s.

8   Hugh also holds 2 c. of land in WALCOTE  from Robert.
Land for 2 ploughs. In lordship 1.
   Ulf with his men has the other.
The value was 20d; now 6s.
   Oslac held these two lands freely.

9   Robert holds 3 c. of land in COSBY from Robert. Land for 3 ploughs.
In lordship 1, with 1 slave.
   3 villagers with 3 Frenchmen and 5 smallholders have 2 ploughs.
The value was 5s; now 20s.

10   Geoffrey holds 1 c. and 1 virgate of land in BARLESTONE  from
Robert. Land for 1½ ploughs.
   2 villagers with 3 smallholders have 1 plough.
The value was 8s; now 10s.

11   Warin holds 3½ c. of land in SWINFORD  from Robert.
Before 1066, 4½ ploughs.
   2 of his men have 2 ploughs.
The value was 21s; now 20s.
   3 thanes held it.

12   Hugh holds 3½ c. of land less 1 virgate from Robert. Before
1066, 5 ploughs. In lordship 1 plough, with 1 slave.
   3 villagers with 3 smallholders have 1 plough.
The value was 10s; now 20s.

Lanbt ten de.R.in eað uilla.iii.car træ ☐ſoliđ.

7 iiii.parte uni v.T.R.E.erant ibi.iii.cař.In dnio.e
.i.cař.7 iii.uilti cū.iii.borđ hnt.i.cař.Valuit.ii.ſol.
Modo.xx.ſoliđ.

De pđictis.viii.car træ ten Alſi.�.car træ 7 dimiđ.
7 iiii.parte uni v.In dnio.e una cař.cū.i.uilto 7 i.borđ.
Ibi.xv.ac pti.Valet.v.ſoliđ.

Suauis ten de.R.ii.car træ 7 ii.bouat in BARESWERDE.
Tra.e.ii.cař.Ibi ht.i.uiltm 7 ii.borđ cū.i.car.
Valu.ii.ſoliđ.Valet.v.ſoliđ.

Ingeld ten de.R.dim car træ in NELVESTONE.Ibi.e
una car cū.i.ſocho 7 ii.borđ.Ibi.ii.ac pti.Valuit.ii.ſol

Ide ten de.R.in SLAGESTONE.i.v træ ☐Modo.v.ſoliđ.
uaſta.Valuit.iiii.denar.7 ualet.

Roger ten de R.iii.car træ 7 ii.bouat in TORP.T.R.E.erant
ibi.iii.car.In dnio.e una car cū.i.ſeruo.7 ii.uilti cū.viii.
borđ hnt.ii.cař.Ibi.iiii.ac pti.Valuit.viii.ſol.M.x.ſol.

Giſlebt ten.vi.car træ de.R.in WALENDEHA.T.R.E.
erant ibi.v.cař.In dnio ſt.ii.7 vii.uilti cū pbro hnt.ii.
cař.Ibi moliñ de.iii.ſoliđ.7 xlii.ac pti.Valuit.iii.ſol
Modo.xxv.ſoliđ.Radulf comes tenuit.

Goduin 7 Frano ten.ii.car træ 7 dim in SLACHESTONE.
T.R.E.erant ibi.v.cař.In dnio.e una.7 iiii.uilti cū.iiii.borđ
☐hnt.i.cař.Valuit.iii.ſol.
M.xvi.

*In GOSECOTE WAPENT.*
Ingeld ten de.R.in RERESBI.ii.car
træ.ii.bouat min.T.R.E.erant.ii.cař ibi.
In dnio.e una.7 dimiđ parte molini
de.ii.ſoliđ.7 viii.ac pti.Valuit.iii.ſoliđ.
Modo.x.ſoliđ.Alnod tenuit cū ſaca 7 ſoca.

13 Lambert holds 3 c. of land and the fourth part of 1 virgate in the same village from Robert. Before 1066, 3 ploughs. In lordship 1 plough.
> 3 villagers with 3 smallholders have 1 plough.

The value was 2s; now 20s.

14 Of the said 8 c. of land Alfsi holds 1½ c. of land and the fourth part of 1 virgate. In lordship 1 plough, with
> 1 villager and 1 smallholder.
> Meadow, 15 acres.

Value 5s.

[In GARTREE Wapentake]

15 Swafi holds 2 c. and 2 b. of land in (Husbands) BOSWORTH from Robert. Land for 2 ploughs. He has
> 1 villager and 2 smallholders with 1 plough.

The value was 2s; now 5s.

16 Ingold holds ½ c. of land in ILLSTON from Robert. 1 plough, with
> 1 Freeman and 2 smallholders.
> Meadow, 2 acres.

The value was 2s; now 5s.

17 He also holds 1 virgate of land in SLAWSTON from Robert. Waste.

The value was and is 4d.

18 Roger holds 3 c. and 2 b. of land in THORPE (Langton) from Robert. Before 1066, 3 ploughs. In lordship 1 plough, with 1 slave.
> 2 villagers with 8 smallholders have 2 ploughs.
> Meadow, 4 acres.

The value was 8s; now 10s.

19 Gilbert holds 6 c. of land in WELHAM from Robert. Before 1066, 5 ploughs. In lordship 2.
> 7 villagers with a priest have 2 ploughs.
> A mill at 3s; meadow, 42 acres.

The value was 3s; now 25s.
> Earl Ralph held it.

20 Godwin and Fran hold 2½ c. of land in SLAWSTON. Before 1066, 5 ploughs. In lordship 1.
> 4 villagers with 4 smallholders have 1 plough.

The value was 3s; now 16s.

In GOSCOTE Wapentake

21 Ingold holds 2 c. of land less 2 b. in REARSBY from Robert.    234 c
Before 1066, 2 ploughs. In lordship 1.
> ½ part of a mill at 2s; meadow, 8 acres.

The value was 3s; now 10s.
> Alnoth held it with full jurisdiction.

Gerard ten de.R.iii.car træ in GRIMESTONE.T.R.E. erant ibi.iii.car 7 dimid.In dnio ;e una car.7 v.uilli cu.ii.sochis hnt.iii.car.Valuit.iii.sol.Modo.x.sol.

Rotbt ten de.R.ii.car træ in SEGRAVE.T.R.E.erant ibi.ii.car.In dnio.e una.7 iii.uilti cu.iii.bord. Ibi.vii.ac pti.Valuit.xii.den.Modo.v.solid.

Ide ten de.R.xii.car træ in LVDINTONE.T.R.E.erant ibi.xii.car.In dnio.e una.7 v.sochi cu.iii.uittis 7 iii.bord hnt.i.car 7 dimid.Ibi molin de.xvi.den. De hac tra ten Gerard medietate.7 ibi ht.i.car in dnio. 7 iiii.sochi 7 iiii.uilti cu.iiii.bord hnt.ii.car 7 dimid. Ibi.xx.ac pti.Silua dimid leu lg.7 iiii.qrent lat. Valuit.v.solid.Modo.xx.solid.

Ansfrid ten.i.car træ in DALBI de.R.Tra.e.i.car. Ibi st.iii.uilti cu.i.bord.7 x.ac pti.Valuit.xii.den

Hugo ten de.R.vi.car træ in RAGENDELE ʃ Modo.iii.sol. T.R.E.erant ibi.vi.car.In dnio.e una.7 iiii.sochi hnt alia.Ibi.xxx.ac pti.Valuit.xvi.den.Modo.xx.sol.

Ide.H.ten.ii.car træ in WILGES.Vastæ st.7 tam uat

Warin ten de.R.iiii.car træ in OVRETONE.ʃxii.den. T.R.E.erant ibi.vi.car.In dnio.e una 7 ii.uilti cu.i.bord hnt.i.car.Silua.ii.qrent lg.7 una qʒ lat. Valuit.xii.den.Modo.iiii.solid.

Vxor Rotbi burdet ten de.R.ii.car træ in RADE CLIVE.T.R.E.erant ibi.iiii.car.Ibi.iii.uilti cu.ii.bord hnt.i.car.Ibi molin de.iii.sol.7 xii.ac pti.

22    Gerard holds 3 c. of land in GRIMSTON from Robert.
Before 1066, 3½ ploughs. In lordship 1 plough.
   5 villagers with 2 Freemen have 3 ploughs.
The value was 3s; now 10s.

23    Robert holds 2 c. of land in SEAGRAVE from Robert.
Before 1066, 2 ploughs. In lordship 1.
   3 villagers with 3 smallholders.
   Meadow, 7 acres.
The value was 12d; now 5s.

24    He also holds 12 c. of land in LODDINGTON from Robert.
Before 1066, 12 ploughs. In lordship 1.
   5 Freemen with 3 villagers and 3 smallholders have 1½ ploughs.
   A mill at 16d.
   Gerard holds half of this land. He has 1 plough in lordship.
   4 Freemen and 4 villagers with 4 smallholders have 2½ ploughs.
   Meadow, 20 acres; woodland ½ league long and 4 furlongs wide.
The value was 5s; now 20s.

25    Ansfrid holds 1 c. of land in (Great) DALBY from Robert.
Land for 1 plough.
   3 villagers with 1 smallholder.
   Meadow, 10 acres.
The value was 12d; now 3s.

26    Hugh holds 6 c. of land in RAGDALE from Robert.
Before 1066, 6 ploughs. In lordship 1.
   4 Freemen have another.
   Meadow, 30 acres.
The value was 16d; now 20s.

27    Hugh also holds 2 c. of land in 'WILLOWS'. Waste.
Value however, 12d.

28    Warin holds 4 c. of land in COLEORTON from Robert.
Before 1066, 6 ploughs. In lordship 1.
   2 villagers with 1 smallholder have 1 plough.
   Woodland 2 furlongs long and 1 furlong wide.
The value was 12d; now 4s.

29    Robert Burdet's wife holds 2 c. of land in RATCLIFFE (-on-the-Wreak) from Robert. Before 1066, 4 ploughs.
   3 villagers with 2 smallholders have 1 plough.
   A mill at 3s; meadow, 12 acres.

Girard ten de.R.v.car træ IN FRANELVND WAPENT.

in HOLEWELLE.7 in CHETELBI.VI.car træ.T.R.E.eraꝧ
ibi.x.car.In dñio st.II.car.7 VII.uilli cū.IIII.borđ
cū pbro 7 VI.fochis hñt.v.car.ptū ibi.III.q̊ꝥ lg.
7 dimiđ q̊ꝥ lat.Valuit.VIII.fol.Modo.LX.foliđ.

Idē.G.ten de.R.in HERTEBI.I.car træ.Tra.e.I.car.
Hanc hñt ibi.II.fochi cū.III.borđ.Val.v.fol.

Ansfrid ten de.R.III.car træ 7 dim in WIMVNDESHA.
T.R.E.erant ibi.III.car.In dñio.e una.7 v.uilli 7 IIII.
fochi cū.II.borđ hñt.III.car.Ibi.xxx.ac pti.

Valuit.II.foliđ.Modo.xxx.foliđ.

Radulf ten de.R.vi.car træ.in GOLTEBI.7 dim car
træ in SCALDEFORD.T.R.E.erant ibi.vi.car 7 dimiđ.
In dñio.e una car.7 vi.fochi cū.I.borđ hñt.II.car.
Valuit.vi.fol.Modo.XXII.foliđ.Ibi.xx.vi.ac pti.

Has tras q̊ tenuer T.R.E.quo uoluer ire potuer.pter uñ
Serie uocat.q̊ in Ragendel tenuit.III.car træ.fed non
poterat cū ea alicubi recedere.


.XVIII.TERRA ROGERIJ DE BVSLI. IN GERETREV WAPENT.

ROGERIVS DE BVSLI ten de rege.II.car træ in CLOSINTONE.
T.R.E.erant ibi.II.car.Ibi.IIII.fochi cū.II.uillis 7 II.borđ.
hñt.II.car.Ibi.IIII.ac pti.Silua.II.q̊rent lg.7 I.q̊ꝥ lat.
Huj filuæ.IIII.pars.e cujdā fochi regis.Valuit x.fol.
Modo.VIII.foliđ.                    IN GOSECOTE WAPENT.

Rogeri ten de.R.II.car træ in WIMVNDESWALD.T.R.E.
                              eraꝧ ibi.III.car.

234 d

Has hñt ibi.vi.uilli cū.II.francig.Ibi.xxx.ac pti.Valet

In FRAMLAND Wapentake

30 Gerard holds 5 c. of land in HOLWELL and 6 c. of land in (Ab)KETTLEBY from Robert. Before 1066, 10 ploughs.
In lordship 2 ploughs.
> 7 villagers with 4 smallholders with a priest and 6 Freemen have 5 ploughs.
> Meadow 3 furlongs long and ½ furlong wide.

The value was 8s; now 60s.

31 Gerard also holds 1 c. of land in HARBY from Robert.
Land for 1 plough.
> 2 Freemen with 3 smallholders have it.

Value 5s.

32 Ansfrid holds 3½ c. of land in WYMONDHAM from Robert.
Before 1066, 3 ploughs. In lordship 1.
> 5 villagers and 4 Freemen with 2 smallholders have 3 ploughs.
> Meadow, 30 acres.

The value was 2s; now 30s.

33 Ralph Pippin holds 6 c. of land in GOADBY (Marwood) and ½ c. of land in SCALFORD from Robert. Before 1066, 6½ ploughs. In lordship 1 plough.
> 6 Freemen with 1 smallholder have 2 ploughs.

The value was 6s; now 22s.

> Meadow, 26 acres.

The holders of these lands before 1066 could go where they would, except for one called Saeric, who held 3 c. of land in RAGDALE but could not withdraw elsewhere with them.

## 18      LAND OF ROGER OF BULLY

In GARTREE Wapentake

1 Roger of Bully holds 2 c. of land in KNOSSINGTON from the King.
Before 1066, 2 ploughs.
> 4 Freemen with 2 villagers and 2 smallholders have 2 ploughs.
> Meadow, 4 acres; woodland 2 furlongs long and 1 furlong wide.
>> A fourth part of this woodland is a King's Freeman's.

The value was 10s; now 8s.

In GOSCOTE Wapentake

2 Roger holds 2 c. of land in WYMESWOLD from Roger.
Before 1066, 3 ploughs.
> 6 villagers with 2 Frenchmen have them.      234 d
> Meadow, 30 acres.

Value 10s.

Ipfe Rogeri ten *SALTEBI*. Ibi ſt *IN FRANLVND WAPENT*.
.II. hidæ 7 III. car træ. T.R.E. erant ibi. xxviii. car. In dnio
ſt. vi. car. 7 xvi. ſerui. 7 xxiiii. uilli. 7 xxiii. ſocħ cū. xiiii.
borđ hnt. xx. car. Ibi. ii. molini de. viii. ſoliđ. 7 xl
ac p̄ti. Valuit. ix. liƀ. Modo. x. liƀ. Morcar tenuit.
Ricard ten de Rog *WIVORDEBIE*. Ibi ſt. v. car træ
7 iiii. bouatæ 7 dimiđ. T.R.E. erant ibi. v. car.
In dnio. ē una. 7 vii. ſerui. 7 xii. uilli cū. viii. borđ hnt
v. car 7 dimiđ. Ibi. xiiii. ac p̄ti. 7 ii. molini de. x. ſol.
Valuit 7 ual. xl. ſoliđ.
Idē ten de. R. iii. car træ in *BVRTONE*. T.R.E. erant ibi
iiii. car. In dnio. ē una. 7 v. uilli cū. iiii. borđ hnt. ii.
car. Ibi. iii. ac p̄ti. Valuit 7 ual. xx. ſoliđ.

.XIX TERRA ROBERTI DISPENSATOR. *IN GVTLACISTAN WAPENT*.
ROTBERTVS Diſpenſator ten de rege. v. car træ in *LEGRE*.
Tra. ē. iii. car. In dnio. ē una 7 dim. 7 iiii. uilli cū pƀro
7 ii. borđ hnt. i. car 7 dimiđ. Ibi. xl.viii. ac p̄ti. Valuit
Idē ten. vi. car træ in *STANTONE*. ſ7 ual xx. ſol.
Tra. ē        Ibi. vii. uilli cū. iii. borđ. hnt. iii. car. 7 ibi
ſt. iiii. liƀi hoēs. 7 xii. ac p̄ti. Silua. iii. q̄ʒ lḡ. 7 i. q̄ʒ lat.
Idē ten. i. car træ in *TORP*. ſ Valuit 7 ual. xx. ſol.
Tra. ē. i. car. Ibi. iii. uilli cū. iii. borđ hnt dimiđ car.
Ibi. vi. ac p̄ti. Valuit 7 ual. v. ſoliđ. Æilmar liƀe tenuit.
Idē ten. i. car træ in *SVTONE*. Tra. ē.        Ibi. ii. ſocħi
hnt dim car. Silua. iii. q̄rent lḡ. 7 ii. q̄ʒ lat. Valuit
Idē ten. ii. car træ in *REDECLIVE*. ſ7 ual. ii. ſol.
Tra. ē        In dnio. ē una. 7 ii. ſerui. 7 vi. uilli cū. ii.
borđ hnt. i. car. Valuit 7 ual. xx. ſoliđ.

In FRAMLAND Wapentake

3 Roger holds SALTBY himself. 2 hides and 3 c. of land.
Before 1066, 28 ploughs. In lordship 6 ploughs; 16 slaves.
   24 villagers and 23 Freemen with 14 smallholders have 20 ploughs.
   2 mills at 8s; meadow, 40 acres.
The value was £9; now £10.
   Morcar held it.

4 Richard holds WYFORDBY from Roger. 5 c. and 4½ b. of land.
Before 1066, 5 ploughs. In lordship 1; 7 slaves.
   12 villagers with 8 smallholders have 5½ ploughs.
   Meadow, 14 acres; 2 mills at 10s.
The value was and is 40s.

5 He also holds 3 c. of land in BURTON (Lazars) from Roger.
Before 1066, 4 ploughs. In lordship 1.
   5 villagers with 4 smallholders have 2 ploughs.
   Meadow, 3 acres.
The value was and is 20s.

# 9 LAND OF ROBERT THE BURSAR

In GUTHLAXTON Wapentake

1 Robert the Bursar holds 5 c. of land in LEIRE from the King.
Land for 3 ploughs. In lordship 1½.
   4 villagers with a priest and 2 smallholders have 1½ ploughs.
   Meadow, 48 acres.
The value was and is 20s.

He also holds

2 in (Stoney) STANTON 6 c. of land. Land for [...ploughs].
   7 villagers with 3 smallholders have 3 ploughs; 4 free men.
   Meadow, 12 acres; woodland 3 furlongs long and 1 furlong wide.
The value was and is 20s.

3 in PRIMETHORPE 1 c. of land. Land for 1 plough.
   3 villagers with 3 smallholders have ½ plough.
   Meadow, 6 acres.
The value was and is 5s.
   Aelmer held it freely.

4 in SUTTON (-in-the-Elms) 1 c. of land. Land for [...ploughs].
   2 Freemen have ½ plough.
   Woodland 3 furlongs long and 2 furlongs wide.
The value was and is 2s.

5 in RATCLIFFE (Culey) 2 c. of land. Land for [...ploughs].
In lordship 1; 2 slaves.
   6 villagers with 2 smallholders have 1 plough.
The value was and is 20s.

Idē ten. ı . car̄ træ 7 dim in *SACRESTONE* . T̄ra . ē

Ibi . v . uilli hn̄t . ı . car̄.　Ibi faifiuit Rob̄t . ı . car̄ træ.

7 dimid . Henric caluniat͂ ſup eū . Ibi . x . ac̄ p̄ti. ^fereires 9

Valuit 7 ual . v . ſolid.

Idē ten dim car̄ træ in *CVNINGESTONE* . Ibi . un uillſ

cū . ı . bord hr̄ dimid car̄ . Valuit 7 ual . ıı . ſolid.

Idē ten . ı . car̄ træ in *SNARCHETONE* . H̄ uaſta . ē.

Idē ten . ı . car̄ træ in *ODESTONE* . T̄ra . ē　　Ibi . ıııı.

ſochi hn̄t . ı . car̄ . Ibi . vı . ac̄ p̄ti . Valuit 7 ual . x . ſot.

Hanc tr̄a caluniat͂ . H . de fereires . Soca . ıı . car̄ har̄

jacet ad ſup̄ſcriptā uillā.　　　　　Γxıı . den.

Idē ten . ı . car̄ træ in *FLECHENIE* . Vaſta . ē . 7 tam ual

Idē ten . ııı . car̄ træ in *ESMEDITONE* . T̄ra . ē

In dn̄io . ē . ı . car̄ . 7 ııı . ſochi cū . ıı . uillis 7 ı . bord hn̄t . ı.

car̄ . Ibi . ı . ac̄ p̄ti . Valuit 7 ual . x . ſolid. *IN GERTREV WAP.*

Idē ten . ııı . car̄ træ in *FLECHENIO* . T̄ra . ē　　In dn̄io

ē una car̄ . 7 ıı uilli cū . ı . bord hn̄t . ı . car̄ . P̄tū ibi . ıı.

q̄rent lḡ . 7 ı . q̄꜕ lat . Valet . xx . ſot.

Idē ten . xı . car̄ træ 7 ııı . bouat in *WISTANESTOV.*

T.R.E . erant ibi . vııı . car̄ . In dn̄io ſt . ıı . cū . ı . ſeruo.

7 v . uilli cū . v . bord 7 ıx . ſochis hn̄t . ıııı . car̄ . 7 ıı . francig

ſt ibi . 7 molin de . ıı . ſolid . 7 x . ac̄ p̄ti . Valuit . xx . ſot.

Idē ten . v . car̄ træ 7 . vı . bouat in *CHIBVRDE* . Γ Modo . l . ſot.

T.R.E . erant ibi . v . car̄ . Ibi . vııı . uilli cū . vı . bord hn̄t

. ıı . car̄ . Ibi . xıı . ac̄ p̄ti . Valuit . x . ſot . Modo . xxx . ſolid.

Has . ııı . tras tenuit libe Eduin Alferd cū ſaca 7 ſoca.

6    in SHACKERSTONE 1½ c. of land. Land for [...ploughs].
5 villagers have 1 plough.
Robert took possession of 1½ c. of land; Henry of Ferrers
claims it against him.
Meadow, 10 acres.
The value was and is 5s.

7    in CONGERSTONE ½ c. of land.
1 villager with 1 smallholder has ½ plough.
The value was and is 2s.

8    in SNARESTONE 1 c. of land. Waste.

9    in ODSTONE 1 c. of land. Land for [...ploughs].
3 Freemen have 1 plough.
Meadow, 6 acres.
The value was and is 10s.
Henry of Ferrers claims this land.
The jurisdiction of 2 c. of these lies with the above-written village.

[In GARTREE Wapentake]

10    in FLECKNEY 1 c. of land. Waste.
Value however, 12d.

11    in SMEETON (Westerby) 3 c. of land. Land for [...ploughs].
In lordship 1 plough.
3 Freemen with 2 villagers and 1 smallholder have 1 plough.
Meadow, 1 acre.
The value was and is 10s.

In GARTREE Wapentake

12    in FLECKNEY 3 c. of land. Land for [...ploughs].
In lordship 1 plough.
2 villagers with 1 smallholder have 1 plough.
Meadow 2 furlongs long and 1 furlong wide.
Value 20s.

13    in WISTOW 11 c. and 3 b. of land. Before 1066, 8 ploughs.
In lordship 2, with 1 slave.
5 villagers with 5 smallholders and 9 Freemen have 4 ploughs;
2 Frenchmen.
A mill at 2s; meadow, 10 acres.
The value was 20s; now 50s.

14    in KIBWORTH (Beauchamp) 5 c. and 6 b. of land.
Before 1066, 5 ploughs.
8 villagers with 6 smallholders have 2 ploughs.
Meadow, 12 acres.
The value was 10s; now 30s.
Edwin Alfrith held these three lands freely with full jurisdiction.

Idē Robt ten . vi . car træ in *CHIBVRDE* . T.R.E . erant ibi

.iii . car . In dnio st . ii . car 7 dim . 7 iii . serui . 7 ix . uilti cū . ii.

bord hnt . ii . car 7 dim . Ibi . xii . ac pti . Valuit xxx . solid.

Idē ten . i . car træ . 7 ii . bouat in *WITENESTO* ⌐ Modo . xl . sot.

Vasta . ē . 7 tam ualet . ii . solid.

Idē ten . iii . car tre in *TILETONE* . In dnio st ibi . ii . car.

7 xiii . uilti cū pbro 7 i . bord hnt . iii . car . Ibi . viii . ac pti.

Valuit 7 ual . xx . solid . Has tras tenuit Ælmar cū saca

Idē ten in *NORTONE* . iiii . car træ 7 dim.       ⌐7 soca.

In dnio . ē . i . car . 7 vi . uilti cū . ii . sochis 7 iii . bord hnt . ii.

car 7 dimid . Ibi molin de . ii . sot . 7 ii . ac pti . 7 iii . ac siluæ.

Valuit 7 ual . xx . solid.         *IN FRANLVND WAP.*

Idē ten . v . car træ 7 iii . bouat in *SVMERDEBERIE*.

In dnio . ē una car . 7 vi . uilti cū . iii . bord hnt . i . car.

Ibi . x . ac pti . Valuit 7 ual . x . sot . Vlnod libe tenuit.

Idē ten in *WICORE* . i . car træ 7 dim . H uasta . ē . Ibi . ii.

ac pti . Silua . i . qrent 7 dim lg . 7 una qꝣ lat . Val . xii . den.


## .XX. TERRA ROBERTI HOSTIARIJ.

ROTBERT Hostiarius

ten de rege . ii . car træ . in *HOWES* . Tra . ē . iii . car.

In dnio . ē . i . car . 7 iii . serui . 7 viii . uilti cū . i . bord hnt . ii.

car . Ibi . vii . ac pti . Valuit 7 ual . xx . sot.

Turstin ten de . R . ii . car træ 7 dim in *HOWES* . Tra . ē

ii . car . In dnio . ē una . 7 ii . serui . 7 vi . uilti cū . ii . bord

hnt . i . car 7 dim . Ibi . ix . ac pti . Valuit 7 ual . xx . solid.

15 Robert also holds 6 c. of land in KIBWORTH (Beauchamp).    235 a
Before 1066, 3 ploughs. In lordship 2½ ploughs; 3 slaves.
9 villagers with 2 smallholders have 2½ ploughs.
Meadow, 12 acres.
The value was 30s; now 40s.

He also holds
16 in WISTOW 1 c. and 2 b. of land. Waste.
Value however, 2s.

[In GOSCOTE Wapentake]
17 in TILTON 3 c. of land. In lordship 2 ploughs.
13 villagers with a priest and 1 smallholder have 3 ploughs.
Meadow, 8 acres.
The value was and is 20s.
Aelmer held these lands with full jurisdiction.

18 in (East) NORTON 4½ c. of land. In lordship 1 plough.
6 villagers with 2 Freemen and 3 smallholders have 2½ ploughs.
A mill at 2s; meadow, 2 acres; woodland, 3 acres.
The value was and is 20s.

In FRAMLAND Wapentake
19 in SOMERBY 5 c. and 3 b. of land. In lordship 1 plough.
6 villagers with 3 smallholders have 1 plough.
Meadow, 10 acres.
The value was and is 10s.
Wulfnoth held it freely.

20 in WITHCOTE 1½ c. of land. Waste.
Meadow, 2 acres; woodland 1½ furlongs long and 1 furlong wide.
Value 12d.


20          **LAND OF ROBERT USHER**

1 Robert Usher holds 2 c. of land in HOSE from the King.
Land for 3 ploughs. In lordship 1 plough; 3 slaves.
8 villagers with 1 smallholder have 2 ploughs.
Meadow, 7 acres.
The value was and is 20s.

2 Thurstan holds 2½ c. of land in HOSE from Robert.
Land for 2 ploughs. In lordship 1; 2 slaves.
6 villagers with 2 smallholders have 1½ ploughs.
Meadow, 9 acres.
The value was and is 20s.

Idē ten de.R.IIII.car̄ træ in *CLACHESTONE*.Tra.ē.II.
car̄.Has hn̄t ibi.III.fochi cū.II.uillis.7 II.bord̄.
Ibi.VIII.ac̄ p̄ti.Valuit 7 ual.x.folid̄.
Tetbald ten de.R.II.car̄ tre in *CLACHESTONE*.
In dn̄io.ē.I.car̄.cū.I.feruo.7 III.uilli cū.I.bord̄ hn̄t.I.
car̄.Ibi.VI.ac̄ p̄ti.Valuit 7 ual.x.folid̄.

## .XXI. TERRA RADVLFI DE MORTEMER.

RADVLFVS De Mortemer ten de rege *SBERNESTVN*.
7 Rogeri de eo.Ibi ſt.IIII.car̄ træ.Tra.IIII.car̄.In
dn̄io.ē una.7 II.ferui.7 x.uilli cū.II.car̄.Silua.VII.q̄ɀ
lḡ.7 III.q̄ɀ lat̄.Valuit.xxx.fol.Modo.XL.folid̄.
Idē Rog ten de.R.*WESTONE*.Ibi ſt.V.car̄ træ 7 dimid̄.
Tra.ē.V.car̄.In dn̄io ſt.II.7 IIII.ferui.7 XII.uilli cū.I.
focho hn̄t.III.car̄ 7 dimid̄.Valet.LXX.fol.Vafta fuit.
Edric 7 Edged has.II.tras libe tenuer̄.

## .XXII TERRA RADVLFI FILIJ HVBTI. *IN GOSECOTE WAPENT*.

RADVLFVS filius Hubti ten de rege.IX.car̄ træ in
*DALBI*.7 Robt de eo.Tra.ē.XII.car̄.In dn̄io.ē una.
7 unus miles cū.II.fochis 7 XIII.uillis 7 VIII.bord̄ hn̄t
VII.car̄.Pratū ibi.I.leuū lḡ.7 dim leu lat̄.Spinetū
II.q̄rent lḡ.7 una q̄ɀ lat̄.Valuit.III.lib̄.Modo.IIII.lib̄.

## XXIII. TERRA WIDON DE RENBVDCVRT. *IN GOSEGOTE WAPENT*.

WIDO de Reinbudcurt ten de rege.XVIII.car̄ træ
in *TVRSTANESTONE*.Tra.ē.XII.car̄.In dn̄io ſt.II.car̄.
7 xxx.fochi cū.IIII.uillis 7 III.bord̄ hn̄t.XI.car̄.Ibi molin̄
de.VIII.folid̄.7 XVI.ac̄ p̄ti.Valuit xx.fol.Modo.IIII.lib̄.

3 He also holds 4 c. of land in (Long) CLAWSON from Robert.
Land for 2 ploughs.
3 Freemen with 2 villagers and 2 smallholders have them.
Meadow, 8 acres.
The value was and is 10s.

4 Theobald holds 2 c. of land in (Long) CLAWSON from Robert.
In lordship 1 plough, with 1 slave.
3 villagers with 1 smallholder have 1 plough.
Meadow, 6 acres.
The value was and is 10s.

## LAND OF RALPH OF MORTIMER

[In GUTHLAXTON Wapentake]

1 Ralph of Mortimer holds OSBASTON from the King and Roger from
him. 4 c. of land. Land for 4 ploughs. In lordship 1; 2 slaves;
10 villagers with 2 ploughs.
Woodland 7 furlongs long and 3 furlongs wide.
The value was 30s; now 40s.

2 Roger also holds 'WESTON' from Ralph. 5½ c. of land.
Land for 5 ploughs. In lordship 2; 4 slaves.
12 villagers with 1 Freeman have 3½ ploughs..
Value 70s; it was waste.
Edric and Edith held these two lands freely.

## LAND OF RALPH SON OF HUBERT

In GOSCOTE Wapentake

1 Ralph son of Hubert holds 9 c. of land in (Old) DALBY from the
King and Robert from him. Land for 12 ploughs. In lordship 1.
1 man-at-arms with 2 Freemen, 13 villagers and 8 smallholders
have 7 ploughs.
Meadow 1 league long and ½ league wide; spinney 2 furlongs
long and 1 furlong wide.
The value was £3; now £4.

## LAND OF GUY OF RAIMBEAUCOURT

In GOSCOTE Wapentake

1 Guy of Raimbeaucourt holds 18 c. of land in THRUSSINGTON
from the King.
Land for 12 ploughs. In lordship 2 ploughs.
30 Freemen with 4 villagers and 3 smallholders have 11 ploughs.
A mill at 8s; meadow, 16 acres.
The value was 20s; now £4.

Benedict abb ten de Widone . ix . caſ *IN GVTLACISTAN WAP.*

traͤ in *STORMEORDE.* Tra . ē . vi . caſ . Ibi . xii . ſochi hūt . ii . caſ.

H̄ tra p̄tiñ ad *STANFORD* in Nordh̄antoneſcire ; Valuit

xxx . ſolid . Modo . lx . ſolid . Leuric tenuit T.R.E.

Idē abb ten de . W . i . caſ traͤ in *MENSTRETONE.*

Tra . ē . i . caſ 7 dimid . Vaſta . ē . Val tam̄ . ii . ſolid . *IN GERTREV*

Idē abb ten . ii . caſ traͤ 7 ii . bouat in *BARREHORDE*  ⸢*WAP;*

de Widone . Tra . ē . i . caſ . In dn̄io tam̄ . ē una . 7 iiii ; uilli

cū . iii . bord hūt . i . caſ . Ibi . viii . ac p̃ti . Valuit ; vi ; ſol.

Modo . xx . ſolid ; Has tras emit abb Bened a Widone.

Robt ten de . W . ii . caſ traͤ 7 dim in *CLEVELIORDE;*

Tra . ē . i . caſ 7 dim . Ibi ; vii ; ſochi cū . iiii ; bord hūt . ii ; caſ.

Ibi . vi ; ac p̃ti . Valuit . v ; ſol . Modo . x . ſol.

Idē ten de . W . xi . caſ traͤ 7 dimid in *BARESWORDE.*

Tra . ē . xii . caſ . Ibi . xx . ſochi cū ; v . bord . hūt . vi . caſ.

Ibi . xx . ac p̃ti ; Valuit . xxx ; ſol ; Modo ; xx ; ſolid ; He . ii.

traͤ p̄tiñ ad *STANFORD* . Leuric tenuit


.XXII. TERRA WIDON̄ DE CREDVN. *IN FRANELVN WAPENT.*

WIDO DE CREDVN ten de rege . viii . caſ traͤ in *STOVE*

*NEBI* . T.R.E. fueſ ibi . viii . caſ . In dn̄io ſt ; iiii . caſ . 7 vii.

ſerui . 7 iiii . uilli cū ; v . bord 7 xi . ſochis hūt . vi ; caſ.

Ibi ; lx . ac p̃ti ; Valuit ; xx ; ſolid . Modo . lx . ſolid.

Idē ten in Waltham . ii ; caſ traͤ cū ſaca 7 ſoca.

7 dim caſ traͤ ſine ſoca 7 ſaca . Huj traͤ pecunia

ſupius . ē annumerata.

Warin ten de ; W . in *SPROTONE* . iii ; caſ traͤ ; Tra . ē

iii . caſ . In dn̄io . ē una ; 7 ii ; ſerui ; 7 vii . ſochi cū ; i . uillo

hūt . ii . caſ . Ibi moliñ de . iiii . ſol . 7 xv ; ac p̃ti ;

Valuit ; xx . ſol ; Modo . xl . ſolid.

In GUTHLAXTON Wapentake

2 Abbot Benedict holds 9 c. of land in 'STORMESWORTH' from Guy.
Land for 6 ploughs.
  12 Freemen have 2 ploughs.
  This land belongs to Stanford in Northamptonshire.           235 b
The value was 30s; now 60s.
  Leofric held it before 1066.

3 The Abbot also holds 1 c. of land in MISTERTON from Guy.
Land for 1½ ploughs. Waste.
Value however, 2s.

In GARTREE Wapentake

4 The Abbot also holds 2 c. and 2 b. of land in (Husbands) BOSWORTH
from Guy. Land for 1 plough. However, 1 in lordship.
  4 villagers with 3 smallholders have 1 plough.
  Meadow, 8 acres.
The value was 6s; now 20s.
  Abbot Benedict bought these lands from Guy.

5 Robert holds 2½ c. of land from Guy in KILWORTH. Land for 1½ ploughs.
  7 Freemen with 4 smallholders have 2 ploughs.
  Meadow, 6 acres.
The value was 5s; now 10s.

6 He also holds 11½ c. of land in (Husbands) BOSWORTH from Guy.
Land for 12 ploughs.
  20 Freemen with 5 smallholders have 6 ploughs.
  Meadow, 20 acres.
The value was 30s; now 20s.
  These two lands belong to Stanford. Leofric held them.


24          **LAND OF GUY OF CRAON**


In FRAMLAND Wapentake

1 Guy of Craon holds 8 c. of land in STONESBY from the King.
Before 1066, 8 ploughs. In lordship 3 ploughs; 7 slaves.
  4 villagers with 5 smallholders and 11 Freemen have 6 ploughs.
  Meadow, 60 acres.
The value was 20s; now 60s.

2 He also holds 2½ c. of land in WALTHAM (on-the-Wolds) with full
jurisdiction and ½ c. of land without full jurisdiction. The
stock of this land is enumerated above.

3 Warin holds 3 c. of land in SPROXTON from Guy.
Land for 3 ploughs. In lordship 1; 2 slaves.
  7 Freemen with 1 villager have 2 ploughs.
  A mill at 4s; meadow, 15 acres.
The value was 20s; now 40s.

Willelm pevrel ten de rege *Fostone*. Ibi. ẽ dimiđ
hida. Tra. ẽ. v. cař. In dňio sť. 11. 7 11. ſerui. 7 1. ancilla.
7 xi. ſochi cũ. viii. uiłłis 7 1111. borđ hñt. v. cař. Ibi. xvi.
ac pti. Valuit. xl. ſoliđ. Modo. l. ſoliđ.

Idẽ. W. ten dimiđ hiđ 7 111. bouat træ in *Erendesbi.*
Tra. ẽ. vii. cař. Ibi. 11. hoẽs Wiłłi cũ xiiii. uiłłis 7 1111.
borđ hñt. vii. cař. pťũ ibi. 1111. q̃rent lḡ. 7 tntđ lat.
Valuit. xx. ſoliđ. Modo. l. ſoliđ. In Ledeceſtre. ẽ un
burḡſis pťin ad hanc uiłła.

Pagen ten de. W. vi. cař træ 7 v. bouat in *Lvpestor.*
Tra. ẽ. 1111. cař. In dňio sť. 11. 7 x. uiłłi 7 vi. borđ q̃ cũ. 11.
ſochis in Brandeſtorp manentib. 11. cař 7 v. boues hñt
arantes. Hi. ii. ſochi hñt. v. bouat træ. Ibi. xl. ac pti.
Silua infructuoſa. vi. q̃z lḡ. 7 una q̃z lat.
Valuit. l. ſol. Modo. 1111. liḃ.

Ricolf ten de. W. in *Carbi*. 111. cař træ. 111. bouat min.
7 pťin ad Lupeſtorp. Tra. ẽ. 11. cař. In dňio. ẽ una. 7 vi.
uiłłi cũ. 11. borđ hñt. 1. cař. Ibi. viii. ac pti. Silua. 1111.
q̃rent lḡ. 7 11. q̃z lat. Valuit. v. ſol. Modo. xxx. ſol.
Sasfriđ ten de. W. in *Essebi*. xvi. cař tre. 11. bouat
min. Tra. ẽ. vii. cař. In dňio sť. 111. cař 7 11. ſerui.
7 xiii. ſochi cũ. 1. uiłło 7 x. borđ hñt. 1111. cař. 7 dim. Ibi. xl.
ac pti. Valuit. xx. ſol. Modo. lx. ſoliđ.

Witłs buenuaſłet ten. 11. cař træ in *Ravenestorp*. Vaſta
fuit 7 eſt.

# LAND OF WILLIAM PEVEREL

In GUTHLAXTON Wapentake

1  William Peverel holds FOSTON from the King. ½ hide. Land for
5 ploughs. In lordship 2; 2 male and 1 female slaves.
    11 Freemen with 8 villagers and 4 smallholders have 5 ploughs.
    Meadow, 16 acres.
The value was 40s; now 50s.

2  William also holds ½ hide and 3 b. of land in ARNESBY.
Land for 7 ploughs.
    2 of William's men with 14 villagers and 3 smallholders have
       7 ploughs.
    Meadow 4 furlongs long and as many wide.
The value was 20s; now 50s.
    In Leicester a burgess who belongs to this village.

3  Payne holds 6 c. and 5 b. of land in LUBBESTHORPE from William.
Land for 4 ploughs. In lordship 2.
    10 villagers and 6 smallholders who, with 2 Freemen dwelling
       in 'Bromkinsthorpe' have 2 c. and 5 oxen ploughing.
    These 2 Freemen have 5 b. of land.
    Meadow, 40 acres; barren woodland 6 furlongs long and
       1 furlong wide.
The value was 50s; now £4.

4  Riculf holds 3 c. of land less 3 b. in KIRBY (Muxloe) from William;
they belong to Lubbesthorpe. Land for 2 ploughs. In lordship 1.
    6 villagers with 2 smallholders have 1 plough.
    Meadow, 8 acres; woodland 4 furlongs long and 2 furlongs wide.
The value was 5s; now 30s.

5  Saxfrid holds 16 c. of land less 2 b. in ASHBY (Magna) from William.
Land for 7 ploughs. In lordship 3 ploughs; 2 slaves.
    13 Freemen with 1 villager and 10 smallholders have 4½ ploughs.
    Meadow, 40 acres.
The value was 20s; now 60s.

# LAND OF WILLIAM BONVALLET

In GOSCOTE Wapentake

1  William Bonvallet holds 2 c. of land in RAVENSTONE.
It was and is waste.

# .XXVII TERRA WILLI LOVETH.

WILLELM Loveth ten de rege . III . car træ de *DIVVORT*.

Tra . e . III . car . In dnio . e una . 7 VI . uilli cu . VI . bord hnt . II.
car . Valuit . x . fol . Modo . xxx . folid.

Ide . W . ten *TEDIWORDE* . Ibi erant T.R.E . II . car . Ibi . II . fochi
cu alijs . II . hoibz hnt . I . car . Ibi . x . ac pti . Valuit . III . folid.
Huj træ Soca jacet ad Bugedone co regis.           *F* Modo . x . fol.

Ide . W . ten . v . car træ in *SEWESTEN* . T.R.E . erant ibi . v . car.
In dnio . e . I . car . 7 VI . uilli . cu . I . fochi hnt . I . car 7 dimid.
Valuit . III . folid . Modo . x . folid . H tra . e *IN FRANELVN WAP*.

# .XX. VIII. TERRA GOISFRIDI ALSELIN: *IN GEREKEV WAPENT*.

GOISFRID ALSELIN ten de rege . VI . car 7 træ in *ALCTONE*.
7 Normann de eo . T.R.E . erant ibi . VIII . car . In dnio st . II . car.
7 II . ferui . 7 XIX . uilli cu . I . focho 7 I . libo hoc 7 III . bord hnt
VI . car . Silua ibi . IIII . qrent lg . 7 II . qz lat.
Valuit . LX . folid . Modo . c . folid.

Ide . N . ten de . G . in *GOVTEBI* . III . car træ . T.R.E . erant
ibi . II . car . In dnio . e dimid car cu . I . feruo . 7 IIII . uilli cu . II.
bord hnt . I . car . Silua . IIII . qrent lg . 7 II . qz lat.
Valuit 7 ual . xx . folid.

Ide . N . ten de . G . in *CHEITORP* . I . car træ . Ibi fuit . I . car . T.R.E.
Ibi . I . fochs cu . II . uillis 7 I . bord hnt . I . car . Ibi . x . ac filuæ.
Valuit . v . fol . Modo . VI . folid.

# LAND OF WILLIAM LOVETT

1  William Lovett holds 3 c. of land in DISEWORTH from the King.
Land for 3 ploughs.  In lordship 1.
  6 villagers with 6 smallholders have 2 ploughs.
The value was 10s; now 30s.

[In GARTREE Wapentake]

2  William also holds THEDDINGWORTH.  Before 1066, 2 ploughs.
  2 Freemen with 2 other men have 1 plough.
  Meadow, 10 acres.
The value was 3s; now 10s.
  The jurisdiction of this land lies with the King's manor of Bowden.

[In FRAMLAND Wapentake]

3  William also holds 5 c. of land in SEWSTERN.  Before 1066,
5 ploughs.  In lordship 1 plough.
  6 villagers with 1 Freeman have 1½ ploughs.
The value was 3s; now 10s.
  This land is in FRAMLAND Wapentake.

4  In *STOFALDE* 3 parts of 1 virgate.  Waste.

# LAND OF GEOFFREY ALSELIN

In GARTREE Wapentake

1  Geoffrey of Alselin holds 6 c. of land in HALLATON  from the King
and Norman from him.  Before 1066, **8** ploughs.
In lordship 2 ploughs; 2 slaves.
  19 villagers with 1 Freeman, 1 free man and 3 smallholders
    have 6 ploughs.
Woodland 4 furlongs long and 2 furlongs wide.
The value was 60s; now 100s.

2  Norman also holds 3 c. of land in GOADBY from Geoffrey.
Before 1066, 2 ploughs.  In lordship ½ plough, with 1 slave.
  4 villagers with 2 smallholders have 1 plough.
  Woodland 4 furlongs long and 2 furlongs wide.
The value was and is 20s.

3  Norman also holds 1 c. of land in KEYTHORPE from Geoffrey.
Before 1066, 1 plough.
  1 Freeman with 2 villagers and 1 smallholder have 1 plough.
  Woodland, 10 acres.
The value was 5s; now 6s.

Idē.N.teñ de G.xii.car̄ træ in *BILLESDONE*.T.R.E.eraɴ
ibi.xii.car̄.In dñio nil fuit nec.ē.Ibi.iiii.fochi cū.iii.
uiltis 7 ii.bord hñt.ii.car̄.Ibi.x.ac̄ p̃ti.

De hac tra teñ.iii.milites.vii.carucat 7 dim.7 in dñio
hñt.iii.car̄.7 xi.uiltos cū.ii.bord hñtes.ii.car̄ 7 dimid.
Totū ualuit.lv.folid.Modo.lx.folid.

Idē.N.teñ de.G.x.car̄ træ in *ROVESTONE*.T.R.E.erant
ibi.vi.car̄.In dñio.ē.i.car̄.7 uñ miles cū.vii.uiltis 7 i.bord
hñt.iii.car̄.Ibi.viii.ac̄ p̃ti.Valuit.xx.fol.Modo.xxv.folid.
Hanc tra totā tenuit Tochi cū faca 7 foca


.XXIX TERRA GOISFRIDI DE WIRCE.
Goisfrid De Wirce teñ de rege.iii.car̄ træ in *STAN*
*TONE*.T.R.E.erant ibi.iiii.car̄.In dñio.ē.i.car̄.7 xiii.
uilli cū.v.bord hñt.iii.car̄.Silua ibi.i.leuū lḡ.7 dim leu
lat̄.Valuit 7 ual.xx.fol.Hanc tra ded rex.W.Goisfrido
p cōmutatione uillæ q̃ uocat Turchileftone.7 hanc fequentē
Idē.G.teñ.iiii.car̄ træ 7 dim in *NORTONE*.T.R.E.erant ibi.iii.
car̄.In dñio.ē.i.car̄ 7 dim.7 iii.uilli cū.i.focho 7 i.bord hñt
.i.car̄.Ibi moliñ de.ii.folid.7 iii.ac̄ p̃ti.7 iii.ac̄ filuæ.
Valuit 7 ual.x.fol.Aluuin libe teñ *IN FRANELVND WAPENT*.
Ipfe.G.teñ *MEDELTONE*.Ibi ſt.vii.hidæ 7 una car̄ træ
7 una bouata.In una q̃q̃ hida.ſt.xiiii.car̄ træ 7 dimid.
In dñio ſt.iiii.car̄.7 iiii.ferui.7 xx.uilli cū.ii.p̃bris 7 xiiii.
bord hñt.vi.car̄ 7 dim.Mercat redd.xx.fol.7 ii.molini
xxv.folid.Ibi.xx.ac̄ p̃ti.Silua.i.q̃rent lḡ.7 i.q̃ʒ lat̄.
Valuit.c.folid.Modo.viii.lib.Huic Ꝋ adjac ĥ mēbra.

235 c

4    Norman also holds 12 c. of land in BILLESDON from Geoffrey.
Before 1066, 12 ploughs. None were nor are in lordship.
  4 Freemen with 3 villagers and 2 smallholders have 2 ploughs.
  Meadow, 10 acres.
  3 men-at-arms hold 7½ c. of this land. In lordship
they have 3 ploughs and
  11 villagers with 2 smallholders who have 2 ploughs.
The value of the whole was 55s; now 60s.

5    Norman also holds 10 c. of land in ROLLESTON from Geoffrey.
Before 1066, 6 ploughs. In lordship 1 plough.
  1 man-at-arms with 7 villagers and 1 smallholder have 3 ploughs.
  Meadow, 8 acres.
The value was 20s; now 25s.
  Toki held all this land with full jurisdiction.

29         LAND OF GEOFFREY OF LA GUERCHE

[In GUTHLAXTON Wapentake]
1    Geoffrey of La Guerche holds 3 c. of land in STANTON (-under-
Bardon) from the King. Before 1066, 4 ploughs.
In lordship 1 plough.
  13 villagers with 5 smallholders have 3 ploughs.
  Woodland 1 league long and ½ league wide.
The value was and is 20s.
  King William gave this land and the following, likewise, to
Geoffrey in exchange for the village called Thurcaston.

[In GOSCOTE Wapentake]
2    Geoffrey also holds 4½ c. of land in (East) NORTON.
Before 1066, 3 ploughs. In lordship 1½ ploughs.
  3 villagers with 1 Freeman and 1 smallholder have 1 plough.
  A mill at 2s; meadow, 3 acres; woodland, 3 acres.
The value was and is 10s.
  Alwin and Ulf held it freely.

In FRAMLAND Wapentake
3    Geoffrey holds MELTON (Mowbray) himself. 7 hides, 1 c.
and 1 b. of land. In each hide are 14½ c. of land.
In lordship 4 ploughs; 4 slaves.
  20 villagers with 2 priests and 14 smallholders have 6½ ploughs.
  A market which pays 20s; 2 mills, 25s; meadow, 20 acres;
    woodland 1 furlong long and 1 furlong wide.
The value was 100s; now £8.
  These members are attached to this manor.

In Fredebi.x.car træ.7 xxx.ac p̄ti.

In Wordebi.i.car træ 7 dim.7 dimid bouata.7 vi.ac p̄ti.

In Burtone.xii.car træ.i.bouata min.7 xii.ac p̄ti.

In Chitebie.viii.car træ.7 vi.ac p̄ti.

In Chirchebi.xvii.car træ.In Siſtenebi.ii.car træ 7 dimid.

In Eſteuuelle.vi.car træ.7 x.ac p̄ti.In Goutebi.vi.car træ

In his tris.T.R.E.fuer.xlviii.car. £7 xx.ac p̄ti

Modo ſt ibi.c.ſochi cū.x.uiſtis 7 xiii.bord hntes.xl.iii.car.

Valuit tot q̄do recep̄.iiii.lib 7 x.ſol.Modo.xv.lib 7 x.ſol.

Hanc trā tenuit Leuric.f.Leuuini T.R.E.cū ſaca 7 ſoca.

235 d

In *ALEBIE* ſt.viii.car træ.ii.bouat min.q ptin ad Medel
tone.Ibi fuer.v.car.Modo.xvi.ſochi hnt ibi.v.car.7 vi.
acs p̄ti.Valuit.x.ſolid.Modo.xl.ſolid. *IN GVTLACISTAN WAP.*

Walter ten de.G.viii.car træ in *VLESTORP*.Ibi fuer.vi.
car.In dñio ſt.ii.7 iiii.ſerui.7 ix.uiſti 7 iiii.bord cū.ii.car.
Ibi molin de.xvi.den.7 xvi.ac p̄ti.Valuit.x.ſol.m̊.xxx.ſol.

Alfrid ten de.G.ii.car træ in *LILINGE*.Ibi fuer.iiii.car.
In dñio.ē.i.car.7 ii.ſerui.7 ix.uiſti cū.iii.bord hnt.ii.car.
Valuit.x.ſol.Modo.xx.ſolid.

Robt ten de.G.in *BETMESWELLE*.i.car træ.Ibi.ē.i.bord.
Valuit 7 ual.xii.denar.

Aluuin ten de.G.in *STORMODE*.i.car træ.Ibi fuit.i.car.
7 modo ſimilit.ē cū.ii.uiſtis 7 i.bord.Valuit 7 ual.v.ſolid.

Aluuin ten de G.in *SVINFORD*.i.car træ.Vaſta.ē.Val tam

Buterus ten de.G.xiiii. *IN GERETREV WAPENT.* £ii.ſol.
car træ in *PICHEWELLE* 7 *LVVESTORP*.Ibi fuer.x.car.In dñio
ſt.iiii.car.7 xiiii.ſerui.7 vii.uiſti cū p̄bro 7 xxvi.ſochis
7 ix.bord hnt.xiii.car.Ibi molin de.iiii.den.7 l.ac p̄ti.
Valuit.xl.ſolid.Modo.iiii.lib.Ordmar libe tenuit.T.R.E.

In FREEBY 10 c. of land. Meadow, 30 acres.
In WYFORDBY 1½ c. and ½ b. of land. Meadow, 6 acres.
In BURTON (Lazars) 12 c. of land less 1 b. Meadow, 12 acres.
In (Eye) KETTLEBY 8 c. of land. Meadow, 6 acres.
In KIRBY (Bellars) 17 c. of land.
In SYSONBY 2½ c. of land.
In EASTWELL 6 c. of land. Meadow, 10 acres.
In GOADBY (Marwood) 6 c. of land. Meadow, 20 acres.
In these lands there were 48 ploughs before 1066.
> Now 100 Freemen with 10 villagers and 13 smallholders who
>> have 43 ploughs.
Total value when acquired £4 10s; now £15 10s.
> Before 1066 Leofric son of Leofwin held this land with
full jurisdiction.

4   In WELBY 8 c. of land less 2 b. which belong to Melton.      235 d
There were 5 ploughs.
> Now 16 Freemen have 5 ploughs.
Meadow, 6 acres.
The value was 10s; now 40s.

In GUTHLAXTON Wapentake
5   Walter holds 8 c. of land in ULLESTHORPE from Geoffrey.
There were 6 ploughs. In lordship 2; 4 slaves.
> 9 villagers and 4 smallholders with 2 ploughs.
> A mill at 16d; meadow, 16 acres.
The value was 10s; now 30s.

6   Alfred holds 2 c. of land in *LILINGE* from Geoffrey.
There were 4 ploughs. In lordship 1 plough; 2 slaves.
> 9 villagers with 3 smallholders have 2 ploughs.
The value was 10s; now 20s.

7   Robert holds 1 c. of land in BITTESWELL from Geoffrey.
> 1 smallholder.
The value was and is 12d.

8   Alwin holds 1 c. of land in 'STORMESWORTH' from Geoffrey.
There was 1 plough. Now likewise, with
> 2 villagers and 1 smallholder.
The value was and is 5s.

9   Alwin holds 1 c. of land in SWINFORD from Geoffrey.
Waste. Value however, 2s.

In GARTREE Wapentake
0   Buterus holds 14 c. of land in PICKWELL and LEESTHORPE
from Geoffrey. There were 10 ploughs. In lordship 4 ploughs;
14 slaves.
> 7 villagers with a priest, 26 Freemen and 9 smallholders
>> have 13 ploughs.
A mill at 4d; meadow, 50 acres.
The value was 40s; now £4.
> Ordmer held it freely before 1066.

In Godtorp sī . III . caī trǣ 7 dim . Soca *IN FRANLVND WAP*.

de Picheuuelle 7 de Sūmerdebie . Ibi fueī . III . caī . Ibi . ē m̄

.I. caī cū . II . borđ . 7 III . ac̄ p̄ti . Valuit 7 ual . x . soliđ.

In Burgo . ē . I . caī trǣ . Ibi fuit . I . caī . Soca de Picheuuelle.

Valuit 7 ual . v . soliđ.          *IN GOSECOTE WAPENT*.

Willſ ten de . G . in *CVNIBVRG* . IX . caī trǣ . Ibi fueī . VIII .

caī . In dñio sī . II . 7 XXVIII . uilli cū . VII . borđ hn̄t . VII . caī.

Ibi molin̄ de . x . soł . 7 XL . ac̄ p̄ti . Valuit . III . lib̄ . Modo . IIII . lib̄.

Idem ten de . G . *Bvrtone* cū soca 7 saca . Ibi sī . v . caī trǣ.

Ibi fueī . III . caī . Ibi . IX . sochi hn̄t . IIII . caī . Ibi . XL . ac̄ p̄ti.

Valuit . v . soł . Modo . xx . soł . Leuuin libe tenuit.

Albicus ten de . G . in *NIWETONE* . VI . caī trǣ . Ibi fueī . IIII.

caī . In dñio . ē una . 7 v . sochi cū . II . uilłis 7 . II . borđ hn̄t . III .

caī . Ibi . XVI . ac̄ p̄ti . Valuit . XII . soł . Modo . xx . soliđ.

Ħ q̄q̄ tra . ē de cōmutatione Turchileſtone.

Radulf ten de . G . in *CHERCHEBI* . VII . caī trǣ 7 hī in dñio

III . caī . 7 VI . uiłłos cū . IIII . borđ hn̄tes . I . caī . Ibi . xx . ac̄ p̄ti.

Rainer ten de . G . in *SISTENEBI* . II . caī trǣ ⌐ Valet . VII . lib̄.

7 hī in dñio . I . caī 7 dim . 7 II . sochi cū . IIII . uiłłis hn̄t . I . caī 7 dim .

Ibi . x . ac̄ p̄ti . Valet . xx . soliđ.

Willſ 7 Roger ten de . G . VIII . caī trǣ 7 II . bouat in *STACHE*

*TONE* . 7 jac̄ ad Medeltone . Ibi fueī . v . caī . In dñio . ē dim

caī . 7 XVI . sochi cū . II . borđ hn̄t . v . caī . Ibi . xxx . ac̄ p̄ti.

Valuit . xxx . soł . Modo . xL . soliđ . Leuric . f . Leuuini libe tenuit.

In FRAMLAND Wapentake

1 In *GODTORP* 3½ c. of land. Jurisdiction of Pickwell and Somerby.
There were 3 ploughs. Now 1 plough, with
2 smallholders.
Meadow, 3 acres.
The value was and is 10s.

2 In BURROUGH (-on-the-Hill) 1 c. of land. There was 1 plough.
Jurisdiction of Pickwell.
The value was and is 5s.

In GOSCOTE Wapentake

3 William holds 9 c. of land in QUENIBOROUGH from Geoffrey.
There were 8 ploughs. In lordship 2.
28 villagers with 7 smallholders have 7 ploughs.
A mill at 10s; meadow, 40s.
The value was £3; now £4.

4 He also holds BURTON (-on-the-Wolds) from Geoffrey with
full jurisdiction. 5 c. of land. There were 3 ploughs.
9 Freemen have 4 ploughs.
Meadow, 40 acres.
The value was 5s; now 20s.
Leofwin held it freely.

5 Aubrey holds 6 c. of land in (Cold)NEWTON from Geoffrey.
There were 4 ploughs. In lordship 1.
5 Freemen with 2 villagers and 2 smallholders have 3 ploughs.
Meadow, 16 acres.
The value was 12s; now 20s.
This land is also of the Thurcaston exchange.

[In FRAMLAND Wapentake]

6 Ralph holds 7 c. of land in KIRBY (Bellars) from Geoffrey.
In lordship he has 3 ploughs and
6 villagers with 4 smallholders who have 1 plough.
Meadow, 20 acres.
Value £7.

7 Rainer holds 2 c. of land in SYSONBY from Geoffrey.
He has 1½ ploughs in lordship.
2 Freemen with 4 villagers have 1½ ploughs.
Meadow, 10 acres.
Value 20s.

8 William and Roger hold 8 c. and 2 b. of land in STATHERN from
Geoffrey. It lies with Melton (lands) There were 5 ploughs.
In lordship ½ plough.
16 Freemen with 2 smallholders have 5 ploughs.
Meadow, 30 acres.
The value was 30s; now 40s.
Leofric son of Leofwin held it freely.

Roḃt ten de.G.in *DALBI*.IIII.car    *IN FRANLVND WAPENT.*

træ 7 dim . Ibi fuer . III . car 7 dim . In dnio . e . I . car . 7 IIII . fochi

cū . v . uiłłis 7 I . borđ hnt . II . car . Ibi . x . ac p̃ti . Valuit . v . fol . m

Aluuold ten de.G.in *WICOC* . I . car træ 7 dimiđ.    ⌐xx . folid.

Ibi fuit . I . car . Modo . e ibi . I . uiłłs 7 II . ac p̃ti . 7 v . ac filuæ.

Valuit 7 uał . v . fol . Hæ . II . træ sī de cõmutatione Tvrchileſtone.

ut hões . G . dicunt . Aluuold liḃe tenuit.    ⌐Valet . x . fol.

In *DALBI* sī . II . car træ 7 dim . 7 ibi . III . fochi . Soca de Picheuuelle.


## .XXX. TERRA GODEFRIDI DE CĀBRAI *IN FRANLVND WAPENT.*

Godefriđ De Cambrai . ten de rege . II . car træ in *SPROTONE.*

Ibi fuer . II . car ⸵ Ibi . VII . fochi cū . I . uiłło 7 I . borđ hnt . I . car.

Ibi molin de . v . fol 7 IIII . den ⸗ IIII . ac p̃ti . Valuit . VIII . fol . m . XII . fol.


## .XXXI. TERRA GVNFRIDI DE CIOCHES. *IN GERETREV WAPENT.*

Gvnfriđ De Cioches ten de rege . III . car træ in *MVSELAI.*

Ibi hī . I . car in dnio cū . I . feruo . 7 IIII . uiłłi cū . II . borđ hnt . I . car.

Ibi . VIII . ac p̃ti . Valet . xx . folid . Vaſta fuit . Tedḃt ten de Gunfr.

.II.
236 a
## .XXX. TERRA HVNFRIDI CAMERARIJ. *IN GOSECOT WAPENT.*

Hvnfriđ Camerarius ten de rege in *DALBI* . I . car træ.

Ibi fuer . II . car 7 dimiđ . In dnio . e una . 7 III . uiłłi hnt dim car.

In FRAMLAND Wapentake

19 Robert holds 4½ c. of land in (Little) DALBY from Geoffrey.
There were 3½ ploughs. In lordship 1 plough.
4 Freemen with 5 villagers and 1 smallholder have 2 ploughs.
Meadow, 10 acres.
The value was 5s; now 20s.

20 Alfwold holds 1½ c. of land in WITHCOTE from Geoffrey.
There was 1 plough. Now there is
1 villager.
Meadow, 2 acres; woodland, 5 acres.
The value was and is 5s.
These two lands are of the Thurcaston exchange, as Geoffrey's
men state.
Alfwold held them freely.

21 In (Little) DALBY 2½ c. of land.
3 Freemen.
Jurisdiction of Pickwell.
Value 10s.

30 **LAND OF GODFREY OF CAMBRAI**

In FRAMLAND Wapentake

1 Godfrey of Cambrai holds 2 c. of land in SPROXTON from the King.
There were 2 ploughs.
7 Freemen with 1 villager and 1 smallholder have 1 plough.
A mill at 5s 4d; meadow, 4 acres.
The value was 8s; now 12s.

31 **LAND OF GUNFRID OF CHOCQUES**

In GARTREE Wapentake

1 Gunfrid of Chocques holds 3 c. of land in MOWSLEY from the King.
He has 1 plough in lordship, with 1 slave.
4 villagers with 2 smallholders have 1 plough.
Meadow, 8 acres.
Value 20s. It was waste.
Theodbert holds from Gunfrid.

32 **LAND OF HUMPHREY THE CHAMBERLAIN** 236 a

In GOSCOTE Wapentake

1 Humphrey the Chamberlain holds 1 c. of land in (Great) DALBY
from the King. There were 2½ ploughs. In lordship 1.
3 villagers have ½ plough.
Meadow, 6 acres.

Idē ten in *BARNESBI*.1.car̄ træ.Ibi fuer̄ ⌐Ibi.vi.ac̄ p̄ti.
11.car̄ 7 dimid.In dn̄io.ē una.7 111.uiłłi hn̄t dim car̄.Ibi.vi.ac̄ p̄ti.
Hæ.11.træ ualuer̄.viii.soł.Modo.xx.solid.Aluuin liƀe tenuit.

## .XXX. .III. TERRA GISLEBERTI DE GAND. *IN GERETREV WAP.*

GISLEBERTVS De Gand ten de rege.v.car̄ træ in *BARES*
*WERDE*.7 Wiłłs peurel de eo.Ibi fuer̄.111.car̄.In dn̄io.ē una
car̄.7 un uiłłs cū.11.bord.Ibi.xvi.ac̄ p̄ti.Valuit.vi.den
q̄do recep̄.Modo.xx.solid.

## .XXX. .IIII. TERRA GIRBERTI   *IN GVTLACIST WAP.*

GIRBERTVS ten de rege.1111.car̄ træ 7 dim in *ESSEBI*.
Ibi fuer̄.111.car̄.In dn̄io.ē una car̄.cū.111.uiłłis ibi mantib.
Valuit.xv.soł.Modo.x.solid.
Idē ten.1111.car̄ træ in *MVSELAI*.Ibi fuer̄.111.car̄.Ibi.ē m̄
un uiłłs 7 x.ac̄ p̄ti.Valuit.v.soł.Modo.xii.denar̄.

## .XXX. .v. TERRA DVRANDI MALET.

DVRAND Malet ten de rege in *BVRTONE*.v.car̄ træ.
Ibi fuer̄.1111.car̄.In dn̄io.ē.1.car̄.7 11.sochi cū.11.uiłłis
7 1.bord hn̄t.1.car̄.Ibi.xl.ac̄ p̄ti.Valuit.111.soł.Modo
Huic træ p̄tin.1.car træ 7 dim.una bouata min ⌐x.solid.
in *PRESTEWOLDE*.Ibi fuit dim car̄.Ibi.ē.1.sochs.Vał.11.soł.
Idem.D.ten.1.car̄ træ in *WIMVNDESWALE*.Vasta.ē.
Ibi st̄.v.ac̄ p̄ti.Roulf 7 Eduin tenuer̄.

2   He also holds 1 c. of land in BARSBY. There were 2½ ploughs.
In lordship 1.
>   3 villagers have ½ plough.
>   Meadow, 6 acres.

The value of these two lands was 8s; now 20s.
>   Alwin held them freely.

## LAND OF GILBERT OF GHENT

In GARTREE Wapentake

1   Gilbert of Ghent holds 5 c. of land in (Husbands) BOSWORTH
from the King and William Peverel from him.
There were 3 ploughs. In lordship 1 plough;
>   1 villager with 2 smallholders.
>   Meadow, 16 acres.

Value when acquired 6d; now 20s.

## LAND OF GERBERT

In GUTHLAXTON Wapentake

1   Gerbert holds 4½ c. of land in ASHBY (Magna) from the King.
There were 3 ploughs. In lordship 1 plough, with
>   3 villagers who live there.

The value was 15s; now 10s.

[In GARTREE Wapentake]

2   He also holds 4 c. of land in MOWSLEY. There were 3 ploughs.
>   Now 1 villager.
>   Meadow, 10 acres.

The value was 5s; now 12d.

## LAND OF DURAND MALET

[In GOSCOTE Wapentake]

1   Durand Malet holds 5 c. of land in BURTON (-on-the-Wolds) from
the King. There were 4 ploughs. In lordship 1 plough.
>   2 Freemen with 2 villagers and 1 smallholder have 1 plough.
>   Meadow, 40 acres.

The value was 3s; now 10s.
>   1½ c. of land less 1 b. in PRESTWOLD belong to this land.

There was ½ plough.
>   1 Freeman.

Value 2s.

2   Durand also holds 1 c. of land in WYMESWOLD. Waste.
>   Meadow, 5 acres.
>   Rolf and Edwin held it.

TERRA DROGON DE BEVRERE *IN FRANLVND WAPENT.*

DROGO de Beurere ten de rege. XII. car træ in *OVRETONE.*
7 Fulco de eo. Ibi fuer. XII. car. In dnio. e. I. car. 7 VIII. uilli
cu pbro 7 IIII. soch 7 IIII. bord hnt. v. car. Ibi. xxx. ac pti.
7 totid nemoris. Valuit 7 ual. L. solid. *IN GOSECOT WAPENT.*
Adelelm ten de Drog. IIII. car træ 7 II. bouat in *HOBIE.*
Ibi fuer. IIII. car. In dnio. e. I. car. 7 VIII. uilli cu. IIII. bord
hnt. I. car. Ibi. VI. ac pti. Valuit. II. sol. Modo. XX. solid.
Vlf tenuit cu soca 7 saca.


.XXXVII. TERRA MAINNON BRITONIS.

MAINQ Brito ten de rege *LVTRESVRDE.* Ibi st. XIII. car
træ. Ibi fuer. IX. car. In dnio st. III. car. 7 II. serui. 7 I. ancilla
7 VI. uilli cu. VII. bord 7 XII. sochi hnt. IIII. car. Ibi. XII. ac pti.
Valuit 7 ual. VII. lib. Radulf com tenuit has. III. tras.
Ide ten. II. car træ in *MINSTRETONE.* Ibi fuer. II. car. Nc
un sochs cu. I. bord ht ibi. I. car. Valuit 7 ual. xx. solid.
Ide ten in *TORP.* II. car træ. Ibi fuer. II. car. Nc in dnio
ht. I. car 7 dim. 7 molin de. II. solid. Valuit 7 ual. xx. solid.


.XXXVIII. TERRA OGERIJ BRITONIS. *IN GVTLAGISTAN WAP.*

OGERVS Brito ten de rege. II. partes uni hidæ. idest
XII. car træ. Ibi fuer. VIII. car. In dnio st. II. car. 7 II. serui.
7 IX. uilli cu. VII. bord 7 x. sochis hnt. IIII. car. Ibi molin
de. II. solid. 7 XII. ac pti. Valuit 7 ual. XL. solid. Eur libe
tenuit T.R.E.

6      # LAND OF DROGO OF LA BEUVRIERE

**In FRAMLAND Wapentake**

1    Drogo of La Beuvriere holds 12 c. of land in (Cold) OVERTON from the
King and Fulk from him. There were 12 ploughs. In lordship 1 plough.
     8 villagers with a priest, 4 Freemen and 4 smallholders
       have 5 ploughs.
     Meadow, 30 acres; as much wood.
   The value was and is 50s.

**In GOSCOTE Wapentake**

2    Aethelhelm holds 4 c. and 2 b. of land in HOBY from Drogo
There were 4 ploughs. In lordship 1 plough.
     8 villagers with 4 smallholders have 1 plough.
     Meadow, 6 acres.
   The value was 2s; now 20s.
     Ulf held it with full jurisdiction.

7      # LAND OF MAINOU THE BRETON

**[In GUTHLAXTON Wapentake]**

1    Mainou the Breton holds LUTTERWORTH from the King. 13 c. of
land. There were 9 ploughs. In lordship 3 ploughs;
2 male and 1 female slaves.
     6 villagers with 7 smallholders and 12 Freemen have 4 ploughs.
     Meadow, 12 acres.
   The value was and is £7.
     Earl Ralph held these 3 lands.

2    He also holds 2 c. of land in MISTERTON. There were 2 ploughs.
     Now 1 Freeman with 1 smallholder has 1 plough.
   The value was and is 20s.

3    He also holds 2 c. of land in CATTHORPE. There were 2 ploughs.
Now in lordship he has 1½ ploughs.
     A mill at 2s.
   The value was and is 20s.

8      # LAND OF OGER THE BRETON

**In GUTHLAXTON Wapentake**

1    Oger the Breton holds 2 parts of 1 hide in KILBY from the King,
that is 12 c. of.land. There were 8 ploughs.
In lordship 2 ploughs; 2 slaves.
     9 villagers with 7 smallholders and 10 Freemen have 4 ploughs.
     A mill at 2s; meadow, 12 acres.
   The value was and is 40s.
     Everard held it freely before 1066.

.XXXIX. TERRA NIGELLI DE ALBINGI *In Gosecot Wapentac.*

NIGELLVS de ALBINGI teñ de rege in *Sela* . II . car trae.

7 Hunfrid de eo. Ibi . I . car in dñio . ē . Valuit . XII . deñ . M . v . folid.

Turchil teñ de Nigello in *Dvntone* . III . hid.

Tra . VI . car . Ibi . ē uñ uitts 7 IIII . ac pti . Silua dim leu lg . 7 IIII.

qrent lat . Valuit . XX . fot . Modo . II . fot . Vafta recep.

236 b

:XL. TERRA JVDITAE COMITISSE. *In Gvtlacistan Wap.*

JVDITA Comitiffa teñ in *Oldebi* . IX . car tre . 7 II . bouat.

Ibi fuer . IX . car : 7 tot car hñt ibi . XLVI . fochi cu XI.

bord . 7 III . feruis : Ibi . XXX . ac pti . Valuit XL . fot . m . LX . fot.

Ead comit teñ in *Petlinge* . IIII . car trae . Ibi fuer . II . car.

Nc . IIII . fochi cu . II . bord hñt ibi . I . car . Ibi . VIII . ac pti.

Ead comit teñ in *Cossebi* . VIII . car trae . Ibi fuer . VI . car.

Nc . XXVI . fochi hñt ibi . V . car . Ibi . XX . ac pti . Valuit XXX . fot.

Modo ual hae . II : trae . c . folid.

In *Frellesworde* . teñ comit . VI . car trae . Ibi . VI . car fuer.

Nc . XIIII . fochi hñt ibi . V . car . 7 VIII . acs pti . Val . XL . fot

In *Scerneford* . teñ . Co . I . car trae . Valuit 7 ual XXXII . deñ.

In *Wilechebi* . teñ . Co . v . car trae una v min . Ibi . V . car

fuer . Nc XIII . fochi hñt ibi . III . car . 7 XII . acs pti.

Valuit . XXX . folid . Modo ; XL . folid.

In *Hadre* . teñ . Co . IIII . car trae . Ibi . II . car fuer . Nc . IIII.

uitti hñt ibi . I . car . Valuit . XVI . deñ . Modo . XX . folid.

Hanc tra tota Wallef com tenuit . 7 Sbern . I . lib hō.

# LAND OF NIGEL OF AUBIGNY

In GOSCOTE Wapentake

1    Nigel of Aubigny holds 2 c. of land in SEAL from the King
and Humphrey from him. In lordship 1 plough.
The value was 12d; now 5s.

2    Thorkell holds 3 hides in DONINGTON (Le Heath) from Nigel.
Land for 6 ploughs.
     1 villager.
     Meadow, 4 acres; woodland ½ league long and 4 furlongs wide.
The value was 20s; now 2s.
     Acquired waste.

# LAND OF COUNTESS JUDITH

In GUTHLAXTON Wapentake

1    Countess Judith holds 9 c. and 2 b. of land in OADBY.
There were 9 ploughs.
     46 Freemen with 11 smallholders and 3 slaves have as many ploughs.
     Meadow, 30 acres.
The value was 40s; now 60s.

2    The Countess also holds 4 c. of land in PEATLING (Magna).
There were 2 ploughs.
     Now 4 Freemen with 2 smallholders have 1 plough.
     Meadow, 8 acres.

3    The Countess also holds 8 c. of land in COSBY. There were 6 ploughs.
     Now 26 Freemen have 5 ploughs.
     Meadow, 20 acres.
The value was 30s; now the value of these two lands, 100s.

   The Countess holds

4    in FROLESWORTH 6 c. of land. There were 6 ploughs.
     Now 14 Freemen have 5 ploughs.
     Meadow, 8 acres.
Value 40s.

5    in SHARNFORD 1 c. of land.
The value was and is 32d.

6    in WILLOUGHBY (Waterless) 5 c. of land less 1 virgate.
There were 5 ploughs.
     Now 13 Freemen have 3 ploughs.
     Meadow, 12 acres.
The value was 30s; now 40s.

7    in HEATHER 4 c. of land. There were 2 ploughs.
     Now 4 villagers have 1 plough.
The value was 16d; now 20s.
     Earl Waltheof, and 1 Freeman Esbern, held all this land.

Hvgo de Grentemaifnil ten de Judita . iiii . car træ
                              comitiffa

in *Broctone* . Ibi . ii . car fuer . Nc . viii . fochi cu . ii . bord

hnt ibi . iii . car . Valuit . x . fot . Modo . xx . folid.

Ide ten . ii . car træ in *Merchenefeld* . Ibi . ii . car fuer.

Nc ft ibi . ii . bord . Silua . vi . qrent lg . 7 iiii . qrent lat.

Valuit tot . ii . fot . Modo . x . fot . Vlf tenuit libe T.R.E.

Ide . H . ten . ii . car træ in *Elvelege* . Ibi . ii . car fuer.

Nc in dnio ht . i . car . cu . ii . feruis . 7 ibi ft . ii . uitti.

Silua . iiii . qʒ lg . 7 ii . qʒ lat . Valuit . ii . fot . Modo . x . fot.

Ide . H . ten in *Ricoltorp* . ii . car træ 7 ii . bouat . Ibi . ii.

car fuer . Nc . ii . uitti ibi . 7 molin de . iiii . fot . 7 viii . ac pti.

Valuit 7 ual . x . folid.

Hugo burdet ten de comitiffa . ii . car træ 7 dimid

in *Reresbi* . Ibi . e . i . car in dnio . 7 pbr cu . i . uitto

7 iii . bord . 7 molin de . ii . folid . 7 x . ac pti . Valuit . x . fot.

Ide ten . vi . car træ 7 dimid in *Alebi*.          Modo . xx . fot.

Ibi . iiii . car fuer . Nc in dnio . e . i . car 7 dim . 7 vii . uitti

cu . ii . fochis 7 iii . bord hnt . i . car 7 dim . De parte

molini . iii . folid . 7 xii . ac pti . Valuit . x . fot . Modo . xx . fot.

Ide ten dimid car træ in *Sixtenebi* . Ibi . i . fochs ht . i.

car . Valuit . viii . den . Modo . ii . folid . Alden libe tenuit.

Robt de Buci ten de Comitiffa *In Geretrev Wap*.

vii . car træ in *Lobenho* . Ibi . vi . car fuer . Nc . ii . car ft

in dnio . 7 iii . ferui . 7 viii . uitti cu . iii . bord 7 ii . francig

hnt . iiii . car . Ibi . xx . ac pti . Valuit . x . fot . Modo . lx . fot.

In GUTHLAXTON Wapentake

8  Hugh of Grandmesnil holds 4 c. of land in BROUGHTON (Astley) from Countess Judith. There were 2 ploughs.
Now 8 Freemen with 2 smallholders have 3 ploughs.
The value was 10s; now 20s.

9  He also holds 2 c. of land in MARKFIELD. There were 2 ploughs.
Now 2 smallholders.
Woodland 6 furlongs long and 4 furlongs wide.
The value of the whole was 2s; now 10s.
Ulf held it freely before 1066.

10  Hugh also holds 2 c. of land in *ELVELEGE*.
There were 2 ploughs. Now in lordship he has 1 plough, with 2 slaves.
2 villagers.
Woodland 4 furlongs long and 2 furlongs wide.
The value was 2s; now 10s.

[In FRAMLAND Wapentake]

11  Hugh also holds 2 c. and 2 b. of land in 'RINGLETHORPE'.
There were 2 ploughs.
Now 2 villagers.
A mill at 4s; meadow, 8 acres.
The value was and is 10s.

[In GOSCOTE Wapentake]

12  Hugh Burdet holds 2½ c. of land in REARSBY from the Countess.
In lordship 1 plough;
a priest with 1 villager and 3 smallholders.
A mill at 2s; meadow, 10 acres.
The value was 10s; now 20s.

[In FRAMLAND Wapentake]

13  He also holds 6½ c. of land in WELBY. There were 4 ploughs.
Now in lordship 1½ ploughs.
7 villagers with 2 Freemen and 3 smallholders have 1½ ploughs.
From part of a mill 3s; meadow, 12 acres.
The value was 10s; now 20s.

14  He also holds ½ c. of land in SYSONBY.
1 Freeman has 1 plough.
The value was 8d; now 2s.
Haldane held it freely.

In GARTREE Wapentake

15  Robert of Bucy holds 7 c. of land in LUBENHAM from the Countess.
There were 6 ploughs. Now 2 ploughs in lordship; 3 slaves.
8 villagers with 3 smallholders and 2 Frenchmen have
4 ploughs.
Meadow, 20 acres.
The value was 10s; now 60s.

Idē.R.teń.vii.car̄ træ 7 dimiđ in *FOXTONE* Ibi.vi.car̄
fuer̄.Nc̄ st̄.ii.car̄ in dñio 7 v.ſerui 7 i.ancilla.7 iii.ſochi
cū pβro 7 xviii.uiłłis 7 iii.borđ hn̄t.ix.car̄.Ibi.xx.
ac̄ p̄ti.Valuit.xx.ſoliđ.Modo.iiii.liβ.
Idē teń.ix.car̄ træ in *GVTMVNDESLEA*.Ibi.vi.car̄ fuer̄.
Nc̄.ē in dñio.i.car̄.7 ii.ſerui 7 vi.uiłłi cū pβro 7.v.
borđ 7 uno liβo hōē hn̄t.v.car̄.Ibi.xx.ac̄ p̄ti.
Valuit.x.ſoliđ.Modo.xl.ſoliđ.Tres taini liβe tenuer̄.
Idē teń.iii.car̄ træ in *BVGEDONE*.Ibi.iiii.car̄ fuer̄.
Nc̄ in dñio.i.car̄.7 iiii.uiłłi cū.viii.borđ hn̄t.ii.car̄.
Ibi.xv.ac̄ p̄ti.Valuit.x.ſoł.Modo.xx.ſoliđ.
Idē teń.ii.car̄ træ 7 dimiđ in *ACTORP*.Ibi.iii.car̄ fuer̄.
Nc̄ in dñio st̄.ii.car̄.7 viii.uiłłi cū.ii.ſochis 7 iiii.borđ
hn̄t.ii.car̄.

236 c

Ibi.ix.ac̄ p̄ti.Silua.ii.q̄ʒ lḡ.7 una q̄ʒ lat̄.Valuit.viii.
Idē Robt̄ ten de Comitiſſa.i.car̄ træ ſoł.m̄.xl.ſoł.
in *BLADESTONE*.Ibi.ē un uiłłs.Valuit.x.den̄.M̄.ii.ſoł.
Soca huj træ ht̄ Robt̄ de Todeni.
Idē teń.iii.car̄ træ in *STOCTONE*.Ibi.iiii.car̄ fuer̄.
Nc̄ in dñio.i.car̄.7 ii.uiłłi cū.i.ſocho hn̄t.i.car̄.Ibi mo
linū de.ii.ſoł.7 viii.ac̄ p̄ti.Silua.v.q̄rent̄ lḡ.7 ii.q̄ʒ lat̄.
Valuit.vii.ſoliđ.Modo.xx.ſoliđ.
Hugo de Grentem teń de Comitiſſa.iii.car̄ træ in *GLOR*
*STONE*.Ibi.iii.car̄ fuer̄.Nc̄ in dñio.i.car̄.7 vi.uiłłi
cū.ii.borđ hn̄t.ii.car̄.Ibi.iiii.ac̄ p̄ti.Silua.iii.q̄rent
lḡ.7 una q̄ʒ lat̄.Valuit.iii.ſoł.Modo.xxx.ſoliđ.
Robt̄ ten de.Co.xi.car̄ træ in *SCALDEFORD*.Ibi.xii.
car̄ fuer̄.Nc̄ in dñio.i.car̄ 7 dim.7 v.uiłłi cū.xi.ſochis
7 xiii.borđ hn̄t.vi.car̄.Ibi.xxx.ac̄ p̄ti.Valuit.x.ſoł.
Modo.lx.ſoliđ.Quinq̄ taini liβe tenuer̄.T.R.E.

236 b, c

Robert also holds 7½ c. of land in FOXTON. There were 6 ploughs.
Now 2 ploughs in lordship; 5 male and 1 female slaves.
   3 Freemen with a priest, 18 villagers and 3 smallholders
      have 9 ploughs.
   Meadow, 20 acres.
The value was 20s; now £4.

He also holds
in GUMLEY 9 c. of land. There were 6 ploughs.
Now in lordship 1 plough; 2 slaves.
   6 villagers with a priest, 5 smallholders and 1 free man
      have 5 ploughs.
   Meadow, 20 acres.
The value was 10s; now 40s.
   3 thanes held it freely.

in (Great) BOWDEN 3 c. of land. There were 4 ploughs.
Now in lordship 1 plough.
   4 villagers with 8 smallholders have 2 ploughs.
   Meadow, 15 acres.
The value was 10s; now 20s.

in OTHORPE 2½ c. of land. There were 3 ploughs.
Now in lordship 2 ploughs.
   8 villagers with 2 Freemen and 4 smallholders have 2 ploughs.
   Meadow, 9 acres; woodland 2 furlongs long and 1 furlong wide.   236 c
The value was 8s; now 40s.

Robert also holds 1 c. of land in BLASTON from the Countess.
   1 villager.
The value was 10d; now 2s.
   Robert of Tosny has the jurisdiction of this land.

He also holds 3 c. of land in STOCKERSTON. There were 4 ploughs.
Now in lordship 1 plough.
   2 villagers with 1 Freeman have 1 plough.
   A mill at 2s; meadow, 8 acres; woodland 5 furlongs long
      and 2 furlongs wide.
The value was 7s; now 20s.

Hugh of Grandmesnil holds 3 c. of land in GLOOSTON from the
Countess. There were 3 ploughs. Now in lordship 1 plough.
   6 villagers with 2 smallholders have 2 ploughs.
   Meadow, 4 acres; woodland 3 furlongs long and 1 furlong wide.
The value was 3s; now 30s.

[In FRAMLAND Wapentake]
Robert holds 11 c. of land in SCALFORD from the Countess.
There were 12 ploughs. Now in lordship 1½ ploughs.
5 villagers with 11 Freemen and 13 smallholders have 6 ploughs.
   Meadow, 30 acres.
The value was 10s; now 60s.
   5 thanes held it freely before 1066.

Hugo burdet ten de Comitiſſa.ix.car trǣ in GLOWESBI.

Ibi.vi.car fuer.Nc in dnio.ii.car.7 vii.ſochi cu pbro

7 vi.uillis 7 v.bord hnt.v.car.Ibi molin de.ii.ſolid.

7 xxiiii.ac pti.Silua.i.qrent lg.7 i.lat.Valuit 7 ual

Robt ten de.Co.ii.car trǣ.ii.bouat min ⌜xl.ſolid.

in OLDEBI 7 WICHINGESTONE.Ibi fuit.i.car 7 dimid.

Nc.e ibi.i.bord.Valuit 7 ual.ii.ſolid.

Grimbald ten de.Co.vii.car trǣ in OSVLVESTONE.

Ibi.xii.car fuer.Nc in dnio.ii.car.7 xv.uilli cu.iiii.

bord hnt.vi.car.Ibi.i.francig ht.i.car cu.iiii.bord.

Ibi.xxx.ac pti.Silua.v.qrent lg.7 una qʒ lat.

Valuit.l.ſot.Modo.iii.lib.Turchil tenuit cu ſaca 7 ſoca.

Grimbald ten de.Co.v.car trǣ in ADELACHESTONE.

Ibi.v.car fuer.Nc in dnio.i.car.7 iiii.uilli cu.iiii.

bord hnt.i.car.Ibi molin de.ii.ſolid.Valuit.x.ſolid.

Osbn ten de.Co.ii.car trǣ in STANTONE.⌜Modo.xx.ſot.

Ibi.i.car fuit.Nc in dnio dim car.7 x.ac pti.Val.ii.ſot.

Azo ten de.Co.ii.car trǣ in CRAWEHO.Ibi.iii.car fuer.

Nc in dnio.i.car.7 iiii.uilli hnt alia.Ibi.iiii.ac pti.

Silua.iiii.qrent lg.7 ii.qʒ lat.Valuit.viii.ſot.M.xx.

Gislebt ten.i.car trǣ in WELEHA.Vaſta.e.7 tam ual

Gunduin ten.ii.car trǣ in DEDIGWORDE.⌜iii.ſolid.

Ibi.i.car fuit.Nc.i.uills ibi ht dim car.Ibi.ii.ac pti

7 dimid.Valuit.xii.den.Modo.x.ſolid.

[In GOSCOTE Wapentake]
Hugh Burdet holds 9 c. of land in LOWESBY from the Countess.
There were 6 ploughs. Now in lordship 2 ploughs.
  7 Freemen with a priest, 6 villagers and 5 smallholders
    have 5 ploughs.
  A mill at 2s; meadow, 24 acres; woodland 1 furlong long
    and 1 wide.
The value was and is 40s.

[In GUTHLAXTON Wapentake]
Robert holds 2 c. of land less 2 b. in OADBY and WIGSTON (Magna)
from the Countess. There was 1½ ploughs.
  Now 1 smallholder.
The value was and is 2s.

[In GARTREE Wapentake]
Grimbald holds 7 c. of land in OWSTON from the Countess.
There were 12 ploughs. Now in lordship 2 ploughs.
  15 villagers with 3 smallholders have 6 ploughs. 1 Frenchman
    has 1 plough with 3 smallholders.
  Meadow, 30 acres; woodland 5 furlongs long and 1 furlong wide.
The value was 50s; now £3.
  Thorkell held it with full jurisdiction.

[In GOSCOTE Wapentake]
Grimbald holds 5 c. of land in ALLEXTON from the Countess.
There were 5 ploughs. Now in lordship 1 plough.
  4 villagers with 4 smallholders have 1 plough.
    A mill at 2s.
The value was 10s; now 20s.

[In GARTREE Wapentake]
Osbern holds 2 c. of land in STONTON (Wyville)  from the Countess.
There was 1 plough. Now in lordship ½ plough.
  Meadow, 10 acres.
Value 4s.

Azor holds 2 c. of land in CRANOE from the Countess.
There were 3 ploughs. Now in lordship 1 plough.
  4 villagers have another.
  Meadow, 4 acres; woodland 4 furlongs long and 2 furlongs wide.
The value was 8s; now 20(s).

Gilbert holds 1 c. of land in WELHAM. Waste.
Value however , 3s.

Gundwin holds 2 c. of land in THEDDINGWORTH. There was 1 plough.
  Now 1 villager has ½ plough.
  Meadow, 2½ acres.
The value was 12d; now 10s.

Radulf' ten de Co . iiii . car' træ in _Ascbi_ . Ibi . viii . car'
fueʀ . Nc in dñio . ii . car' .7 ii . ſerui .7 xxiiii . uilli cũ pƀro
7 iii . borđ hñt . vi . car' . Ibi moliñ de . iiii . ſot .7 xl . ac pti.
Spinetũ . i . q̃ʒ lḡ .7 i . lat . Valuit 7 uat . iiii . liƀ

Idē ten de . Co . i . car' træ 7 dim' in _Niwebold_ . Ibi . i . car'
fuit . Nc in dñio . i . car' .7 un uills cũ . iiii . borđ hŧ aliã.
Ibi . iii . ac pti . Valuit 7 uat . xx . ſolid.

Feggo ten de . Co . i . car' tre 7 dim' in _Gadesbi_ . Ibi . i . car'
fuit . Nc in dñio . i . car' cũ . i . borđ . Ibi moliñ de . xii . den.
7 iii . ac pti . Valuit 7 uat . v . ſolid.

Othingar' ten de . Co . dim' car' træ in _Gadesbi_ . Ibi fuit
dimiđ car' .7 m̃ eſt .7 ii . ac pti .7 dimiđ pars molini . de . ii . ſot.

Wlſi ten de . Co . in _Brochesbi_ ⌐ Valuit 7 uat . v . ſot.
vi . bouat træ . Ibi . i . car' fuit . Nc in dñio . i . car' cũ . ii . borđ.
7 iiii . ac pti . Valuit 7 uat . iiii . ſot. ⌐ ualet . iii . ſot.

Goduin ten . i . car' træ 7 ii . bouat in _Alebi_ . Vaſta . ē . Tam

236 d

Radulf' ten de Comitiſſa dimiđ car' træ in _Alebi_ . Vaſta . ē
Valet tam̃ . ii . ſolid. _In Gosecote Wapent._

Grimbald ten de . Co . dim' car' træ in _Adelachestone_.
In dñio . ē ibi d|im car' .7 moliñ de . xvi . den . Valet . v . ſolid.

Hugo muſard ten de . Co . v . car' _In Franlvnd Wapent._
træ in _Saxebi_ . Ibi . vi . car' fueʀ . Nc in dñio . i . car' .7 ii . uilli
cũ . vi . ſochis hñt . iii . car' . Ibi . lx . ac pti .7 moliñ de . iiii . ſot.
Valuit 7 uat . xx . ſolid.

[In GOSCOTE Wapentake]

32  Ralph holds 4 c. of land in ASHBY (Folville) from the Countess.
There were 8 ploughs. Now in lordship 2 ploughs; 2 slaves.
    24 villagers with a priest and 3 smallholders have 6 ploughs.
    A mill at 4s; meadow, 40 acres; spinney 1 furlong long and 1 wide.
The value was and is £4.

33  He also holds 1½ c. of land in NEWBOLD (Folville) from the
Countess. There was 1 plough. Now in lordship 1 plough.
    1 villager with 4 smallholders has another.
    Meadow, 3 acres.
The value was and is 20s.

34  Feggi holds 1½ c. of land in GADDESBY from the Countess.
There was 1 plough. Now in lordship 1 plough, with
    1 smallholder.
    A mill at 12d; meadow, 3 acres.
The value was and is 5s.

35  Odincar holds ½ c. of land in GADDESBY from the Countess.
There was and now is ½ plough.
    Meadow, 2 acres; ½ part of a mill at 2s.
The value was and is 5s.

36  Wulfsi holds 6 b. of land in BROOKSBY from the Countess.
There was 1 plough. Now in lordship 1 plough, with
    2 smallholders.
    Meadow, 4 acres.
The value was and is 4s.

[In FRAMLAND Wapentake]
37  Godwin holds 1 c. and 2 b. of land in WELBY. Waste.
Value however, 3s.

38  Ralph holds ½ c. of land in WELBY from the Countess.        236 d
Waste. Value however, 2s.

In GOSCOTE Wapentake
39  Grimbald holds ½ c. of land in ALLEXTON from the Countess.
In lordship ½ plough;
    A mill at 16d.
Value 5s.

In FRAMLAND Wapentake
40  Hugh Musard holds 5 c. of land in SAXBY from the Countess.
There were 6 ploughs. Now in lordship 1 plough.
    2 villagers with 6 Freemen have 3 ploughs.
    Meadow, 60 acres; a mill at 4s.
The value was and is 20s.

Idē teñ de. Co. VIII. car̄ træ in *SPROTONE* . Ibi. VI. car̄ eraÿ.
Nc in dñio. I. car̄. 7 XVI. foċhi cū. v. uiłłis 7 pbro hñt. IIII.
car̄. Ibi moliñ de. IIII. folid. 7 p̄tū. II. q̇z̄ lḡ. 7 tñtd lat̄.
Valuit. xx. fol. Modo. L. fol. Algar tenuit cū foca 7 faca.


## .XLI. TERRA ADELIZ VXORIS HVGONIS DE GRENTM.

ADELIZ uxor Hugonis teñ de rege. I. car̄ træ in *MERDE*
*GRAVE*. Tra. ē dim car̄. Hanc hñt ibi. III. uiłłi. Valuit. v. fol.
Leuric teñ de ea. VIII. car̄ træ 7 dimid͑     Modo. IIII. fol.
in alia *PETLINGE*. Tra. ē. IIII. car̄. Nc in dñio. I. car̄. 7 IX.
uiłłi cū pbro 7 IIII. foċħ 7 VII. bord hñt. IIII. car̄ 7 dimid͑.
Ibi moliñ de. XVI. deñ. 7 X. ac̄ p̄ti. Valuit 7 uał XL. folid͑.
Idē teñ de ead in *BARCHEBI*. I. car̄ træ 7 dim. Tra. ē. II. car̄.
Nc in dñio. I. car̄. cū. I. feruo. 7 VI. uiłłi cū. v. bord hñt
II. car̄. Ibi moliñ. XII. deñ. 7 v. ac̄ p̄ti. Valuit 7 uał. xxx. fol.
Siuuard libe tenuit.


## .XLII. TERRE SERVIENT REGIS. *IN GERETREV WAPENT*.

HERBERT teñ de rege. IIII. car̄ træ in *BVRC*. Ibi. v. car̄
fuer̄. Nc in dñio. I. car̄ 7 dim. 7 IIII. ferui. 7 VI. bord cū. I. foċħ
hñt. III. car̄. Ibi. xx. ac̄ p̄ti. Silua. XIII. q̇rent lḡ. 7 IIII. lat̄.
Valuit. x. fol. Modo. xxx. fol.
Idē teñ dimid͑ car̄. træ in *NIWETONE*. In dñio ħt ibi dim car̄
7 II. uiłłos. 7 II. ac̄s p̄ti. Valuit. II. fol. Modo. v. fol.

41 He also holds 8 c. of land in SPROXTON from the Countess.
There were 6 ploughs. Now in lordship 1 plough.
  16 Freemen with 5 villagers and a priest have 4 ploughs.
  A mill at 4s; meadow 2 furlongs long and as many wide.
The value was 20s; now 50s.
  Algar held it with full jurisdiction.

41 # LAND OF ADELAIDE WIFE OF HUGH OF GRANDMESNIL

[In GOSCOTE Wapentake]

1 Adelaide wife of Hugh holds 1 c. of land in BELGRAVE from the
King. Land for ½ plough.
  3 villagers have it.
The value was 5s; now 4s.

[In GUTHLAXTON Wapentake]

2 Leofric holds 8½ c. of land in another PEATLING (Parva).
Land for 4 ploughs. Now in lordship 1 plough.
  9 villagers with a priest, 4 Freemen and 7 smallholders
    have 4½ ploughs.
  A mill at 16d; meadow, 10 acres.
The value was and is 40s.

[In GOSCOTE Wapentake]

3 He also holds 1½ c. of land in BARKBY from her. Land for 2 ploughs.
Now in lordship 1 plough, with 1 slave.
  6 villagers with 5 smallholders have 2 ploughs.
  A mill at 12d; meadow, 5 acres.
The value was and is 30s.
  Siward held it freely.

42 # LAND OF THE KING'S SERVANTS

In GARTREE [FRAMLAND] Wapentake

1 Herbert holds 4 c. of land in BURROUGH (on-the-Hill) from the King.
There were 5 ploughs. Now in lordship 1½ ploughs; 4 slaves.
  6 smallholders with 1 Freeman have 3 ploughs.
  Meadow, 20 acres; woodland 13 furlongs long and 4 wide.
The value was 10s; now 30s.

[In GOSCOTE Wapentake]

2 He also holds ½ c. of land in (Cold) NEWTON. In lordship he
has ½ plough and
  2 villagers.
  Meadow, 2 acres.
The value was 2s; now 5s.

Idē ten. iii. car̄ træ in *NETONE*. Ibi fuer̄. iii. car̄ 7 dimid̄.

Nc̄ in dn̄io. ii. car̄.7 fr̄. H. hr̄ ibi. ii. car̄. cū. i. feruo.7 ix. uilti

hn̄t. ii. car̄. Ibi. viii. ac̄ p̄ti. Valuit. v. fot. Modo. xx. fot.

Idē ten de foca. vi. bouat træ    *IN FRANLVND WAP.*

in *BVRG*. Vafta. ē. Valuit 7 uat. ii. folid̄.

R<sup>de Lorz</sup>OBERTVS ten de rege. v. car̄ træ in *HOLETONE*. Ibi. iiii.

car̄ fuer̄. Ibi nc̄. ii. uilti 7 p̄tū. i. q̃ɀ lḡ.7 dim q̃ɀ lat̄.

Idē ten. ii. car̄ træ            ⌐Robt ui poffidet.

in *WIMVNDESWALE*. Nc̄ ibi. i. uilts cū. i. bord̄ hr̄ dim car̄.

Ibi. v. ac̄ p̄ti. Hæ. ii. træ ualent. vii. fot.

Aschil ten de rege in *ESTWELLE*. v. car̄ træ 7 ii. bouat̄.

Tra. ē. iiii. car̄. Nc̄ in dn̄io. i. car̄.7 vii. uilti cū. iii. bord̄ hn̄t

. iii. car̄. Ibi. xx. ac̄ p̄ti. Valuit 7 uat̄. xxiiii. fot.

RAVEN ten de rege in *RICOLTORP*. ii. car̄ træ. ii. bouat̄

min. Tra. ē. ii. car̄. Ibi. i. uilts cū. i. bord̄ hr̄ dim car̄.

Ibi. vi. ac̄ p̄ti. Valuit. viii. fot. Modo. x. folid̄.

R<sup>framen</sup>ADVLFVS ten de rege in cōmdatione. iii. car̄ træ 7 dim in *ESSEBERIE*.

Ibi ſt̄. ii. uilti hn̄tes. vi. car̄.7 xii. ac̄ p̄ti.    Vat̄. x. folid̄.

Turchil ten de rege dimid̄ car̄ træ in *SCERNEFORD*. Ibi ſt̄. iii.

bord̄ hn̄tes. vi. āalia. uat̄. iiii. folid̄.

<sup>237 a</sup>
.XLIII. TERRA HVGONIS COMITIS. *IN GVTLACISTAN WAP.*

COMES HVGO ten de rege *BARHOV*. Ibi ſt̄. xv. car̄ træ.

In dn̄io hr̄. iiii. car̄ 7 dimid̄.7 ii. feruos cū. i. ancilla.

3  He also holds 3 c. of land in NEWTON. There were 3½ ploughs.
Now in lordship 2 ploughs.
A free man has 2 ploughs, with 1 slave; 9 villagers have 2 ploughs.
Meadow, 8 acres.
The value was 5s; now 20s.

In FRAMLAND Wapentake

4  He also holds 6 b. of land from the jurisdiction in BURROUGH
(on-the-Hill). Waste.
The value was and is 2s.

[In GOSCOTE Wapentake]

5  Robert of Jort holds 5 c. of land in HOTON from the King.
There were 4 ploughs.
Now 2 villagers.
Meadow 1 furlong long and ½ furlong wide.
Robert occupies it by force.

6  He also holds 2 c. of land in WYMESWOLD.
Now 1 villager with 1 smallholder has ½ plough.
Meadow, 5 acres.
Value of these two lands, 7s.

[In FRAMLAND Wapentake]

7  Askell holds 5 c. and 2 b. of land in EASTWELL from the King.
Land for 4 ploughs. Now in lordship 1 plough.
7 villagers with 3 smallholders have 3 ploughs.
Meadow, 20 acres.
The value was and is 24s.

8  Raven holds 2 c. of land less 2 b. in 'RINGLETHORPE' from the King.
Land for 2 ploughs.
1 villager with 1 smallholder has ½ plough.
Meadow, 6 acres.
The value was 8s; now 10s.

[In GOSCOTE Wapentake]

9  Ralph Framen holds 3½ c. of land in ASFORDBY in commendation
from the King.
2 villagers who have 6 ploughs.
Meadow, 12 acres.
Value 10s.

[In GUTHLAXTON Wapentake]

10  Thorkell holds ½ c. of land in SHARNFORD from the King.
3 smallholders who have 6 cattle.
Value 5s.

# 43  LAND OF EARL HUGH  237 a

In GUTHLAXTON [GOSCOTE] Wapentake

1  Earl Hugh holds BARROW (on-Soar) from the King. 15 c. of land.
In lordship he has 4½ ploughs; 2 male with 1 female slaves.

7 xl . uilli cu . xiii . bord hnt . xi . car . Ibi . iii . molini de . xxx.

folid .Silua . i . leu lg .7 iiii . qrent lat . q redd . v . folid.

Hoc co tenuit Herald comes . cu append infrafcriptis.

In Dvnintone . v . car træ 7 iii . q̇ pti lg .7 i . q̇ lat.

In Cofintone . vi . car træ. In Hohtone . vi . car træ

In Setgraue . ii . car træ 7 x . ac pti. In Siglebi . i . car træ.

In Redrefbi . ii . car træ . i . bouata min .7 viii . ac pti.

In Brochefbi . ii . car træ .7 vii . ac pti .7 Molin . v . folid.

In Frifebi . i . car træ 7 dim .7 iiii . ac pti.  ⌈ lg .7 v . q̇ lat.

In Prefteuuald . ii . car træ . ptu . iii . q̇ lg .7 i . q̇ lat . Silua . vi . q̇

In Cernelega . iiii . car træ . Vafta . e.                    rq pciu

In Gadefbi . i . car træ .7 iiii . ac pti .7 molin . iii . folid.

In Redebi . iii . car træ . ii . bouat min .7 iii . ac pti.

In Frifebi . i . car træ 7 dimid .7 iiii . ac pti .7 molin . xxviii . den.

De his tris ten . iiii . milites de comite . xii . carucatas træ.

In his ht ipfe com in dnio . iiii . car 7 dim .7 xxx . fochos.

7 xx . v . uillos 7 xiii . bord hntes xv . car 7 dimid . cu . i . feruo.

Milites ej hnt in dnio . iii . car .7 xii . uillos cu . i . focho 7 ii . bord

hntes . iii . car.

In *Lvctebvrne* ten Rogeri de comite . viii . car træ.

Radulf . iii . car træ 7 dim . Hugo . iii . car træ 7 dimid . ⊙

Godric . iii . car træ 7 dim . Rogeri dimid car træ.

In dnio ft . v . car .7 viii . uilli cu . xv . fochis 7 xvi . bord . hnt

xii . car 7 dimid . Ibi . ii . molini de . x . folid .7 xlv . ac pti.

Silua . vii . qrent lg .7 iii . q̇ lat . Quinq taini libe tenuer.

Leuuin ten de comite . i . hid in *Bvrtone* . Soca ptin ad

Lucteburne . In dnio . e . i . car .7 un uilts cu . ii . bord .7 xx . ac pti.

In ead uilla ten Godric de Comite . ii . car træ .7 ibi ht . i . car

in dnio .7 xx . acs pti . Huj træ foca reclamat . H . de Grentemaifn.

40 villagers with 13 smallholders have 11 ploughs.

3 mills at 30s; woodland 1 league long and 4 furlongs wide
    which pays 5s.

Earl Harold held this manor with the dependencies written below.

In (Castle) DONINGTON 5 c. of land.

Meadow 3 furlongs long and 1 furlong wide.

In COSSINGTON 6 c. of land.

In HOTON 6 c. of land.

In SEAGRAVE 2 c. of land. Meadow, 10 acres. In SILEBY 1 c. of land.

In REARSBY 2 c. of land less 1 b. Meadow, 8 acres.

In BROOKSBY 2 c. of land. Meadow, 7 acres. A mill, 5s.

In FRISBY (on-the-Wreak) 1½ c. of land. Meadow, 4 acres.

In PRESTWOLD 2 c. of land. Meadow 3 furlongs long and
    1 furlong wide; woodland 6 furlongs long and 5 furlongs wide.

In CHARLEY 4 c. of land. Waste.         *Find out the assessment.*

In GADDESBY 1 c. of land. Meadow, 4 acres; a mill, 3s.

In ROTHERBY 3 c. of land less 2 b. Meadow, 3 acres.

In FRISBY (on-the-Wreak) 1½ c. of land. Meadow, 4 acres;
    a mill, 28d.

4 of the Earl's men-at-arms hold 12 c. of land from these
lands. In these the Earl himself has in lordship 4½ ploughs and
    30 Freemen, 25 villagers and 13 smallholders who have
        15½ ploughs with 1 slave.

His men-at-arms have in lordship 3 ploughs and
    12 villagers with 1 Freeman and 2 smallholders who have 3 ploughs.

2   In LOUGHBOROUGH Roger holds 8 c. of land from the Earl;
Ralph 3½ c. of land; Hugh 3½ c. of land; Godric 3½ c. of land;
Roger ½ c. of land. In lordship 5 ploughs.
    8 villagers with 15 Freemen and 16 smallholders have 12½ ploughs.
    2 mills at 10s; meadow, 45 acres; woodland 7 furlongs long
      and 3 furlongs wide.
    5 thanes held them freely.

3   Leofwin holds 1 hide in BURTON (on-the-Wolds) from the Earl.
The jurisdiction belongs to Loughborough. In lordship 1 plough;
    1 villager with 2 smallholders.
    Meadow, 20 acres.

4   In the same village Godric holds 2 c. of land from the Earl.
He has 1 plough in lordship.
    Meadow, 20 acres.
    Hugh of Grandmesnil claims the jurisdiction of this land.

Roger ten . v . car træ de . H . in *TEDINGESWORDE*.

Ibi hŧ . i . car in dñio 7 iiii . uiłłi cũ . iiii . borđ hñt . ii . car . Ibi

moliñ . vi . denar 7 vi . ac p̃ti . H̃ tra . e in calũnia regis . Herald

Roƀt ten de comite . H . xv . car træ in *COGEWORDE*. ſ tenuit.

Ibi hŧ . v . car in dñio . cũ . i . ſeruo 7 ii . anciłł . 7 xxv . uiłłi cũ

xiii . borđ hñt . x . car . Herald tenuit.

Huic ᙏ p̃tiñ . iii . car træ in *AVEDERNE* 7 in *DEXLEIA* . Ibi sŧ

xx . ac p̃ti . Silua . i . q̃ʒ 7 dim in lg̃ . 7 una q̃ʒ lat.

In his oῖibʒ p̃ſcriptis tris fueŧ . qt xx . car . T.R.E.

Toŧ Valuit 7 uał . xl . liƀ . Q̃do recep̃ coῖ . ualƀ . x . liƀ

In *BORTONE* ten Hugo de comite . ii . car træ . i . bouata miñ.

Vaſta . e . H̃ cõputat cũ ſupioribʒ.

Rogeri ten de comite . H . in . . . . . . . . Ibi . e dimiđ car

. . . . . 7 iiii . uiłłi cũ . ii . borđ hñt . . . . dimiđ Alnod tenuit.

Robertvs filius . W . hoſtiarij ten de rege in *HOWES* . ii . car

Ibi hŧ . i . car in dñio 7 iii . ſeru 7 viii . uiłłi cũ . i . borđ hñtes . ii . car.

Ibi . vii . ac p̃ti . Valuit 7 uał . xx . ſoliđ.

Turſtiñ ten de . Ro . in *HOWES* . ii . car træ 7 dim . Ibi hŧ . i . car.

7 ii . ſeru . 7 vi . uiłł 7 ii . borđ cũ . i . car 7 dimiđ . Ibi . ix . ac p̃ti.

Idē Turſtiñ ten de . Rꝋ . In *CLACHESTONE* ſ Valuit 7 uał . xx . ſoł.

iiii . car træ . 7 Tetbald . ii . car træ . Ibi . e in dñio . i . car.

7 iii . ſocħi 7 v . uiłłi 7 iiii . borđ cũ . iii . car . 7 i . ſeruo . Ibi . xiiii.

ac p̃ti . Valuit 7 uał totũ . xx . ſoliđ.

Has tras tenueŧ T . R . E . Outi 7 Arnui cũ ſaca 7 ſoca.

[In GARTREE Wapentake]

5   Roger holds 5 c. of land in THEDDINGWORTH from Earl Hugh.
He has 1 plough in lordship.
> 4 villagers with 4 smallholders have 2 ploughs.
> A mill, 6d; meadow, 6 acres.
> This land is in the King's claim.

Earl Harold held it.


[In GOSCOTE Wapentake]

6   Robert holds 15 c. of land in KEGWORTH from Earl Hugh.
He has 5 ploughs in lordship, with 1 male and 2 female slaves.
> 25 villagers with 13 smallholders have 10 ploughs.

Earl Harold held it.
To this manor belong 3 c. of land in HATHERN and DISHLEY.
> Meadow, 20 acres; woodland 1½ furlongs in length and
>   1 furlong wide.

In all these lands above written there were 80 ploughs before 1066.
The value of the whole was and is £40. When the Earl acquired it
the value was £10.


7   In BURTON (on-the-Wolds) Hugh holds 2 c. of land less 1 b. from
the Earl. Waste. It is accounted for with those above.


8   Roger of Bully holds 1 c. of land in ...... from Earl Hugh. ½ plough ......
> 4 villagers with 2 smallholders have 2½ ploughs.

Alnoth held it.


[In FRAMLAND Wapentake]

9   Robert son of William the Usher holds 2 c. of land in HOSE from
the King. He has 1 plough in lordship; 3 slaves.
> 8 villagers with 1 smallholder who have 2 ploughs.
> Meadow, 7 acres.

The value was and is 20s.


10   Thurstan holds 2½ c. of land in HOSE from Robert.
He has 1 plough; 2 slaves;
> 6 villagers and 2 smallholders with 1½ ploughs.
> Meadow, 9 acres.

The value was and is 20s.


11   Thurstan also holds 4 c. of land in (Long) CLAWSON from Robert and
Theobald. 2 c. of land. In lordship 1 plough;
> 3 Freemen, 5 villagers and 4 smallholders with 3 ploughs
>   and 1 slave.
> Meadow, 14 acres.

The value of the whole was and is 20s.
> Auti and Ernwy held these lands with full jurisdiction before 1066.

## .XLII. TERRA HOMINŬ COMITIS *In Gvtlæcistan Wap.* De Mellent

Dᴇ Cᴏᴍɪᴛᴇ Dᴇ Mᴇʟʟᴇɴᴛ. ten Turald tra. ɪɪɪɪ. uitto̗

7 ibi ht in dnio tra. ɪ. car. 7 v. sochos cu. ɪ. uitto 7 ɪɪ. bord

hntes. ɪɪ. car. Ibi. v. ac p̃ti. Valet. xx. sot. H̃ tra jacet in *Aɪʟᴇsᴛᴏɴ*.

Vlnod ten de com. ɪɪɪɪ. car træ p̃tin ad *Aɪʟᴇsᴛᴏɴᴇ*.

In dnio ht. ɪ. car. 7 ɪɪ. uitti cu. ɪɪɪ. bord hnt. ɪ. car. Ibi. ɪɪ. ac

brocæ de qb̗ ht Witts peurel soca. ɪɪ. den p ann. Tot uat. xx. sot.

Leuuin tenuit T.R.E.

Wɪᴛᴛs ten de com dimid hid. 7 una car træ 7 dimid. in *Bʟᴀᴅɪ*

Ibi fuer. ɪx. car. Nc in dnio. ɪ. car cu. ɪ. seruo. 7 xxvɪɪɪ.

sochi 7 ɪɪɪɪ. uitti cu. ɪɪɪɪ. bord hnt. vɪ. car. Ibi molin

de. ɪɪ. sot. 7 xxx. ac p̃ti. Valuit. xxx. sot. Modo. ʟ. solid.

Bricmar 7 Vlf tenuer.

Rᴀᴅᴜʟf ten de. Co. *Wᴇsᴛʜᴀ̃*. Ibi. dimid hida 7 ɪ. car træ.

Ibi fuer. vɪ. car. Nc in dnio. ɪɪ. car. 7 ɪɪ. serui. 7 xxɪɪɪɪ.

sochi 7 xɪ. uitti cu. v. bord hnt. v. car. Ibi. e un miles.

7 molin de. ɪɪ. solid. 7 xvɪ. ac p̃ti. Valuit. xxv. sot. M̃. ʟx. sot.

Rᴏʙᴛ ten de. Co. ɪɪɪɪ. car træ 7 dim in *Pᴇᴛʟɪɴɢᴇ*. Ibi fuit

una car. Ibi. ɪɪɪ. sochi hnt dim car. Ibi. x. ac p̃ti.

Valuit. ɪɪɪɪ. sot. Modo. v. solid. Osmar libe tenuit.

Iᴅᴇ̃ ten de. co. *Bʀᴀɴᴅɪɴᴇsᴛᴏʀ*. Ibi st. ɪɪ. partes uni hidæ.

idest. xɪɪ. car træ. Ibi fuer. vɪ. car. Nc in dnio. ɪɪ. car.

7 ɪɪ. serui. 7 ɪx. sochi 7 ɪɪɪ. uitti cu. vɪ. bord hnt. ɪɪɪ. car.

Ibi. xvɪ. ac p̃ti. De hac tra ten Osbn. ɪɪɪ. car træ. 7 ibi ht. ɪ. car.

Valuit. xxx. solid. Modo. xʟ. solid. Boui libe tenuit.

In GUTHLAXTON Wapentake

1　Thorold holds land for 4 villagers from the Count of Meulan.
In lordship he has land for 1 plough and
　5 Freemen with 1 villager and 2 smallholders who have 2 ploughs.
　Meadow, 5 acres.
Value 20s.
　This land lies in Aylestone.

From the Count

2　Wulfnoth holds 4 c. of land which belong to AYLESTONE.
In lordship he has 1 plough.
　2 villagers with 3 smallholders have 1 plough.
　Watermeadow, 2 acres of which William Peverel has the
　　jurisdiction of 2d a year.
Value of the whole, 20s.
　Leofwin held it before 1066.

3　William holds ½ hide and 1½ c. of land in BLABY.  There were 9
ploughs.  Now in lordship 1 plough, with 1 slave.
　28 Freemen and 4 villagers with 4 smallholders have 6 ploughs.
　A mill at 2s; meadow, 30 acres.
The value was 30s; now 50s.
　Brictmer and Ulf held it.

4　Ralph holds WHETSTONE.  ½ hide and 1 c. of land.  There were 6
ploughs.  Now in lordship 2 ploughs; 2 slaves.
　24 Freemen and 11 villagers with 5 smallholders have 5 ploughs.
　　1 man-at-arms.
　A mill at 2s; meadow, 16 acres.
The value was 25s; now 60s.

5　Robert holds 4½ c. of land in PEATLING (Magna).
There was 1 plough.
　3 Freemen have ½ plough.
　Meadow, 10 acres.
The value was 4s; now 5s.
　Osmer held it freely.

6　He also holds  BRUNTINGTHORPE.  2 parts of one hide, that is 12 c.
of land.  There were 6 ploughs.  Now in lordship 2 ploughs; 2 slaves.
　9 Freemen and 3 villagers with 6 smallholders have 3 ploughs.
　Meadow, 16 acres.
　Of this land Osbern holds 3 c. of land.  He has 1 plough.
The value was 30s; now 40s.
　Bovi held it freely.

Fulco ten de.Co.viii.car̃ træ in *CLAIBROC*.Ibi fuer̃.ix.car̃.
Nc in dñio.i.car̃.7 ii.ſerui.7 ix.ſochi 7 ix.uilli 7 ii.milit
cū.vi.bord hñt.v.car̃.Valuit.x.ſol.Modo.lv.ſolid.
Robt ten de.Co.*SAWELLE*.Ibi ſt.ix.car̃ træ.Ibi fuer̃
vii.car̃.7 vi.ſerui.7 xxiii.uilli cū.xi.bord hñt.vi.car̃.
Ibi molin de.ii.ſol.7 lx.ac̃ p̃ti.Valuit.xl.ſol.M.lx.ſol.
Saxi libe tenuit T.R.E.
Robt ten de.Co.|iiii.car̃ In PLOTELEI træ.Ibi fuer̃.iiii.car̃.Nc in dñio
.ii.car̃.7 ii.ſerui.7 iiii.uilli cū.i.bord hñt.i.car̃.Ibi.ii.
ac̃ p̃ti.Valuit.x.ſolid.Modo.xxx.ſolid.Leuric tenuit.
Radulf ten de.co.ix.car̃ træ in *BAGEWORDE*.Ibi fuer̃
vii.car̃.Nc in dñio ſt.ii.cū.i.ſeruo.7 xxiiii.uilli 7 iii.
ſochi cū.vii.bord hñt.v.car̃.Silua.i.leu l̃g.7 dim leū lat.
Valuit.xl.ſol.Modo.iiii.lib.Saxi libe tenuit.
Ingenulf ten de Co.vi.car̃ træ in *IBESTOCHE*.Ibi fuer̃
iiii.car̃.Nc in dñio.i.car̃.7 x.ſochi cū.xi.bord hñt.iiii.
car̃.Valuit.v.ſol.M.xl.ſol.Soca jac ad ſupiore uillã.Bag
Radulf ten de.Co.ii.car̃ træ 7 dim in *CHIVELESWORDE*.
Ibi fuer̃.ii.car̃.Nc.i.car̃ in dñio cū.i.ſeruo.7 ii.uilli cū.v.
bord hñt.i.car̃.Ibi.viii.ac̃ p̃ti.Valuit 7 ual.xx.ſol.Vlchetel
Ide ten de Co...car̃ træ 7 ii.bouat in ead uilla. ⌐libe tenuit.
Ibi fuit dim car̃.7 tant ibi.e in dñio.cū.i.ſocho 7 ii.bord.7 una
ancilla.Ibi molin de.ii.ſol.7 iiii.ac̃ p̃ti.Valuit.ii.ſol.m.x.ſolid.
Ide Vlchetel tenuit.

Fulk holds 8 c. of land in CLAYBROOKE. There were 9 ploughs.
Now in lordship 1 plough; 2 slaves.
   9 Freemen, 9 villagers and 2 men-at-arms with 6
      smallholders have 5 ploughs.
The value was 10s; now 55s.

Robert holds SHAWELL. 9 c. of land. There were 7 ploughs;
6 slaves.
   23 villagers with 11 smallholders have 6 ploughs.
   A mill at 2s; meadow, 60 acres.
The value was 40s; now 60s.
   Saxi held it freely before 1066.

Robert holds 4 c. of land in *PLOTELEI*. There were 4 ploughs.
Now in lordship 2 ploughs; 2 slaves.
   4 villagers with 1 smallholder have 1 plough.
   Meadow, 2 acres.
The value was 10s; now 30s.
   Leofric held it.

Ralph holds 9 c. of land in BAGWORTH. There were 7 ploughs.
Now in lordship 2, with 1 slave.
   24 villagers and 3 Freemen with 7 smallholders have 5 ploughs.
   Woodland 1 league long and ½ league wide.
The value was 40s; now £4.
   Saxi held it freely.

Ingenwulf holds 6 c. of land in IBSTOCK. There were 4 ploughs.
Now in lordship 1 plough.
   10 Freemen with 11 smallholders have 3 ploughs.
The value was 5s; now 40s.
   The jurisdiction lies in the above village, Bagworth.

Ralph holds 2½ c. of land in (North)KILWORTH.
There were 2 ploughs. Now in lordship 1 plough, with 1 slave.
   2 villagers with 5 smallholders have 1 plough.
   Meadow, 8 acres.
The value was and is 20s.
   Ulfketel held it freely.

He also holds 5 c. and 2 b. of land in the same village.
There was ½ plough and as many are there in lordship, with
   1 Freeman, 2 smallholders and 1 female slave.
   A mill at 2s; meadow, 4 acres.
The value was 2s; now 10s.
   Ulfketel also held it.

# LEICESTERSHIRE HOLDINGS
# ENTERED ELSEWHERE IN THE SURVEY

*The Latin text of these entries is given in the county volumes concerned. With the exception of Thringstone these places were transferred to Leicestershire during the late 19th century. They are here included so that the description of the modern county may be complete.*

## In DERBYSHIRE

| 1 | LAND OF THE KING | 272 d |
|---|---|---|

**E 1**  21 S.  In WILLESLEY 2 c. of land taxable. Land for 2 ploughs. Jurisdiction.
2 Freemen, 7 villagers and 1 smallholder have 2½ ploughs.
Meadow, 16 acres; woodland pasture 1 furlong long
and 1 furlong wide.

**E 2**  23 S.  In THRINGSTONE ½ c. of land taxable. Land for 4 oxen.

**E 3**  24 B.  In MEASHAM 2 c. of land taxable.  Land for 3 ploughs. Waste.
Meadow, 20 acres; underwood 1 furlong and 1 furlong wide.

**E 4**  25 B.  In CHILCOTE 3 c. of land taxable. Land for 3 ploughs.
3 villagers have 2 ploughs.
Meadow, 12 acres.
Value before 1066, 40s; now 10s.
It belongs to Clifton (Campville), in Stafford.

| 3 | LAND OF THE ABBEY OF BURTON | 273 b |
|---|---|---|

**E 5**  2 M.  In APPLEBY the Abbot of Burton had 5 c. of land taxable. Land
for 5 ploughs. Of this land Abbot Leofric leased 1 c. of land to
Countess Goda; the King has it now.
In the same village, now in lordship 2 ploughs.
8 villagers and 1 smallholder with 1 plough.
Value before 1066, 20s; now 60s.

| 6 | LAND OF HENRY OF FERRERS | 274 b |
|---|---|---|

**E 6**  16 M.  In STRETTON (-en-le-Field) Aelfric had 1 c. of land taxable.
Land for 1 plough.
4 villagers have 2 ploughs.
1 mill, 5s; meadow, 10 acres.
Value before 1066, 20s; now 15s.
Roger holds it.

**E 7**  20 M.  In WILLESLEY  Aelfric had 1 c. of land taxable. Land for 1 plough.
Waste.
3 villagers have 5 ploughing oxen.
Value before 1066, 20s; now 16s.

**E 8**    8 M.    In RAVENSTONE   Godric had 1 c. of land taxable. Land for 1 plough. Waste.
> Meadow, 8 acres.
> Value before 1066, 15s; now 12d.

**E 9**    9 M.    In DONISTHORPE   Carl had 1 c. of land taxable. Land for ½ plough. Waste.
> Value before 1066, 5s; now 12d.

**E 10**    10 M.    In OAKTHORPE   Ernwin had 6 b. of land taxable. Land for ½ plough. Waste.
> Value before 1066, 5s; now 4d.

**E 11**    11 M.    In THRINGSTONE   Alnoth had ½ c. of land taxable. Waste.
> Value before 1066, 5s; now 2d.

**In NORTHAMPTONSHIRE**

**E 12**    19    (Humphrey) also holds 2 hides and 1 virgate of land and the third part of 1 virgate in (Little) BOWDEN. Land for 6 ploughs.
> In lordship 1, with 1 slave.
> 11 villagers with 1 smallholder have 2 ploughs.
> A mill at 16d; meadow, 8 acres.
> 3 Freemen with 2 ploughs.
> The value was 64d; now 30s.
> Godwin and wulfwin held it.

# NOTES

ABBREVIATIONS used in the notes. DB ... Domesday Book. DG ... H.C. Darby and G.R. Versey *Domesday Gazetteer* Cambridge 1975. Mon. Ang. ... Sir William Dugdale *Monasticon Anglicanum* 1846. MS ... Manuscript. OEB ... G. Tengvik *Old English Bynames* Uppsala 1938. PNDB ... O. von Feilitzen *Pre-Conquest Personal Names of Domesday Book* Uppsala 1937. Leic. Surv. ... The Leicestershire Survey ed. C.F. Slade (University of Leicester, 1956). VCH ... Victoria County History (Leicestershire volume 1).

The editor is grateful to Dr. Barrie Cox for his advice on the place-name identifications.

The manuscript is written on leaves, or folios, of parchment (sheepskin), measuring about 15 inches by 11 inches (38 cm by 28 cm), on both sides. On each side are two columns, making four to each folio. The folios were numbered in the 17th century, and the four columns of each are here lettered a,b,c,d. The manuscript emphasises words and usually distinguishes chapters and sections by the use of red ink. Underlining here indicates deletion.

LEICESTERSHIRE. *LEDECESTRESCIRE* in red across both columns on folio 230 ab; *LEDECESTSCIRE* across every other folio. The shire emerged from the district assigned to the maintenance of the Danish army at Leicester in the late 9th century, but was formally organised later, perhaps not until just before the conquest (H.P.R. Finberg *Gloucestershire Studies* Leicester 1957, 17ff).

C 1     ORA. Literally an ounce, in Scandinavia a monetary unit and coin still in use; in DB valued at 16d or, as here, at 20d.
        SESTER. A dry or liquid measure of uncertain capacity; reckoned at 32 ounces for honey.

C 3     £42 10s. DB uses the Old English currency system which endured for a thousand years until 1971. The pound contained 20 shillings, each of 12 pence, abbreviated as £(ibrae), s(olidi), d(enarii).

C 11    HUGH OF GRANDMESNIL. The largest landholder in the Borough and the County. Shortly after the conquest he was created castellan of Leicester, 'Hugoni vero Grentemaisnilo municipatum Legrecestrae commendavit' (The Ecclesiastical History of Orderic Vitalis ed. M. Chibnall vol ii, 264). See below note 9.

C 12    WATFORD in Northamptonshire where Hugh held '3½ hides in WEEDON (Beck) in exchange for Watford', (DB Northants., 23,3). Gilbert Cook held 2 hides at Watford, (DB Northants., 57,2).

C 16    MS error, *ht* for *hnt*, 'has' for 'have',

C 17    CARUCATE. The unit of land measurement in Danish areas; comprising 8 bovates. The abbreviations c. and b. are here used.

C 18    SHERIFFDOM ... COUNTY. Since each county had its sheriff (*vicecomes*), but few had an Earl (*comes*) in 1086, the terms are interchangeable.
        HERESWODE. 'The wood of the army', later Leicester Forest; probably associated with the Danish army at Leicester.

L       EARL HUGH is entered here at number 13 although his lands were omitted in the text and entered later at number 43. The numbering of the text and list of landholders is, therefore, inconsistent until Roger of Bully, entered at number 18 in both text and list of landholders as a result of the omission in the latter of the land of Robert of Bucy.

1,1a    IN FRAMLAND WAPENTAKE'. There were four Leicestershire Wapentakes (later Hundreds) in 1086. Goscote Wapentake was divided during the 14th century, and Sparkenhoe Hundred was in existence by 1129. The relationship between the DB Wapentakes and modern Hundreds is:-

| DB Form | Modern Form |
| --- | --- |
| GOSE(N)COTE | East Goscote |
| | West Goscote |
| GUTLACISTAN | Guthlaxton |
| | Sparkenhoe |
| FRANLAND, FRANDONE | Framland |
| GERTREV(VES) | Gartree |

The Wapentake rubrication is not complete and headings are inserted, within square brackets, on the evidence of the Leicestershire Survey of c. 1129/30.

This document also reveals the existence in Leicestershire of the system of small hundreds, a sub-division of the county between the Wapentake and vill, which are also found in Nottinghamshire, Derbyshire and probably Lincolnshire. They are explained in the Lindsey Survey of c. 1115 and discussed by J.H. Round *Feudal England* (1964 reprint) 69-76, 149-74. Although the Survey remains the sole authority for these Leicestershire hundreds it seems likely that they originated in the period of Danish settlement, and that they illustrate an earlier system of assessment for taxation purposes based on the villar assessment of 12 c., but associated in larger groups of 144 c.

Comparison of assessments in DB and the Survey reveals the existence of places, entered separately in 1129/30 and under a single heading in DB, which are therefore known to have existed in 1086. Instances of DB omission or possible scribal errors are given in the notes. All references to the Survey are to the edition of C.F. Slade (University of Leicester 1956).

| | |
|---|---|
| 1,2 | HUGH SON OF BALDRIC sheriff of Nottinghamshire. |
| 1,4 | Farley *In Graveho i (car) trae . . . In Carletone v(i bov)atae trae*; the missing sections are visible under a slight ink-blot in the MS. |
| 1,5 | *ABEGRAVE.* Identified as 'Prestgrave', a deserted village; the Abbey at Peterborough held land here in the Leic. Surv., 23 which formed part of the grant by Earl Ralph of Hereford. See note 5,2. |
| 1,7 | 'THE BURGH'. A lost village between Whatborough and Launde; it appears as 'Burthveit' in 12th century charters, and 'Burfielde' on map of 1586, W.G. Hoskins *Essays in Leicestershire History*, 95-96. |
| 1,10 | SERVICE OF THE ISLE OF WIGHT. As a contribution to the re-organized system of coastal defence established after the conquest, perhaps c. 1066/67 while Odo and William fitzOsbern, lord of the Isle of Wight, were acting as viceroys during William's absence in Normandy, although more probably after William's death in 1070. |
| | SHEPSHED but probably including Long Watton, Lockington and Hemington, Leic. Surv. 19. |
| 1,12 | BITTESBY. A late addition, in a smaller script, within two rulings to fit the line. |
| 2,6 | MS *villes* for *villis*, corrected by Farley. |
| 2,7 | FRIENDAY. *Friendai* is an OFrisian variant, with the weak inflection of the goddess's name, of the byname *Friday* (OE *Frigedæg*, OG *Frigdag*, etc.) OED s.v. Friday, OEB 218. |
| 3,1 | 2 CHURCHES. Probably St. Margaret and the chapel of St. Mary Magdalene in Knighton, *Registrum Antiquissimum of the Cathedral Church of Lincoln* ed. C.W. Foster I, 139, 190. |
| 3,15 | R ... SON OF WALTER. The name omitted. |
| 5,2 | EARL RALPH GAVE IT. Earl Ralph of Hereford, nephew of King Edward, granted lands to Peterborough c. 1041-1057; 'Raulfus comes propinquus Eduardi dedit Eston et Brinninghurst et Prestgrave et Dreitun et Glathestun', *The Chronicle of Hugh Candidus* ed. W. T. Mellows (1949), 69. |
| 6,1 | 22½ C. OF LAND giving a hide, in Leicestershire, of 18 carucates as also in 38,1. The statement in 29,3 'In each hide are 14½ c. of land' was seen by J.H. Round *Feudal England* (1968 reprint), 77 as a description of an unusual assessment. |
| | WHEN THE ABBEY ACQUIRED IT. Burbage formed part of the original foundation of Earl Leofric of Mercia in or around 1043, although the *valuit* clause here probably refers to a regrant of the Abbey's temporalities by William I in 1070, VCH 284. Where an earlier value is given for Leicestershire it is never stated to be that current in 1066 and indeed many of the larger holdings, notably that of Hugh of Grandmesnil, cannot have been organised much before 1070/71; the period to which the *valuit* entries presumably refer. |
| 6,3 | VALUE 30s. Its position indicated by the use of transposition signs. |
| 9 | COUNT OF MEULAN. Robert of Beaumont, styled Earl of Leicester by 1107. 'The town of Leicester had four lords; the King, the Bishop of Lincoln, Earl Simon and Ivo, son of Hugh. The Count of Meulan, however, cunningly got a foothold there through the share of Ivo, who was castellan and Sheriff and farmed it for the King, and with the King's aid and his own cunning bought the whole town under his control. By this means he became an Earl in England ... ', Orderic Vitalis *The Ecclesiastical History* ed. M. Chibnall vi, 18-21. |
| 9,1 | LEOFWIN (HELD). Tenuit erased on the MS, whether by accident or on purpose. |
| 10 | EARL AUBREY. Of Northumbria, in the early 1080's, 'of little use in difficult circumstances, he went home' to Normandy (Simeon *Historia Regum* Rolls 75, 1885, ii, 199). His extensive holdings in England had not yet been granted to others in 1086. |
| 10,8 | 4 PLOUGHS. The facsimile does not reproduce the first stroke; corrected by Farley. |
| 10,15 | RALPH OF CHARTRES. OEB 133. |
| 10,16 | IN SHOBY, but probably including 5 c. of land entered at Saxelby, a neighbouring village, in the Leic. Surv. 17. |
| 10,17 | ALL THESE LANDS. The word order corrected by interlined a,b. |
| 11 | COUNTESS GODIVA widow of Earl Leofric of Mercia. |
| 12 | COUNTESS AELFEVA wife of Earl Algar of Mercia. |
| 13 | HUGH OF GRANDMESNIL. In or before 1081 King William confirmed a number of grants made to the Abbey of St. Evroul. Hugh of Grandmesnil had given the tithes of |

various manors, with the services of 16 peasants (*rustici*) as collectors, and nine churches with small amounts of land, *The Ecclesiastical History of Orderic Vitalis* ed. M. Chibnall iii, 235-7. The Leicestershire grants are given here:

| DB | Place | Granted to St. Evroul |
|---|---|---|
| 13,4 | Earl Shilton | 3 peasants |
| 13,17 | Carlton Curlieu | 1 peasant with the church and 5 v. of land. |
| 13,18 | Noseley | the church and 2 v. of land. |
| 13,19 | Thurcaston | the church and 2 v. of land. |
| 13,20 | Belgrave | 2 peasants with the church and 11 v. of land. |
| 13,40 | Glenfield | 2 the church and 2 v. of land. |
| 13,52 | Stoughton | 1 peasant |
| 13,57 | Thorpe Langton | 1 peasant |
| 13,62 | Thurmaston | 1 peasant |

The position of these tithe collectors is discussed by R.F. Lennard *Peasant Tithe Collectors* (English Historical Review lxix, 1969). See notes 29,3; 43,2;6.

13,18 WATER MEADOW. *Broc* OE, came to mean 'a brook', but originally the word (like its cognates MDu and Du *broek*, LG *brok*, OHG *bruch*, G *bruch*) meant 'marsh, bog', etc., a sense retained by *brook* 'water-meadow' in ModE dialects of Kent, Sussex, Surrey, and in medieval field names in Cambridgeshire and Essex. See EPNS xxv 51, and OED s.v. *brook*.

13,20 BELGRAVE. Only recently renamed, 'Merthegrave quae nunc alio nomine Belegrava dicitur' (Orderic Vitalis op. cit., 236), although the English name persisted: it appears as Mardegrave in the Survey, 16. DEPN suggests that the first element of the original name, OE *mearþ* 'a marten', would have resembled, to the Norman ear, French *merde*, 'shit'; hence the substitution of *bel* 'fine'.

13,21 BUXTON; thus OEB 223, although 'Buckstone' would be better, but *pbochestan* could be the result of a miscopied spelling for a place-name like Wroxton, Oxfordshire, *Werochestan* DB 159 d, in which w- has been represented by the runic letter *wynn* QUIA. 'That', implying an indirect statement and in use in the Vulgate and Fathers and not, as in VCH 315, a scribal error for *quod*.

13,27 THURLASTON. Probably a detached portion of Gartree Wapentake under which heading it is entered in the Leic. Surv., 23.

13,34 1½ PLOUGHS. No figure given, but probably 1.

13,41 ROBERT BURDET. MS error 'Burdel' for 'Burdet', see 13,53.

13,45 *NEVLEBI*. Dr. Barrie Cox suggests that this is possibly 'Nagli's *by*', with vocalisation of *g* after a back-vowel to form a dipthong with the preceding vowel and AN substitution of *e* for *a*. The OScand p.n. *Nagli* is an original by-name 'nail, spike'. However, the p.n. may be an early Scandinavianisation of OE *Næglestun* (which is Nailstone in Sparkenhoe Hundred). The earliest securely dated form for the latter is otherwise *Naylestone*, 1225. The OE p.n. *Nægl* is unrecorded, but cf. *Nægling* in *Beowulf* 2680; a by-name directly parallel to ON *Nagli*.

13,51 MS error, *In GERBERIE* for *In INGERBERIE*.

13,55 HUGH of Gouville, VCH 291.

13,63 SERVANTS. *Servientes Regis*, the King's Servants (or 'Serjeants'), occur at the end of several counties, in a separate chapter, individually named (as below 42,1-10), with or instead of the King's Thanes or Almsmen. Unnamed *servientes* are also sometimes listed in the villages, as here. Though the Latin is ambiguous, the *Servientes* of Wymeswold were probably not in lordship. They may or may not be comparable with the west-country *radchenistre* or *radmans*, 'riding men', and may not have anything but the name in common with later 'serjeantries'. See also Staffs. 12,17.

13,66 ALTON but probably including Blackfordby and Kilwardby, entered separately in the Leic. Surv., 19.

13,67 EARL WALTHEOF who held land elsewhere in Leicestershire, see 14,16. A possible but less likely alternative is Earl William of Hereford whose lands were forfeited by his son in 1075. The phrase *de Feudo Willi Comitis* describes his holdings in Oxfordshire, see DB Oxon not B5, 59.

14,3 KING'S SHEPSHED. *Regis* interlined in a lighter ink; Shepshed is entered above at 1,10.
ALWIN CLAIMS. The dispute was settled soon after; 'In WORTHINGTON 3 c. according to the King's charter', Leic. Surv., 18. The disputed 1 c. was returned to Shepshed; 'In WORTHINGTON 1 c. of the holding of Shepshed', Leic. Surv., 28.

14,6 *IN DOMINIO* interlined in a lighter ink.

| | |
|---|---|
| 14,18 | MEGINTA. DB *Mechenta* through Anglo-Norman substitution *ch* < *g* (PNDB 113, 128); the continental German feminine pers. n. *Maganza* < *Meginta, Meginza* 10th and 11th century, E. Forstemann, *Altdeutsches Namenbuch,* I *Personennamen* (Bonn 1900), 1072. |
| 14,19-20 | SEAL. Nether Seal and Over Seal were transferred to Derbyshire in 1897, see note 39,1. |
| 14,23 | BISHOP OSMUND of Salisbury, 1078-1099. |
| 14,30 | *WINDESERS. Widesers* Leic. Surv., 19. Dr. Barrie Cox suggests a location in Long Whatton parish, Goscote Wapentake. The valley in which Whatton and Diseworth lie has an east-west axis and would thus be a trap for the winds bringing the poorest weather in this part of the country. OE *wind, ears,* 'the wind's arse', referring to a conformation of land which funnelled the wind. |
| 14,33 | 3 PLOUGHS. The facsimile does not reproduce the final stroke. |
| 15,1 | HORNINGHOLD. Granted by Robert of Tosny to his newly founded priory at Belvoir in 1076, VCH (Lincolnshire) ii, 126. |
| 15,3 | IN HARBY but probably including Plungar, Leic. Surv., 22. |
| 15,16 | BOTTESFORD. MS error, 'h' and 'l' for 'b' and 't'; *HOLESFORD* for *BOTESFORD.* |
| 17,24 | IN LODDINGTON but probably including Launde, Leic. Surv., 36. |
| 19,2-12 | LAND FOR (... PLOUGHS). The MS is left blank; the information not available or unreported. |
| 19,6 | HAVE 1 PLOUGH. There is an erasure in the MS between *car* and *ibi,* possibly *trae*; '5 villagers have 1 c. of land' corrected to '5 villagers have 1 plough'. |
| 19,14 | EDWIN ALFRITH. OEB 213. |
| 20 | LAND OF ROBERT USHER. Entered again below, see note 43,9. |
| 21,2 | 'WESTON'. A deserted village at SK 303027. |
| 23,2 | ABBOT BENEDICT of Selby. Guy of Raimbeaucourt had granted Stanford with its outliers to Selby, 'pro amore Dei, et anima domini mei Willielmi' (Mon. Ang., iii, 499), although reported in DB as a straightforward purchase. See also 23,4 and DB Northamptonshire 41,3. |
| 27,4 | *IN STOFALDE.* 'Stofalde iii p i v W' in the margin, omitted by Farley. The 'W' may alternatively represent W(illielmus). |
| 29,3 | MELTON. Geoffrey of La Guerche had granted two parts of the tithes, a tenth of the market and tolls and a man as a collector to the Abbey of St. Nicholas of Angers in 1077, (Mon. Ang., vi, 996). See above note 13. |
| 29,6 | *LILINGE.* Dr. Barrie Cox suggests a location in the Bitteswell-Ullesthorpe area of Guthlaxton Wapentake near Watling St. OE p.n. Lilla, *ing* 'Lilla's people'. The two Peatlings the only other names in *-ingas* in the county, are a few miles away. |
| 38,1 | EUR. Probably a curtailed form of Eurard, see Hunts. 6,7; PNDB 249. |
| 39,1 | SEAL. Nichols identifies with Over Seal. See also note 14,20. |
| 40 | COUNTESS JUDITH widow of Earl Waltheof of Northamptonshire and Huntingdonshire executed in 1076 following the revolt of the Earls. |
| 40,10 | *ELVELEGE.* The place is lost; the name form either OE p.n. Aelfa, *leah* 'the wood of Aelfa' or OE *elf, leah* 'the wood of the elves'. |
| 40,11 | 'RINGLETHORPE'. Now Goldsmith's Grange in Scalford. Formerly a grange of Garendon Abbey. *Goldsmiths Grange* 1577 IPM, after John Goldsmith, a former owner, died 1467. |
| 40,34 | FEGGO. Most likely represents the ODan pers. n. *Feggi* (originally a by-name meaning 'old man'), identified and discussed by O. von Feilitzen, 'Notes on Some Scandinavian Personal Names in English 12th Century Records', *Personnamns Studier 1964 (Anthroponymica Suecana* 6, Stockholm, 1965), 54, and followed by Gillian Fellows-Jensen *Scandinavian Personal-Names in Lincolnshire and Yorkshire* (Copenhagen 1968), 81. |
| 40,40 | HUGH MUSARD. Possibly related to Hascoit Musard, a Breton and landholder in several counties |
| 42,1 | FRAMLAND. MS Gartree, in error. |
| 42,3 | HERBERT'S BROTHER following VCH 335. Farley reproduces the MS *fr h* as *fr H.* A possible alternative would be either *fr(ancus) h(omo),* 'freeman', or *fr(ancigenus) h(omo),* 'Frenchman', *NETONE.* 'Newton', the first element perhaps showing the influence of OScand *nyr* upon OE *niwe.* A location in Cold Newton, as suggested by C.F. Slade (*Leicestershire Survey* 1956, 37), seems likely. |
| 43,1 | GOSCOTE. MS Guthlaxton, in error. |
| 43,2 | ROGER of Melay and Brisard in a confirmation of the grants of St. Evroul, see above |

note 13. Roger of Melay and Brisard and Robert Pultrel, two of Earl Hugh's men, gave their tithes in Leicestershire.

43,6      ROBERT Pultrel, see above 43,2.

43,8      MS *'comite H in ... i car (trae). Ibi e dimid car*
         *... 7 iiii villi cu ii bord hnt ii car et dimid.'*
         The place name is entirely lost; the gap of 0.7cm would allow 4 or 5 letters.

43,9-11    ROBERT SON OF WILLIAM THE USHER HOLDS. These lands are also entered above at 20,1-4 with the addition here of the identity of Robert's father and the TRE holders of Long Clawson. The coincidence of information recorded in the two entries presupposes a common original and suggests that the entries in DB were abbreviated direct from the original returns, perhaps by the scribe himself (V.H. Galbraith *The Making of Domesday Book* 165, 169, 203).

# INDICES AND MAPS

# INDEX OF PERSONS

Familiar modern spellings are given when they exist. Unfamiliar names are usually given in an approximate late 11th century form, avoiding variants that were already obsolescent or pedantic. Spellings that mislead the modern eye are avoided where possible. Two, however, cannot be avoided: they are combined in the name of 'Leofgeat', pronounced 'Leffyet', or 'Levyet'. The definite article is omitted before bynames, except where there is reason to suppose that they described the individual. The chapter numbers of listed landholders are printed in italics.

| | | | |
|---|---|---|---|
| Adelaide wife of Hugh | | Everard | 38,1 |
| of Grandmesnil | *41* | Feggi | 40,34 |
| Countess Aelfeva | *12* | Framen, see Ralph | |
| Aelfric | 14,28;30 | Fran | 17,20 |
| Aelfric the priest | 8,5 | Frienday | 2,7 |
| Aelmer | 5,1. 10,8. 19,3; 17 | Fulbert | 13,34 |
| Aethelhelm | 36,2 | Fulk | 13,54. 36,1. 44,7 |
| Alfred | 29,6 | Gamel | 14,33 |
| Alfrith, see Edwin | | Geoffrey | 16,4-5. 17,10 |
| Alfsi | 17,14 | Geoffrey Alselin | 28 |
| Alfwold | 14,31-32. 29,20 | Geoffrey of La Guerche | *29.* C 14 |
| Algar | 40,41 | Gerard | 17,22; 24; 30-31 |
| Alnoth | 17,21. 43,8 | Gerbert | 34 |
| Alric son of Mergeat | 16,9 | Gilbert | 15,13; 15. 17,19 |
| Alselin, see Geoffrey | | Gilbert of Ghent | *33* |
| Alwin | 13,3; 28; 59; 73. 14,3 | Gladwin | 14,24 |
| | 17,3. 29,2; 8; 9. 32,2 | Godfrey | 3,12. 16,1 |
| Alwin Buxton | 13,21 | Godfrey of Cambrai | *30* |
| Ansfrid | 17,25; 32 | Countess Godiva | *11* |
| Ardwulf | 14,27 | Godric | 3,10; 12-13. 14,16. |
| Arkell | 2,4-6 | | 43,2; 4 |
| Arnbern the priest | 8,4 | Godwin | 1,9-10. 17,5; 20. |
| Arnold | 13,43; 45-46; 64; | | 40,37 |
| | 66-67 | Godwin the priest | 8,1 |
| Askell | 42,7 | Grimbald | 40,26-27; 39 |
| Aubrey | 29,15 | Gundwin | 40,31 |
| Earl Aubrey | *10* | Gunfrid of Chocques | *31* |
| Auti | 43,11 | Guy of Craon | *24* |
| Azor | 40,29 | Guy of Raimbeaucourt | *23* |
| Baldric | 15,15 | Gytha | 2,7 |
| Baldwin | 13,28 | Haldane | 3,15. 40,14 |
| Baldwin, see Hugh | | Harding | 10,5; 17 |
| Bardi | 3,11 | Earl Harold | 43,1; 5-6 |
| Abbot Benedict | 23,2; 4 | Heldwin | 15,15 |
| Bonvallet, see William | | Henry of Ferrers | *14.* C 16. 19,6; 9 |
| Bovi | 44,6 | Herbert | 2,2. 42,1 |
| Brictmer | 44,3 | Howard | 13,32-33; 52; 74 |
| Burdet, see Robert | | Hubert, see Ralph | |
| Buterus | 29,10 | Hugh | 2,7. 6,7. 13,55-56; |
| Clarebald | 15,15 | | 68; 72-73. 14,17; 33. |
| Drogo of La Beuvriere | *36* | | 17,7-8; 12; 26-27. |
| Durand | 16,3. 35,2 | | 40,10-11. 43,2; 7. |
| Durand Malet | *35* | | *43.* C 8 |
| Edith | 21,2 | Earl Hugh | |
| Queen Edith | 1,9 | Hugh son of Baldwin | 1,2 |
| Edric | 21,2 | Hugh Burdet | 40,12-14; 24 |
| Edwin | 13,49. 35,2 | Hugh of Gouville | C 12 |
| Edwin Alfrith | 19,14 | Hugh of Grandmesnil | *13.* C 5; 11-12. |
| Erneis | 13,40; 52 | | 40,8-11; 22. 43,4 |
| Ernwy | 43,11 | Hugh Musard | 40,40-41 |
| Esbern | 14,23. 40,7 | Humphrey | 39,1 |
| | | Humphrey the | |
| | | Chamberlain | *32.* 1,5 |

Ingold 8,3. 17,16-17; 21
Ingenwulf 44,1
Ivo 13,35; 44; 50-51; 65. 15,12
John 14,26
Countess Judith 40. C 17. 14,16
Kari 14,28
Ketelbern 3,16
Lambert 17,13
Laurence 16,7
Leofnoth 3,14. 14,28
Leofric 14,23. 15,7; 15-16. 23,2;6. 41,2-4. 44,9
Leofric son of Leofwin 29,3; 18
Leofwin 1,12. 9,1. 13,19. 17,4. 29,14. 43,3. 44,2
Leofwin, see Leofric
Lovett 13,58
Lovett, see William
Mainou the Breton 37
Meginta 14,18
Mergeat, see Alric
Count of Meulan 9. 44,1-13
Morcar 18,3
Earl Morcar 1,2
Moriland 16,6
Musard, see Hugh
Nigel 14,10; 23; 30; 34
Nigel of Aubigny 39
Norman 10,6; 11-13. 16,2. 28,1-5
Odard 15,15
Odincar 40,35
Odger the Breton 38
Ordmer 29,10
Osbern C 11. 2,5-6; 13,38; 57. 15,9. 40,28. 44,6
Osgot 1,9
Oslac 2,4. 17,8
Osmer 44,5
Osmund 2,4. 15,7; 14
Bishop Osmund 14,23
Oswulf 15,7
Payne 25,3
Peverel, see William
Pippin, see Ralph
Quentin's wife 8,2
R...... son of Walter 3,15
Rainer 29,17
Ralph 3,5-10; 14. 10,7; 14. 13,46. 29,16. 40,32-33; 38. 43,2. 44,4; 10; 12
Ralph Framen 42,9
Ralph Pippin 17,33
Earl Ralph 5,2. 13,1; 15. 17,19. 37,1
Ralph of Chartres 10,15
Ralph son of Hubert 22
Ralph of Mortimer 21
Ranulf 3,11
Raven 42,8
Richard 18,4
Riculf 25,4
Roald 14,11
Robert 2,3-4. 3,4. 10,9. 13,28; 30; 63. 14,19; 29. 15,15. 17,9; 23. 22,1. 23,5. 29,7; 19. 40,16; 20; 23; 25. 43,6; 10-11. 44,5; 8-9
Robert's wife 13,37
Robert Burdet's wife 17,29
Robert the Bursar 19. C 16
Robert of Bucy 17. 13,27. 40,15
Robert of Jort 42,5
Robert of Tosny 15. 1,4. 40,20
Robert of Vessey 16. C 13
Robert son of William the Usher 43,9
Robert Burdet's son 13,41; 53
Rolf 15,7. 35,2
Roger 3,13. 13,31. 14,13; 15; 25; 28; 31-32. 15,11; 14; 16. 17,18. 18,2. 21,1-2. 29,18. 43,2; 5.
Roger of Bully 18. 43,8
Saeric 17,33
Saxfrid 25,5
Saxi 9,1; 5. 44,8; 10
Serlo 13,42; 63
Siward 41,3
Swafi 17,15
Swein 13,60; 67
Theobald 20,4. 43,11
Theodbert 31,1
Thorkell 39,2. 40,26. 42,10
Thorold 44,1
Thurstan 20,2-3. 43,10-11
Toki 28,5
Ulf 3,10. 13,6; 36; 39. 17,8. 29,2. 36,2. 40,9. 44,3
Ulfketel 44,12-13
Walkelin 2,1-3
Walter, see R ....
Walter 13,47; 69-71. 15,8; 11. 29,5
Earl Waltheof 13,67. 14,16. 40,7
Warin 17,11; 28. 24,3
Wazelin 14,14
Widhard 13,61
William 2,2. 13,62. 15,10-11; 16. 29,13; 18. 44,3
William Bonvallet 26
William Lovett 27
William Peverel 25. 33,1. 44,2
Wulfbert 13,48
Wulfgeat 3,16
Wulfnoth 19,19. 44,2
Wulfric 4,1. 10,2
Wulfsi 40,36

**Churches and Clergy.** Abbot Benedict (of Selby) 23,2; 4. **Archbishop** of York 2. C 7. **Bishop** of Bayeux 1,10. Coutances 4. Lincoln 3. Osmund (of Salisbury) 14,23. **Abbeys** ... Coventry C 9. 6. Crowland C 10. 7. Peterborough 5. (Selby) 23,2; 4. **Churches** ... St. Mary's, Southwell 2,7. St. Mary's, Lincoln 3,3. **Priests** see Aelfric, Arnbern, Godwin.

**Secular Titles and Occupational Names.** Bursar (*dispensator*) .. Robert. Chamberlain (*camerarius*) .. Humphrey. Count (*comes*) .. of Meulan. Countess (*comitissa*) .. Aelfeva, Godiva, Judith. Earl (*comes*) .. Aubrey, Harold, Hugh, Morcar, Ralph, Waltheof. Queen (*regina*) .. Edith. Thane (*tainus*) .. Leofric, Osmund, Oswulf, Rolf. Usher (*hostiarius*) .. William.


## TECHNICAL TERMS

Many words meaning measurements have to be transliterated. But translation may not dodge other problems by the use of obsolete or made-up words which do not exist in modern English. The translations here used are given in italics. They cannot be exact; they aim at the nearest modern equivalent.

BORDARIUS. Cultivator of inferior status, usually with a little land. *s m a l l h o l d e r*

BOVATA. One eighth of a carucate. *b.*

CARUCA. A plough, with the oxen who pulled it, usually reckoned as 8. *p l o u g h*

CARUCATA. The unit of land measurement in Danish areas. *c.*

DOMINIUM. The mastery or dominion of a lord (*dominus*); including ploughs, land men, villages, etc., reserved for the lord's use; often concentrated in a *home farm* or *demesne*, a 'Manor Farm' or 'Lordship Farm'. *l o r d s h i p*

FIRMA. Old English *feorm*, provisions due to the King or lord; a fixed sum paid in place of these and of other miscellaneous dues. *r e v e n u e*

FRANCUS HOMO. Equivalent of *liber homo* (free man). *f r e e m a n*

GELDUM. The principal royal tax, originally levied during the Danish wars, normally at an equal number of pence on each *hide* of land. *t a x*

HIDA. The English unit of land measurement or assessment, often reckoned at 120 acres; see Sussex, Appendix. *h i d e*

LEUGA. A measure of length, usually about a mile and a half. *l e a g u e*

SACA. German *Sache*, English *sake*, Latin *causa*, affair, lawsuit; the fullest authority normally exercised by a lord. *f u l l j u r i s d i c t i o n*

SOCA. 'Soke', from *socn*, to seek, comparable with Latin *quaestio*. Jurisdiction with the right to receive fines and a multiplicity of other dues. District in which such *soca* is exercised; a place in a *soca. j u r i s d i c t i o n*

TAINUS, TEGNUS. Person holding land from the King by special grant; formerly used of the King's ministers and military companions. *t h a n e*

T.R.E. *tempore regis Edwardi*, in King Edward's time. *b e f o r e 1 0 6 6*

VILLA. Translating Old English *tun*, town. The later distinction between a small *village* and a large *town* was not yet in use in 1086. *v i l l a g e* or *t o w n*

VILLANUS. Member of a *villa*, usually with more land than a *bordarius. v i l l a g e r*

VIRGATA. A quarter of a hide, reckoned at 30 acres. *v i r g a t e*

WAPENTAC. Equivalent of the English Hundred in Danish areas. *w a p e n t a k e*

# SYSTEMS OF REFERENCE TO DOMESDAY BOOK

The manuscript is divided into numbered chapters, and the chapters into sections, usually marked by large initials and red ink. Farley, however, did not number the sections. References have therefore been inexact, by folio numbers, which cannot be closer than an entire page or column. Moreover, half a dozen different ways of referring to the same column have been devised. In 1816 Ellis used three separate systems in his indices; (i) on pages i-cvii; 435-518; 537-570; (ii) on pages 1-144; (iii) on pages 145-433 and 519-535. Other systems have since come into use, notably that used by Vinogradoff, here followed. This edition numbers the sections, the normal practicable form of close reference; but since all discussion of Domesday for three hundred years has been obliged to refer to page or column, a comparative table will help to locate references given. The five columns below give Vinogradoff's notation, Ellis' three systems, and that employed by Welldon Finn and others. Maitland, Stenton, Darby and others have usually followed Ellis (i).

| Vinogradoff | Ellis (i) | Ellis (ii) | Ellis (iii) | Finn |
|---|---|---|---|---|
| 152 a | 152 | 152 a | 152 | 152ai |
| 152 b | 152 | 152 a | 152.2 | 152a2 |
| 152 c | 152 b | 152 b | 152 b | 152bi |
| 152 d | 152 b | 152 b | 152b2 | 152b2 |

In Leicestershire, the relation between the Vinogradoff notation, here followed, and the chapters and sections is

| | | | | | | | | | | | |
|---|---|---|---|---|---|---|---|---|---|---|---|
| 230 a | C 1 | - | 18 | 233 a | 13,63 | - | 13,74 | 236 a | 32,1 | - | 39,2 |
| b | Landholders | - | 1,3 | b | 14,1 | - | 14,17 | b | 40,1 | - | 40,19 |
| c | 1,3 | - | 1,7 | c | 14,18 | - | 14,34 | c | 40,19 | - | 40,37 |
| d | 1,7 | - | 3,1 | d | 15,1 | - | 15,13 | d | 40,38 | - | 42,10 |
| 231 a | 3,2 | - | 4,1 | 234 a | 15,14 | - | 16,9 | 237 a | 43,1 | - | 43,11 |
| b | 5,1 | - | 8,5 | b | 17,1 | - | 17,20 | b | 44,1 | - | 44,13 |
| c | 9,1 | - | 10,7 | c | 17,21 | - | 18,2 | | | | |
| d | 10,8 | - | 12,2 | d | 18,2 | - | 19,14 | | | | |
| 232 a | 13,1 | - | 13,15 | 235 a | 19,15 | - | 23,2 | | | | |
| b | 13,16 | - | 13,29 | b | 23,2 | - | 26,1 | | | | |
| c | 13,30 | - | 13,46 | c | 27,1 | - | 29,3 | | | | |
| d | 13,47 | - | 13,63 | d | 29,4 | - | 31,1 | | | | |

# INDEX OF PLACES

The name of each place is followed by (i) the initial of its Wapentake and its location on the Maps in this volume; (ii) its National Grid reference; (iii) chapter and section references in DB. Bracketed figures denote mention in sections dealing with a different place. Unless otherwise stated, the identifications of EPNS and the spellings of the Ordnance Survey are followed for places in England; of OEB for places abroad. The National Grid reference system is explained on all Ordnance Survey maps, and in the Automobile Association handbooks; the figures reading from left to right are given before those reading from bottom to top of the map. Places marked with an asterix (*) are in the 100 kilometre grid square SP. All others are in square SK. The Leicestershire Wapentakes (see note 1,1a) are Gartree (Ga); Goscote (Go); Guthlaxton (Gu); Framland (F). Places entered in Derbyshire in DB are marked with a dagger (†); in Northamptonshire with two daggers (††). Unidentified places are shown in DB spelling, in italics.

| Place | Map | Grid | Text |
|---|---|---|---|
| Allexton | Go 89 | 81 00 | (1,3.) 40,27; 39 |
| Alton | Go 16 | 39 14 | 13,66 |
| Anstey | Go 53 | 55 08 | (C 11.) 13,22 |
| Appleby† | Go 5 | 31 09 | 11,2. 14,22. E 5 |
| Arnesby* | Gu 77 | 61 92 | 4,1. 25,2 |
| Asfordby | Go 46 | 70 19 | (1,3.) 42,9 |
| Ashby de la Zouch | Go 17 | 35 16 | 13,65 |
| Ashby Folville | Go 73 | 70 12 | 14,17. 40,32 |
| Ashby Magna* | Gu 74 | 56 90 | 25,5. 34,1 |
| Ashby Parva* | Gu 71 | 52 88 | 17,5 |
| Aylestone | Gu 55 | 57 01 | 9,1. 12,1. (44,1-2) |
| Baggrave | Ga 3 | 69 08 | (1,3) |
| Bagworth | Gu 12 | 44 08 | 44,10(-11) |
| Barkby | Go 67 | 63 09 | 15,10. 41,3 |
| Barkestone | F 3 | 78 35 | 15,4 |
| Barlestone | Gu 27 | 42 05 | 13,46. 17,10 |
| Barrow-on-Soar | Go 48 | 57 17 | (C 8). 43,1 |
| Barsby | Go 74 | 69 11 | (1,3.) 32,2 |
| Barton-in-the-Beans | Gu 6 | 39 04 | 13,73 |
| Barwell* | Gu 38 | 44 96 | 6,3-4 |
| Beeby | Go 77 | 66 08 | 7,2 |
| Belgrave | Go 68 | 59 06 | (C 11.) 13,20 41,1 |
| Billesdon | Ga 18 | 72 02 | 28,4 |
| Bilstone | Gu 18 | 36 05 | 11,3 |
| Birstall | Go 54 | 59 09 | (C 11.) 13,21; 61 |
| Bittesby* | Gu 79 | 50 85 | 1,12 |
| Bitteswell* | Gu 80 | 53 85 | 10,9. 29,7 44,3 |
| Blaby* | Gu 50 | 57 97 | (1,4. 15,2.) 40,20 |
| Blaston* | Ga 41 | 80 95 | 14,21 |
| Boothorpe | Go 12 | 31 17 | |
| Husbands Bosworth* | Ga 60 | 64 84 | 16,7. 17,15. 23,4; 6. 33,1 |
| Market Bosworth | Gu 25 | 40 03 | 9,5. 13,72 |
| Bottesford | F 1 | 80 39 | 15,5(-7;) 15(-16) |
| Great Bowden* | Ga 54 | 74 88 | 1,4. (27,2.) 40,18 |
| Little Bowden*†† | Ga 58 | 74 87 | E 12 |
| Branston | F 10 | 81 29 | 3,14 |
| Brascote | Gu 29 | 44 02 | 13,11 |
| Braunstone | Gu 53 | 55 02 | (13,5;) 41 |
| 'Bromkinsthorpe' | Gu 54 | 57 03 | (C 11. 13,5. 25,3) |
| Brooksby | Go 62 | 67 16 | 40,36. (43,1... |
| Broughton Astley* | Gu 63 | 52 92 | (C 11. 10,7.) 13,38. 40,8 |
| Nether Broughton | F 13 | 69 26 | 1,2 |
| Bruntingthorpe | Gu 85 | 60 90 | 13,26. 44,6 |
| Buckminster | F 26 | 88 23 | 3,15 |
| Burbage* | Gu 40 | 44 92 | 6,1 |
| 'The Burgh'. | - | - | (1,7) |
| Burrough-on-the Hill | F 42 | 75 10 | 14,32. 29,12... 42,1; 4 |
| Burton Lazars | F 40 | 76 16 | 14,29. 18,5. (29,3) |
| Burton-on-the-Wolds | Go 38 | 59 21 | 29,14. 35,1. 43,3-4; 7 |
| Burton Overy* | Ga 23 | 67 98 | (C 11.) 13,1... |
| Cadeby | Gu 24 | 42 02 | 13,44 |
| Carlton Curlieu* | Ga 28 | 69 97 | (1,4.) 13,17 |
| Castle Donington | Go 26 | 44 27 | 12,2. (43,1) |
| Catthorpe* | Gu 94 | 55 78 | 37,3 |
| Chadwell | F 19 | 78 24 | (1,3) |
| Charley | Go 25 | 48 14 | (43,1) |
| Chilcote† | Go 4 | 28 11 | E 4 |
| Long Clawson | F 12 | 72 27 | 15,12. 20,3-4. 43,11 |
| Claybrooke* | Gu 69 | 49 88 | 44,7 |
| Coleorton | Go 19 | 39 17 | 14,18; 28. 17,28 |
| Congerstone | Gu 19 | 36 05 | 14,13. 19,7 |
| Cosby* | Gu 66 | 54 95 | 9,4. 17,9. 40,3 |
| Cossington | Go 56 | 60 13 | (43,1) |
| Coston | F 25 | 84 22 | 14,5 |
| Cotesbach* | Gu 92 | 53 82 | 13,48-49 |
| Cotes de Val* | Gu 82 | 55 88 | 3,5 |
| Cranoe* | Ga 39 | 76 95 | (1,4.) 40,29 |
| Croft* | Gu 47 | 51 95 | 10,7. 13,37 |

| | Map | Grid | Text |
|---|---|---|---|
| Croxton Kerrial | F 11 | 83 29 | 1,1a |
| South Croxton | Go 75 | 69 10 | 3,13. 15,11 |
| Great Dalby | Go 70 | 74 14 | 3,12. 17,25. 32,1 |
| Little Dalby | F 41 | 77 13 | (C 14.) 14,31 29,19; 21 |
| Old Dalby | Go 40 | 67 23 | 22,1 |
| Desford | Gu 32 | 47 03 | (C 11. 13,5;) 8 |
| Diseworth | Go 29 | 45 24 | 27,1 |
| Dishley | Go 32 | 51 21 | 1,9. (43,6) |
| Donington le Heath | Gu 8 | 42 12 | 39,2 |
| Donisthorpe† | Go 11 | 31 14 | 14,28. E 9 |
| Dunton Bassett* | Gu 73 | 54 90 | 17,4 |
| Earl Shilton* | Gu 44 | 47 98 | (C 11.) 13,4 |
| Great Easton* | Ga 45 | 85 93 | 5,2-3 |
| Eastwell | F 9 | 77 28 | (29,3.) 42,7 |
| Edmondthorpe | F 36 | 85 17 | 14,6 |
| Elvelege | - | - | 40,10 |
| Enderby* | Gu 51 | 53 99 | (C 11.) 13,39 |
| Evington | Ga 10 | 62 02 | 13,50. 17,6 |
| Fenny Drayton* | Gu 21 | 35 97 | 10,8 |
| Fleckney* | Ga 34 | 64 93 | 19,10; 12 |
| Foston* | Gu 67 | 60 95 | 25,1 |
| Foxton* | Ga 53 | 70 90 | (1,4.) 40,16 |
| Freeby | F 31 | 80 20 | (29,3) |
| Frisby | Ga 17 | 70 01 | 13,54 |
| Frisby-on-the-Wreak | Go 60 | 69 17 | (1,3. 43,1) |
| Frolesworth* | Gu 62 | 50 90 | 9,2. (13,2.) 17,3. 40,4 |
| Gaddesby | Go 71 | 68 13 | (1,3.) 40,34-35. (43,1) |
| Galby | Ga 16 | 69 01 | (1,4). 13,53 |
| Gilmorton* | Gu 83 | 57 88 | 16,1 |
| Great Glen* | Ga 22 | 65 97 | 13,58-59 |
| Glenfield | Gu 36 | 53 06 | (13,5;) 40 |
| Glooston* | Ga 30 | 75 95 | 40,22 |
| Goadby* | Ga 25 | 75 98 | 28,2 |
| Goadby Marwood | F 14 | 78 26 | 17,33. (29,3) |
| Godtorp | – | . | 29,11 |
| Gopsall | Gu 3 | 35 06 | 14,11 |
| Grimston | Go 42 | 68 21 | (1,3.) 17,22 |
| Groby | Gu 35 | 52 07 | 13,6 |
| Gumley* | Ga 52 | 67 90 | 16,4. 40,17 |
| Hallaton* | Ga 31 | 78 96 | 28,1 |
| Halstead | Go 85 | 76 05 | (1,3) |
| Harby | F 4 | 74 31 | 15,3. 17,31 |
| Harston | F 7 | 84 31 | 1,1c |
| Hathern | Go 30 | 50 22 | 43,6 |
| Heather | Gu 7 | 39 10 | 40,7 |
| Hereswode | - | - | (C 18) |
| Hinckley* | Gu 39 | 42 93 | 10,3 |
| Hoby | Go 59 | 67 17 | 36,2 |
| Holwell | F 23 | 73 23 | 3,16. 17,30 |
| Holyoaks* | Ga 42 | 84 95 | 3,11 |
| Horninghold* | Ga 32 | 80 97 | 15,1 |
| Hose | F 8 | 73 29 | 15,13. 20,1-2 43,9-10 |
| Hoton | Go 35 | 57 22 | 42,5. (43,1) |

| | Map | Grid | Text |
|---|---|---|---|
| Houghton-on-the-Hill | Ga 11 | 67 03 | 14,16 |
| Humberstone | Go 69 | 62 06 | 13,24 |
| Huncote* | Gu 46 | 51 97 | 9,3-(4) |
| Hungerton | Go 79 | 69 07 | (15,10) |
| Ibstock | Gu 9 | 40 10 | 44,11 |
| Illston-on-the-Hill | Ga 21 | 70 99 | (1,4.) 8,3. 13,13. 17,16 |
| Ingarsby | Ga 8 | 68 05 | (C 11.) 13,51 |
| Kegworth | Go 27 | 48 26 | (C 8.) 43,6 |
| Ab Kettleby | F 22' | 72 23 | 17,30 |
| Eye Kettleby* | F 39 | 73 16 | (29,3) |
| Keyham | Go 78 | 67 06 | (1,3) |
| Keythorpe | Ga 20 | 76 00 | 2,6. 28,3 |
| Kibworth Beauchamp* | Ga 35 | 68 93 | 19,14-15 |
| Kibworth Harcourt* | Ga 36 | 68 94 | (C 13.) 16,8 |
| Kilby* | Gu 68 | 62 95 | 38,1 |
| South Kilworth* | Gu 97 | 60 81 | 16,3. 23,5 |
| North Kilworth* | Gu 98 | 61 83 | 44,12-13 |
| Kimcote* | Gu 87 | 58 86 | 3,9 |
| Kirby Bellars | F 38 | 71 17 | (29,3;) 16 |
| Kirkby Mallory | Gu 30 | 45 00 | 6,7. 13,7; 10; 42 |
| Kirby Muxloe | Gu 33 | 52 04 | 25,4 |
| Knaptoft* | Gu 86 | 63 87 | 10,1 |
| Knighton | Gu 56 | 60 01 | 3,2 |
| Knipton | F 6 | 82 31 | 1,1b. 15,7 |
| Knossington | Ga 7 | 80 09 | 1,11. 18,1 |
| East Langton* | Ga 49 | 72 92 | 2,1. 5,1 |
| Thorpe Langton* | Ga 50 | 74 92 | 13,14; 57. 16,6. 17,18 |
| Tur Langton | Ga 37 | 71 94 | (C 7.) 2,1-2 |
| Laughton* | Ga 55 | 66 89 | 15,8 |
| Leesthorpe | Ga 1 | 79 13 | 29,10 |
| Legham | - | - | (C 11) |
| Leicester | L | 58 04 | C. 3,1; 6. (13,26. 25,2) |
| Leire* | Gu 72 | 52 90 | 3,3. 17,2. 19,1 |
| Letitone | - | - | (C 11) |
| Lilinge | - | - | 29,6 |
| Linton (Derby.) | Go 1 | 27 17 | 14,34 |
| Little Thorpe | Gu 48 | 54 96 | 10,14 |
| Loddington | Go 90 | 78 02 | 17,24 |
| London | - | - | (C 2) |
| Loughborough | Go 34 | 53 19 | (C 8.) 43,2-3 |
| Lowesby | Go 80 | 72 07 | 40,24 |
| Lubbesthorpe | Gu 52 | 53 00 | 25,3-4 |
| Lubenham* | Ga 57 | 70 87 | 2,3-4. 15,9. 40,15 |
| Lutterworth* | Gu 81 | 54 84 | 37,1 |
| North Marefield | Ga 4 | 74 08 | (1,3) |
| South Marefield | Ga 5 | 74 07 | (1,3) |
| Markfield | Gu 11 | 48 10 | 40,9 |
| Potters Marston* | Gu 43 | 49 96 | 6,2 |
| Measham† | Go 9 | 33 12 | E 3 |
| Medbourne* | Ga 44 | 80 93 | (1,4.) 15,2 |
| Melton Mowbray | F 37 | 75 19 | 29,3-4; (18) |
| Misterton* | Gu 90 | 55 84 | 3,7. 23,3. 37,2 |

| | Map | Grid | Text | | Map | Grid | Text |
|---|---|---|---|---|---|---|---|
| Mowsley* | Ga 56 | 64 89 | 31,1. 34,2 13,45 | Sapcote* | Gu 41 | 48 93 | 10,2. 13,2; 34 |
| *Nevlebi* | - | - | (14,17.) | Saxby | F 33 | 81 20 | 14,4. 40,40 |
| Newbold Folville | Go 72 | 70 13 | 40,33 | Saxelby | Go 43 | 70 21 | (1,3) |
| Newbold Saucey | F 45 | 75 08 | 14,33 | Scalford | F 18 | 76 24 | 17,33. 40,23 |
| Newbold Verdon | Gu 28 | 44 03 | 13,11; 74 | Scraptoft | Ga 9 | 64 05 | 6,5 |
| Cold Newton | Go 82 | 71 06 | 29,15. 42,2-3 | Seagrave | Go 49 | 62 17 | (1,3.) 14,7. 17,23 |
| Newton Burgoland | Go 7 | 37 09 | 14,24-25 | Nether Seal | Go 2 | 29 13 | 14,19 |
| Newton Harcourt* | Ga 26 | 63 97 | (C 13).16,9 | Over Seal | Go 3 | 29 15 | 14,20. 39,1 |
| Norton juxta Twycross | Gu 2 | 32 07 | 11,1 | Sewstern | F 27 | 88 21 | 27,3 |
| East Norton | Go 88 | 78 00 | 19,18. 29,2 | Shackerstone | Gu 4 | 37 06 | 19,6 |
| King's Norton | Ga 15 | 68 00 | (1,4) | Shangton* | Ga 29 | 71 96 | (1,4.) 13,55. 16,5 |
| Noseley* | Ga 24 | 73 98 | 13,18 | Sharnford* | Gu 61 | 48 91 | 3,4. (8,5.) 13,3. 40,5. 42,10 |
| Oadby | Gu 57 | 62 00 | 13,31. 40,1; 25 | Shawell* | Gu 93 | 54 79 | 44,8 |
| Oakham (Rutland) | - | - | (1,11) | Shearsby* | Gu 78 | 62 91 | 8,2. 10,6. 13 13,33 |
| Oakthorpe† | Go 10 | 32 13 | E 10 | Sheepy M & P | Gu 16 | 32 01 | 13,47. 14,12 |
| Odstone | Gu 5 | 39 07 | 19,9 | Shenton | Gu 22 | 38 00 | 10,5. 14,15. 16,2 |
| Orton-on-the-Hill | Gu 13 | 30 04 | 14,9 | Shepshed | Go 31 | 47 19 | (C 15.) 1,10. (14,3) |
| Osbaston | Gu 26 | 42 04 | 21,1 | Shoby | Go 44 | 68 20 | 10,16 |
| Osgathorpe | Go 22 | 43 19 | 14,27 | Sibson | Gu 20 | 35 00 | 10,4 |
| Othorpe* | Ga 40 | 77.95 | 40,19 | Sileby | Go 50 | 60 15 | (C 11. 1,3.) 13,64. (43,1) |
| Cold Overton | F 44 | 81 10 | 36,1 | Skeffington | Go 86 | 74 02 | (1,3) |
| Owston | Ga 6 | 77 07 | 40,26 | Slawston* | Ga 43 | 78 94 | 17,17; 20 |
| Packington | Go 14 | 36 14 | 6,6 | Smeeton Westerby* | Ga 48 | 67 92 | (1,4.) 13,26; 29. 19,11 |
| Peatling Magna* | Gu 76 | 59 92 | 8,1. 17,1. 40,2. 44,5 | Smockington* | Gu 59 | 45 90 | 14,14 |
| Peatling Parva* | Gu 84 | 58 89 | 13,32. 41,2 | Snarestone | Gu 1 | 34 09 | 19,8 |
| Peckleton | Gu 31 | 47 00 | 13,12 | Somerby | F 43 | 77 10 | (1,3.) 14,31. 19,19. 29,11 |
| Pickwell | Ga 2 | 78 11 | (C 14.) 29,10 (-12; 21) 44,9 | Sproxton | F 21 | 85 24 | 24,3. 30,1. 40,41 |
| *Plotelei* | - | - | | Stanford-on-Avon (N/hants) | - | - | (23,2; 4-6) |
| Poultney* | Gu 89 | 58 85 | 3,6 | Stanton-under-Bardon | Gu 10 | 46 10 | 29,1 |
| 'Prestgrave'* | Ga 46 | 86 92 | 1,5 | Stapleford | F 34 | 81 18 | 14,1; (4) |
| Prestwold | Go 36 | 57 21 | 35,1. (43,1) | Stapleton* | Gu 37 | 43 98 | (6,4.) 7,1. 13,9 |
| Primethorpe* | Gu 64 | 52 93 | 19,3 | Stathern | F 5 | 77 31 | 15,16. 29,18 |
| Quenby | Go 81 | 70 06 | 15,11 | Staunton Harold | Go 20 | 38 20 | 13,67 |
| Queniborough | Go 64 | 65 12 | 29,13 | Stockerston* | Ga 33 | 83 97 | (C 11.) 13,1 40,21 |
| Ragdale | Go 45 | 66 19 | 17,26; (33) | *Stofalde* | - | - | 27,4 |
| Ratby | Gu 34 | 51 06 | 13,5 | Stonesby | F 20 | 82 24 | 24,1 |
| Ratcliffe Culey* | Gu 15 | 32 99 | 19,5 | Stoney Stanton* | Gu 42 | 49 94 | 19,2 |
| Ratcliffe-on-the-Wreak | Go 57 | 63 14 | 17,29 | Stonton Wyville* | Ga 38 | 73 95 | 13,56. 40,28 |
| Ravenstone† | Go 15 | 40 13 | 26,1. E 8 | 'Stormesworth'* | Gu 96 | 58 80 | 23,2. 29,8 |
| Rearsby | Go 63 | 65 14 | 17,21. 40,1. (43,1) | Stoughton | Ga 12 | 64 02 | 13,52 |
| Redmile | F 2 | 79 35 | 15,6 | Great Stretton | Ga 13 | 65 00 | (1,4) |
| 'Ringlethorpe' | F 24 | 77 23 | 40,11. 42,8 | Little Stretton | Ga 14 | 66 00 | (1,4) |
| Rolleston | Ga 19 | 73 00 | 28,5 | | | | |
| Rotherby | Go 61 | 67 16 | (43,1) | | | | |
| Rothley | Go 51 | 58 12 | 1,3 | | | | |
| Saddington* | Ga 47 | 65 91 | (C 15.) 1,6 | | | | |
| Saltby | F 15 | 85 26 | 18,3 | | | | |

| | Map | Grid | Text |
|---|---|---|---|
| Stretton-en-le-Field (Derbys.) | Go 6 | 30 11 | 14,28. E 6 |
| Sutton Cheney | Gu 23 | 41 00 | 7,1. 13,43 |
| Sutton-in-the-Elms* | Gu 65 | 52 94 | 8,2. (10,7.) 19,4 |
| Swepstone | Go 8 | 36 10 | 14,23 |
| Swinford* | Gu 95 | 57 79 | 3,10. 8,4. 10,10. 13,25. 17,7;11. 29,9 |
| Sysonby | F 29 | 74 20 | (29,3;) 17. 40,14 |
| Syston | Go 65 | 62 11 | 13,60 |
| Theddingworth* | Ga 59 | 66 85 | 10,12-13. 27,2. 40,31. 43,5 |
| Thorpe Acre | Go 33 | 51 20 | (C 15.) 1,8 |
| Thorpe Arnold | F 30 | 77 20 | 13,70-71 |
| Little Thorpe* | Gu 48 | 54 96 | 10,14 |
| Thringstone | Go 23 | 42 17 | E 2; 11 |
| Thrussington | Go 58 | 64 15 | 23,1 |
| Thurcaston | Go 52 | 56 10 | (C 11.) 13,19. (29,1; 15; 20) |
| Thurlaston* | Gu 45 | 50 99 | 13,27-28 |
| Thurmaston | Go 66 | 61 09 | 13,23; 62 |
| Tilton | Go 83 | 74 06 | (1,3.) 2,7. 19,17 |
| Tonge | Go 28 | 41 23 | 14,2 |
| Tugby | Go 87 | 76 01 | (1,3) |
| Tur Langton, see Langton | | | |
| Twycross | Gu 17 | 33 04 | 14,10 |
| Twyford | Go 76 | 73 10 | (1,3.) 13,30 |
| Ullesthorpe* | Gu 70 | 50 87 | 29,5 |
| Walcote* | Gu 91 | 56 83 | 3,8. 17,8 |
| Waltham-on-the-Wolds | F 17 | 80 25 | 13,69. 24,2 |

| | Map | Grid | Text |
|---|---|---|---|
| Walton* | Gu 88 | 59 87 | 10,11 |
| Walton-on-the-Wolds | Go 39 | 59 19 | 10,17 |
| Wanlip | Go 55 | 60 11 | 10,15 |
| Wartnaby | Go 41 | 71 23 | (1,3) |
| Watford (N/hants) | - | - | (C 12) |
| Welby | F 28 | 72 21 | 29,4. 40,13; 37-38 |
| Welham* | Ga 51 | 76 92 | 2,5. 17,19. 40,30 |
| 'Weston' | Gu 14 | 30 02 | 21,2 |
| Whatborough | Go 84 | 77 05 | 1,7 |
| Whetstone* | Gu 49 | 55 97 | 44,4 |
| Whitwick | Go 24 | 43 16 | 13,68 |
| Isle of Wight (Hants) | - | - | (1,10) |
| Wigston Magna* | Gu 58 | 60 99 | (C 11.) 13,1. 40,25 |
| Wigston Parva* | Gu 60 | 46 89 | 8,5 |
| Willesley† | Go 13 | 34 14 | E 1; 7 |
| Willoughby Waterless* | Gu 75 | 57 92 | 13,35-36. 40,6 |
| 'Willows' | Go 47 | 65 18 | 17,27 |
| Windesers | - | - | 14,30 |
| Wistow* | Ga 27 | 64 95 | 19,13; 16 |
| Withcote | F 46 | 79 05 | 19,20. 29,20 |
| Woodcote | Go 18 | 35 17 | 14,26 |
| Worthington | Go 21 | 40 20 | 14,3 |
| Wycomb | F 16 | 77 24 | (1,3) |
| Wyfordby | F 32 | 79 19 | 14,8. 18,4. (29,3) |
| Wymeswold | Go 37 | 60 23 | 13,63. 18,2. 35,2. 42,6 |
| Wymondham | F 35 | 85 18 | 14,6. 17,32 |

**Places not named**
In FRAMLAND Wapentake 15,14. In GUTHLAXTON Wapentake 17,12-14. 43,8. 44,1-2.

**Places not in Leicestershire**
References are to entries in the Indices of Persons and Places

*Elsewhere in Britain*

Buxton, see note 13,21. London. DERBYSHIRE .. Linton. HAMPSHIRE .. Isle of Wight. NORTHAMPTONSHIRE .. Stanford-on-Avon. Watford. RUTLAND .. Oakham. *See also Index of Churches and Clergy*

*Outside Britain*

Aubigny .. Nigel. La Beuvriere .. Drogo. Bucy .. Robert. Bully .. Roger. Cambrai .. Godfrey. Chartres .. Ralph. Chocques .. Gunfrid. Coutances .. Bishop. Craon .. Guy. Ferrers .. Henry. Ghent .. Gilbert. Gouville .. Hugh. Grandmesnil .. Hugh. La Guerche .. Geoffrey. Jort .. Robert. Meulan .. Count. Mortimer .. Ralph. Raimbeaucourt .. Guy. Tosny .. Robert. Vessey .. Robert.

# NORTH LEICESTERSHIRE

## Goscote Wapentake (Go)

1 Linton
2 Nether Seal
3 Over Seal
4 Chilcote
5 Appleby
6 Stretton-en-le-Field
7 Newton Burgoland
8 Swepstone
9 Measham
10 Oakthorpe
11 Donisthorpe
12 Boothorpe
13 Willesley
14 Packington
15 Ravenstone
16 Alton
17 Ashby de la Zouch
18 Woodcote
19 Coleorton
20 Staunton Harold
21 Worthington
22 Osgathorpe
23 Thringstone
24 Whitwick
25 Charley
26 Castle Donnington
27 Kegworth
28 Tonge
29 Diseworth
30 Hathern
31 Shepshed
32 Dishley
33 Thorpe Acre
34 Loughborough
35 Hoton
36 Prestwold
37 Wymeswold
38 Burton-on-the-Wolds
39 Walton-on-the-Wolds
40 Old Dalby
41 Wartnaby
42 Grimston
43 Saxelby
44 Shoby
45 Ragdale
46 Asfordby
47 'Willows'
48 Barrow-on-Soar
49 Seagrave
50 Sileby
51 Rothley
52 Thurcaston
53 Anstey
54 Birstall
55 Wanlip
56 Cossington
57 Ratcliffe-on-the-Wreak
58 Thrussington
59 Hoby
60 Frisby-on-the-Wreak
61 Rotherby
62 Brooksby
63 Rearsby
64 Queniborough
65 Syston
66 Thurmaston
67 Barkby
68 Belgrave
69 Humberstone
70 Great Dalby
71 Gaddesby
72 Newbold Folville
73 Ashby Folville
74 Barsby
75 South Croxton
76 Twyford
77 Beeby
78 Keyham
79 Hungerton
80 Lowesby
81 Quenby
82 Cold Newton
83 Tilton
84 Whatborough
85 Halstead
86 Skeffington
87 Tugby
88 East Norton
89 Allexton
90 Loddington

'The Burgh'
*Windesers*

## Framland Wapentake (F)

1 Bottesford
2 Redmile
3 Barkestone
4 Harby
5 Stathern
6 Knipton
7 Harston
8 Hose
9 Eastwell
10 Branston
11 Croxton Kerrial
12 Long Clawson
13 Nether Broughton
14 Goadby Marwood
15 Saltby
16 Wycomb
17 Waltham-on-the-Wolds
18 Scalford
19 Chadwell
20 Stonesby
21 Sproxton
22 Ab Kettleby
23 Holwell
24 'Ringlethorpe'
25 Coston
26 Buckminster
27 Sewstern
28 Welby
29 Sysonby
30 Thorpe Arnold
31 Freeby
32 Wyfordby
33 Saxby
34 Stapleford
35 Wymondham
36 Edmondthorpe
37 Melton Mowbray
38 Kirby Bellars
39 Eye Kettleby
40 Burton Lazars
41 Little Dalby
42 Burrough-on-the-Hill
43 Somerby
44 Cold Overton
45 Newbold Saucey
46 Withcote

*Godtorp*
*Stofalde*

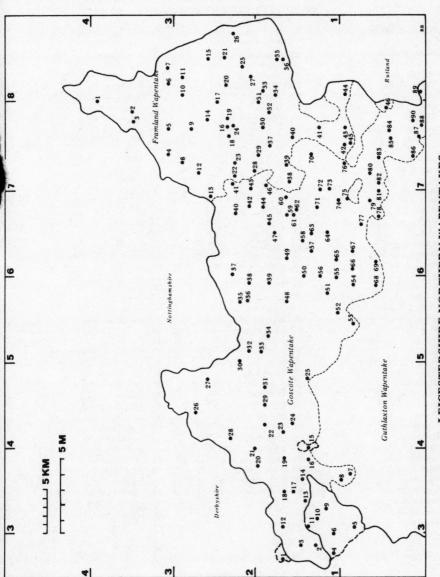

## LEICESTERSHIRE NORTHERN WAPENTAKES

The County Boundary (1086) is marked by thick lines, broken for modern
additions; Hundred boundaries by thin pecked lines.

National Grid 10-kilometre squares are shown on the map border.

# SOUTH LEICESTERSHIRE

## Guthlaxton Wapentake (Gu)

1 Snarestone
2 Norton juxta Twycross
3 Gopsall
4 Shackerstone
5 Odstone
6 Barton-in-the-Beans
7 Heather
8 Donington le Heath
9 Ibstock
10 Stanton-under-Bardon
11 Markfield
12 Bagworth
13 Orton-on-the-Hill
14 'Weston'
15 Ratcliffe Culey
16 Sheepy Magna & Parva
17 Twycross
18 Bilstone
19 Congerstone
20 Sibson
21 Fenny Drayton
22 Shenton
23 Sutton Cheney
24 Cadeby
25 Market Bosworth
26 Osbaston
27 Barlestone
28 Newbold Verdon
29 Brascote
30 Kirkby Mallory
31 Peckleton
32 Desford
33 Kirby Muxloe
34 Ratby
35 Groby
36 Glenfield
37 Stapleton
38 Barwell
39 Hinckley
40 Burbage
41 Sapcote
42 Stoney Stanton
43 Potters Marston
44 Earl Shilton
45 Thurlaston
46 Huncote
47 Croft
48 Little Thorpe
49 Whetstone
50 Blaby
51 Enderby
52 Lubbesthorpe
53 Braunstone
54 'Bromkinsthorpe'

55 Aylestone
56 Knighton
57 Oadby
58 Wigston Magna
59 Smockington
60 Wigston Parva
61 Sharnford
62 Frolesworth
63 Broughton Astley
64 Primethorpe
65 Sutton-in-the-Elms
66 Crosby
67 Foston
68 Kilby
69 Claybrooke
70 Ullesthorpe
71 Ashby Parva
72 Leire
73 Dunton Bassett
74 Ashby Magna
75 Willoughby Waterless
76 Peatling Magna
77 Arnesby
78 Shearsby
79 Bittesby
80 Bitteswell
81 Lutterworth
82 Cotes de Val
83 Gilmorton
84 Peatling Parva
85 Bruntingthorpe
86 Knaptoft
87 Kimcote
88 Walton
89 Poulteney
90 Misterton
91 Walcote
92 Cotesbach
93 Shawell
94 Catthorpe
95 Swinford
96 'Stormesworth'
97 South Kilworth
98 North Kilworth

*Elvelege*
*Lilinge*
*Nevlebi*
*Plotelei*

## Gartree Wapentake (Ga)

1 Leesthorpe
2 Pickwell
3 Baggrave
4 North Marefield

5 South Marefield
6 Owston
7 Knossington
8 Ingarsby
9 Scraptoft
10 Evington
11 Houghton-on-the-Hill
12 Stoughton
13 Great Stretton
14 Little Stretton
15 King's Norton
16 Galby
17 Frisby
18 Billesdon
19 Rolleston
20 Keythorpe
21 Illston-on-the-Hill
22 Great Glen
23 Burton Overy
24 Noseley
25 Goadby
26 Newton Harcourt
27 Wistow
28 Carlton Curlieu
29 Shangton
30 Glooston
31 Hallaton
32 Horninghold
33 Stockerston
34 Fleckney
35 Kibworth Beauchamp
36 Kibworth Harcourt
37 Tur Langton
38 Stonton Wyville
39 Cranoe
40 Othorpe
41 Blaston
42 Holyoaks
43 Slawston
44 Medbourne
45 Great Easton
46 'Prestgrave'
47 Saddington
48 Smeeton Westerby
49 East Langton
50 Thorpe Langton
51 Welham
52 Gumley
53 Foxton
54 Great Bowden
55 Laughton
56 Mowsley
57 Lubenham
58 Little Bowden
59 Theddingworth
60 Husbands Bosworth

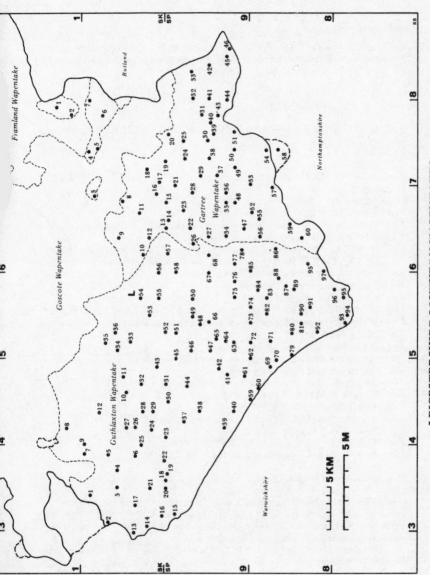

## LEICESTERSHIRE SOUTHERN WAPENTAKES

The County Boundary (1086) is marked by thick lines, broken for modern additions; Hundred boundaries by thin pecked lines.

National Grid 10-kilometre squares are shown on the map border.

# ADDITIONS AND CORRECTIONS to volumes published earlier

## CORNWALL

5,4,19    *Clunewic/Gluinawit.* Mr. Picken points out that this is certainly to be equated with Kilminorth (SX 2353), also in Westwivelshire Hundred ('F'). '?Clinnick' should be deleted. OJP.

## CHESHIRE

C 25    *For* In CHESHIRE the Bishop holds *read* In CHESHIRE the Bishop of that City holds.
A 1    *For* Canon's *read* Canons'.
A 4    *For* smallbolders *read* smallholders.
A 19    *For* In MAELOR CYMRAEG Hundred *read* in MAELOR CYMRAEG Hundred
1,11    *Delete* held it
1,25    *For* serves the Hall *read* serves the Court.
2,23    *For* In EDDISBURY Hundred *read* in EDDISBURY Hundred
5,2    *For* In WIRRAL Hundred *read* in WIRRAL Hundred
5,4    *For* In BUCKLOW (West) Hundred *read* in BUCKLOW (West) Hundred
5,12    *For* In NANTWICH Hundred *read* in NANTWICH Hundred
8,17    *For* he        a freeman *read* he was a freeman.
8,25    *For* 2 ploughman *read* 2 ploughmen.
24,9    *For* ½ virgate paying tax *read* ½ virgate of land paying tax.
26,1    *For* In MACCLESFIELD Hundred *read* [In MACCLESFIELD Hundred]
S3,1    *For* in the other two *Wiches read* in the other*Wiches,*
S2,1    *For* lord's *read* lords'
FT1,1    *For* in the lordship *read* in lordship
FT2,18    *For* the above outliers *read* the above other outliers
R1,10    *For* the values was *read* the value was
R2,1    *For* they call *read* they called
R5,2    *For* Church hold *read* Church held
Y2    *For* BARTON 4 c. *read* BARTON 3 c.
        *Add* another RAWCLIFFE 2 c., the third RAWCLIFFE 3 c.
Y3    *For* HEATON 2 c. *read* HEATON 4 c.
Y4    *For* BURTON [Y] 1 c. *read* BURTON [Y] 4 c.
Y7    *For* another LEECE 6c. *read* another LEECE 2 c.
Y9    *Delete* of land        of
Y12    *For* Gilbert and *read* Gilbert,
Appendix
        *Add after Dee estuary,*  an area along the southern half of the Dee estuary, here called 'Deeside' and the region of Bistre (Mold). The future detached portions of Flintshire (Maelor Saesneg) are abstracted from the entries in Dudestan Hundred (Broxton).
        In modern Denbighshire is the Domesday Hundred of Exestan, later Maelor Cymraeg....